C0-AOC-816

Readings in

EPISTEMOLOGY

Reginald F. O'Neill, S. J.
WESTON COLLEGE

Readings in

EPISTEMOLOGY

Englewood Cliffs, N. J.
PRENTICE-HALL, INC.

Imprimi Potest
James E. Coleran, S.J.
Provincial, New England Province

Nihil Obstat
Russell J. Collins
Diocesan Censor

Imprimatur
† Richard Cardinal Cushing
Archbishop of Boston

March 21, 1961

Second printing...... March, 1963

Library of Congress Catalog Card No.: 61-18427

Printed in the United States of America

75603-C

Preface

The purpose of this volume is to provide, at least on a limited scale, contact with some of the leading philosophers who have studied problems in human knowledge. There is no substitute for a meeting with the "Masters" themselves. Reading about them or perusing digests of their writings can have its value, but students today wish to read what the philosopher himself had to say. At the same time, libraries cannot be expected to provide complete works in quantities sufficient to meet the needs of large classes. Hence there is need for anthologies such as this which provide easy access to some of the outstanding contributions to the history of thought.

The selections offered are, in the opinion of the editor, sufficiently representative of the major themes and ideas in this field, and their arrangement is simply chronological. The emphasis naturally is on the modern period, since it was in the seventeenth century that the problem of knowledge first began to be probed actively and lucidly. So much is this true that some have looked upon the problem of knowledge as *the* problem of modern philosophy. And it is impossible to understand the trends in contemporary thought without some acquaintance with Descartes and with subsequent rationalists and empiricists. This emphasis upon the classical modern period has necessitated some regrettable omissions such as the works of St. Augustine and current Phenomenology; however, to keep the volume within proper limits, these decisions had to be faced.

Most of the selections are accompanied by some introductory notes, and in many cases there are some added footnotes. All such explanatory notes are the editor's, and they have been kept at a minimum because the basic function of this book of readings is to let the authors speak for themselves. However, the introductions may help to point out what the author is seeking to accomplish, and at times these and the footnotes may indicate the direction which an evaluation or critique might take, without going into too much detail. These suggestions are intended to be helpful, and at times they may provide a necessary corrective. Any further explanation would be more appropriate to a history of philosophy or to special studies in the various problems raised. In fact, most of the philosophers represented here have been treated in a little more detail and with more critical evaluation in my own text *Theories of Knowledge* (Prentice-Hall, Inc., 1960), and the student is referred to the second part of that book.

The student may find some of these selections difficult to understand, but persistence should be rewarding. Philosophic thought is far from the level of common sense, and at times it requires repeated reading and serious reflection before the meaning dawns. When that happens, progress is being made and new depth in philosophic experience is reached. Such progress is rewarding and encourages one to try again. At the same time, contact with the leading minds in the history of thought should help the student to develop not only his powers of assimilation but also his powers to evaluate and criticize. Our intellectual inheritance is vastly indebted to the men represented in this volume; personal acquaintance with them will help in the understanding of the contemporary philosophic enterprise.

Reginald F. O'Neill, S.J.

Table of Contents

PART III—THE CONTEMPORARY PERIOD

ANCIENT AND MEDIEVAL PERIODS

Part I

Although the problems of knowledge may not appear to have occupied the minds of the ancient and medieval philosophers with the urgency characteristic of modern philosophy, it is not true to say that they were unconcerned with the nature and meaning of knowledge. In his own times, Plato presented a masterful treatment of the question of Relativism, and his considerations still have importance in the study of the twentieth century varieties. He was also much concerned with the various types of knowledge possible for man, and with the nature of reality corresponding to these types. Here he brought in his analyses of the ideal forms and the relation of the contemplation of these forms or ideas to the elements of universality and necessity in human knowledge.

In his logical considerations, Aristotle went into the various processes of knowing, with special emphasis on demonstration as its ideal. He added to this his studies on the first principles, especially the principle of contradiction.

St. Augustine, facing the Scepticism of his times, developed his doctrine on divine illumination, on the nature of truth, and on the human capacity for truth.

Finally, St. Thomas Aquinas brought to fruition the centuries-old discussion concerning the nature and validity of universal ideas and their originative function in knowledge. Also, his studies on the nature of truth and falsity and their relation to judgment remain classical in their importance and in their impact on philosophy.

Not all these positions can be represented here, but those selected are of first importance and will prove valuable to one interested in the development of philosophic views on the meaning of knowledge.

1

Ideas and the Love of Wisdom

Plato (427-347 B. C.)

In the first selection, Plato presents his views on the role and function of the true philosopher. Any man who merits this title, according to Plato, must be one who loves all wisdom; one who seeks the vision of truth itself and not of any imitation; and one who can distinguish between the "idea" and the "objects which participate in the idea." Finally, he must be one who recognizes the difference between true knowledge and opinion and ignorance. True wisdom, in the Platonic sense, is had only in the contemplation of the absolute, the unchangeable, the ideal Form, the One which is truly Being; whereas the lower sort of knowing, which is opinion, is concerned with the many--with those objects that somehow reflect or participate in the ideal and yet are neither fully being nor non-being.

The second selection beings out this same position in an allegorical way. To prepare for the allegory, Plato illustrates four levels of cognition by means of a line divided into a lower part (representing the visible world) and an upper part (representing the intelligible world). The lower part is subdivided to indicate two levels of knowledge which are concerned with (1) imaginings or appearances and (2) common-sense beliefs; the upper part is also subdivided to represent (1) discursive thinking related to the mathematical sciences and (2) rational intuition or true knowledge of the Forms, especially of the Good. The famous allegory of the cave then illustrates the ascent of the mind from concern with mere appearances and shadows to the contemplation of the Good. A warning that this ascent must be made gradually and only through long training is contained in the dazed condition of the person who comes too quickly into the light.

Further understanding of Plato's theory of knowledge can be gained by a reading of his *Theaetetus*, where he indicates his own position by the negative device of refuting false theories, especially the position that knowledge is sense-perception.

It must be admitted that Plato's views, especially of the meaning and function of the Forms or Ideas, are not easy to understand. Do these constitute a separate world of what is truly "real"? Are the objects of everyday experience merely shadows or reflections rather than real beings? Is knowledge, in its deepest meaning, a contemplation of subsistent Universals? Or are these Forms as much immanent as transcendent, and in what sense? A more detailed consideration of these questions can be found in the historical work done by Reverend Frederick Copleston, S.J.[1]

THE REPUBLIC[2]

Book V

I said:[3] *Until philosophers are kings, or the kings and princes of this world have the spirit [473] and power of philosophy, and political greatness and wisdom meet in one, and those commoner natures who pursue either to the exclusion of the other are compelled to stand aside, cities will never have rest from their evils,—no, nor the human race, as I believe,—and then only will this our State have a possibility of life and behold the light of day.* Such was the thought, my dear Glaucon, which I would fain have uttered if it had not seemed too extravagant; for to be convinced that in no other State can there be happiness private or public is indeed a hard thing.

Socrates, what do you mean? I would have you consider that the word which you have uttered is one at which numerous persons, and very respectable persons too, in a figure pulling off their coats [474] all in a moment, and seizing any weapon that comes to hand, will run at you might and main, before you know where you are, intending to do heaven knows what; and if you don't prepare an answer, and put yourself in motion, you will be "pared by their fine wits," and no mistake.

You got me into the scrape, I said.

And I was quite right; however, I will do all I can to get you out of it; but I can only give you goodwill and advice, and, perhaps, I may be able to fit answers to your questions better than another—that is all. And now, having such an auxiliary, you must do your best to show the unbelievers that you are right.

---

[1]Frederick Copleston, S.J., *A History of Philosophy* (Westminster, Md.: The Newman Press, 1948), Vol. I, Chaps. 19-20, pp. 142-206.

[2]The following three selections are from *The Republic*, V, 473-480 and VI-VII, 507-520, as found in *The Dialogues of Plato*, trans. (1871) by Benjamin Jowett (New York: Random House, Inc., 1937), Vol. I, 737-744, 768-779.

[3]This dialogue or conversation takes place between Socrates and Glaucon, Plato's elder brother. The first speaker is Socrates.

I ought to try, I said, since you offer me such invaluable assistance. And I think that, if there is to be a chance of our escaping, we must explain to them whom we mean when we say that philosophers are to rule in the State; then we shall be able to defend ourselves: There will be discovered to be some natures who ought to study philosophy and to be leaders in the State; and others who are not born to be philosophers, and are meant to be followers rather than leaders.

Then now for a definition, he said.

Follow me, I said, and I hope that I may in some way or other be able to give you a satisfactory explanation.

Proceed.

I dare say that you remember, and therefore I need not remind you, that a lover, if he is worthy of the name, ought to show his love, not to some one part of that which he loves, but to the whole.

I really do not understand, and therefore beg of you to assist my memory.

Another person, I said, might fairly reply as you do; but a man of pleasure like yourself ought to know that all who are in the flower of youth do somehow or other raise a pang or emotion in a lover's breast, and are thought by him to be worthy of his affectionate regards. Is not this a way which you have with the fair; one has a snub nose, and you praise his charming face; the hook-nose of another has, you say, a royal look; while he who is neither snub nor hooked has the grace of regularity: the dark visage is manly, the fair are children of the gods; and as to the sweet "honey pale," as they are called, what is the very name but the invention of a lover who talks in diminutives, and is not adverse to paleness [475] if appearing on the cheek of youth? In a word, there is no excuse which you will not make, and nothing which you will not say, in order not to lose a single flower that blooms in the springtime of youth.

If you make me an authority in matters of love, for the sake of the argument, I assent.

And what do you say of lovers of wine? Do you not see them doing the same? They are glad of any pretext of drinking any wine.

Very good.

And the same is true of ambitious men; if they cannot command an army, they are willing to command a file; and if they cannot be honoured by really great and important persons, they are glad to be honoured by lesser and meaner people, —but honour of some kind they must have.

Exactly.

Once more let me ask: Does he who desires any class of goods, desire the whole class or a part only?

The whole.

And may we not say of the philosopher that he is a lover, not of a part of wisdom only, but of the whole?

Yes, of the whole.

And he who dislikes learning, especially in youth, when he has no power of judging what is good and what is not, such an one we maintain not to be a philosopher or a lover of knowledge, just as he who refuses his food is not hungry, and may be said to have a bad appetite and not a good one?

Very true, he said.

Whereas he who has a taste for every sort of knowledge and who is curious to learn and is never satisfied, may be justly termed a philosopher? Am I not right?

Glaucon said: If curiosity makes a philosopher, you will find many a strange being will have a title to the name. All the lovers of sights have a delight in learning, and must therefore be included. Musical amateurs, too, are a folk strangely out of place among philosophers, for they are the last persons in the world who would come to anything like a philosophical discussion, if they could help, while they run about at the Dionysiac festivals as if they had let out their ears to hear every chorus; whether the performance is in town or country—that makes no difference—they are there. Now are we to maintain that all these and any who have similar tastes, as well as the professors of quite minor arts, are philosophers?

Certainly not, I replied; they are only an imitation.

He said: Who then are the true philosophers?

Those, I said, who are lovers of the vision of truth.

That is also good, he said; but I should like to know what you mean?

To another, I replied, I might have a difficulty in explaining; but I am sure that you will admit a proposition which I am about to make.

What is the proposition?

That since beauty is the opposite of ugliness, they are two?

Certainly.

And inasmuch as they are two [476], each of them is one?

True again.

And of just and unjust, good and evil, and of every other class, the same remark holds: taken singly, each of them is one; but from the various combinations of them with actions and things and with one another, they are seen in all sorts of lights and appear many?

Very true.

And this is the distinction which I draw between the sight-loving, art-loving, practical class and those of whom I am speaking, and who are alone worthy of the name of philosophers.

How do you distinguish them? he said.

The lovers of sounds and sights, I replied, are, as I conceive, fond of fine tones and colours and forms and all the artificial products that are made out of them, but their mind is incapable of seeing or loving absolute beauty.

True, he replied.

Few are they who are able to attain to the sight of this.

Very true.

And he who, having a sense of beautiful things has no sense of absolute beauty, or who, if another lead him to a knowledge of that beauty is unable to follow—of such an one I ask, Is he awake or in a dream only? Reflect: is not the dreamer, sleeping or waking, one who likens dissimilar things, who puts the copy in the place of the real object?

I should certainly say that such an one was dreaming.

But take the case of the other, who recognises the existence of absolute beauty and is able to distinguish the idea from the objects which participate in the idea,[4] neither putting the

---

[4] "Forms" or "Ideas" as they are meant by Plato are not merely subjective modifications of the knower, but have a real existence independent of our minds. This sounds a bit strange in the light of modern terminology, but it must be kept in mind in order to understand Plato. Moreover, quite apart from the inter-

objects in the place of the idea nor the idea in the place of the objects--is he a dreamer, or is he awake?

He is wide awake.

And may we not say that the mind of the one who knows has knowledge, and that the mind of the other, who opines only, has opinion?

Certainly.

But suppose that the latter should quarrel with us and dispute our statement, can we administer any soothing cordial or advice to him, without revealing to him that there is sad disorder in his wits?

We must certainly offer him some good advice, he replied.

Come, then, and let us think of something to say to him. Shall we begin by assuring him that he is welcome to any knowledge which he may have, and that we are rejoiced at his having it? But we should like to ask him a question: Does he who has knowledge know something or nothing? (You must answer for him.)

I answer that he knows something.

Something that is or is not?

Something that is; for how can that which is not ever be known?

And are we assured, after looking at the matter [477] from many points of view, that absolute being is or may be absolutely known, but that the utterly non-existent is utterly unknown?

Nothing can be more certain.

Good. But if there be anything which is of such a nature as to be and not to be, that will have a place intermediate between pure being and the absolute negation of being?

Yes, between them.

And, as knowledge corresponded to being and ignorance of necessity to not-being, for that intermediate between being and not-being there has to be discovered a corresponding intermediate between ignorance and knowledge, if there be such?

Certainly,

Do we admit the existence of opinion?

Undoubtedly.

As being the same with knowledge, or another faculty?

Another faculty.

Then opinion and knowledge have to do with different kinds of matter corresponding to this difference of faculties?

Yes.

And knowledge is relative to being and knows being. But before I proceed further I will make a division.

What division?

I will begin by placing faculties in a class by themselves: they are powers in us, and in all other things, by which we do as we do. Sight and hearing, for example, I should call faculties. Have I clearly explained the class which I mean?

Yes, I quite understand.

Then let me tell you my view about them. I do not see them, and therefore the distinctions of figure, colour, and the like, which enable me to discern the differences of some things, do not apply to them. In speaking of a faculty I think only of its sphere and its result; and that which has the same sphere and the same result I call the same faculty, but that which has another sphere and another result I call different. Would that be your way of speaking?

---

minable discussion as to whether these Forms exist in some world apart, separated from individual things in the sensible world, it should be borne in mind that the insight which Plato seeks to express is that the difference between true and false, beautiful and ugly, good and evil, is not something dependent on and relative to the desires or customs of individual men or groups of men, but is absolute or independent of persons, places, and times.

Yes.

And will you be so very good as to answer one more question? Would you say that knowledge is a faculty, or in what class would you place it?

Certainly knowledge is a faculty, and the mightiest of all faculties.

And is opinion also a faculty?

Certainly, he said; for opinion is that with which we are able to form an opinion.

And yet you were acknowledging a little while ago that knowledge is not the same as opinion?

Why, yes, he said: how can any reasonable [478] being ever identify that which is infallible with that which errs?[5]

An excellent answer, proving, I said, that we are quite conscious of a distinction between them.

Yes.

Then knowledge and opinion having distinct powers have also distinct spheres or subject-matters?

That is certain.

Being is the sphere or subject-matter of knowledge, and knowledge is to know the nature of being.

Yes.

And opinion is to have an opinion?

Yes.

And do we know what we opine? or is the subject-matter of opinion the same as the subject-matter of knowledge?

Nay, he replied, that has been already disproven; if difference in faculty implies difference in the sphere or subject-matter, and if, as we were saying, opinion and knowledge are distinct faculties, then the sphere of knowledge and of opinion cannot be the same.[6]

Then if being is the subject-matter of knowledge, something else must be the subject-matter of opinion?

Yes, something else.

Well then, is not-being the subject-matter of opinion? or, rather, how can there be an opinion at all about not-being? Reflect: when a man has an opinion, has he not an opinion about something? Can he have an opinion which is an opinion about nothing?

Impossible.

He who has an opinion has an opinion about some one thing?

Yes.

And not-being is not one thing but, properly speaking, nothing?

True.

Of not-being, ignorance was assumed to be the necessary correlative; of being, knowledge?

True, he said.

Then opinion is not concerned either with being or with not-being?

Not with either.

And can therefore neither be ignorance nor knowledge?

That seems to be true.

But is opinion to be sought without and beyond either of them, in a greater clearness than knowledge, or in a greater darkness than ignorance?

In neither.

Then I suppose that opinion ap-

---

[5]The difference which Plato here suggests between these "faculties" is one based on the states of mind which they produce. True knowledge cannot err; it is infallible. Mere opinion may be either true or false.

[6]It must be kept in mind that opinion or belief in this context refers to *appearances*, especially to sense perceptions, which can never arrive at grasping objects of thought, such as goodness or beauty.

pears to you to be darker than knowledge, but lighter than ignorance?

Both; and in no small degree.

And also to be within and between them?

Yes.

Then you would infer that opinion is intermediate?

No question.

But were we not saying before, that if anything appeared to be of a sort which is and is not at the same time, that sort of thing would appear also to lie in the interval between pure being and absolute not-being; and that the corresponding faculty is neither knowledge nor ignorance, but will be found in the interval between them?

True.

And in that interval there has now been discovered something which we call opinion?

There has.

Then what remains to be discovered is the object which partakes equally of the nature of being and not-being, and cannot rightly be termed either, pure and simple; this unknown term, when discovered, we may truly call the subject of opinion, and assign each to their proper faculty,—the extremes to the faculties of the extremes and the mean to the faculty of the mean.

True.

This being premised[479], I would ask the gentleman who is of opinion that there is no absolute or unchangeable idea of beauty—in whose opinion the beautiful is the manifold—he, I say, your lover of beautiful sights, who cannot bear to be told that the beautiful is one, and the just is one, or that anything is one—to him I would appeal, saying, Will you be so very kind, sir, as to tell us whether, of all these beautiful things, there is one which will not be found ugly; or of the just, which will not be found unjust; or of the holy, which will not also be unholy?

No, he replied; the beautiful will in some point of view be found ugly; and the same is true of the rest.

And may not the many which are doubles be also halves?—doubles, that is, of one thing, and halves of another?

Quite true.

And things great and small, heavy and light, as they are termed, will not be denoted by these any more than by the opposite names?

True; both these and the opposite names will always attach to all of them.

And can any one of those many things which are called by particular names be said to be this rather than not to be this?

He replied: They are like the punning riddles which are asked at feasts or the children's puzzle about the eunuch aiming at the bat, with what he hit him, as they say in the puzzle, and upon what the bat was sitting. The individual objects of which I am speaking are also a riddle, and have a double sense: nor can you fix them in your mind, either as being or not-being, or both, or neither.

Then what will you do with them? I said. Can they have a better place than between being and not-being? For they are clearly not in greater darkness or negation than not-being, or more full of light and existence than being.

That is quite true, he said.

Thus then we seem to have discovered that the many ideas which the multitude entertain about the beautiful and about all other things are tossing about in some region which is half-way between pure being and pure not-being?

We have.

Yes; and we had before agreed that anything of this kind which we might find was to be described as matter of opinion, and not as matter of knowledge; being the intermediate flux which is caught and detained by the intermediate faculty.

Quite true.

Then those who see the many beautiful, and who yet neither see absolute beauty, nor can follow any guide who points the way thither; who see the many just, and not absolute justice, and the like,—such persons may be said to have opinion but not knowledge?

That is certain.

But those who see the absolute and eternal and immutable[7] may be said to know, and not to have opinion only?

Neither can that be denied.

The one love and embrace the subjects of knowledge, the other those of opinion? The latter are the same, as I dare say you will remember, who listened [480] to sweet sounds and gazed upon fair colours, but would not tolerate the existence of absolute beauty.

Yes, I remember.

Shall we then be guilty of any impropriety in calling them lovers of opinion rather than lovers of wisdom, and will they be very angry with us for thus describing them?

I shall tell them not to be angry; no man should be angry at what is true.

But those who love the truth in each thing are to be called lovers of wisdom and not lovers of opinion.

Assuredly.

* * *

Book VI

And what is the organ with which we see the visible things? [507][8]

The sight, he said.

And with the hearing, I said, we hear, and with the other senses perceive the other objects of sense?

True.

But have you remarked that sight is by far the most costly and complex piece of workmanship which the artificer of the senses ever contrived?

No, I never have, he said.

Then reflect: has the ear or voice need of any third or additional nature in order that the one may be able to hear and the other to be heard?

Nothing of the sort.

No, indeed, I replied; and the same is true of most, if not all, the other senses—you would not say that any of them requires such an addition?

---

[7]Here the difference between the "faculties" is referred to the objects known. True knowledge is of the eternal, the immutable. Mere opinion or belief is of the mutable and of the many.

[8]Plato is now going on to consider knowledge of the "Good" or of "Goodness itself." To introduce his consideration, he discusses human vision and points out that the Sun, as the source of light, is the cause of all vision and of all visibility. In the intelligible order, the Good is analogous to the Sun, because it diffuses and manifests itself in both the moral and physical orders, and it accounts both for moral goodness, the virtues, and for the beauty, harmony, and intelligibility of the world.

Certainly not.

But you see that without the addition of some other nature there is no seeing or being seen?

How do you mean?

Sight being, as I conceive, in the eyes, and he who has eyes wanting to see; colour being also present in them, still unless there be a third nature especially adapted to the purpose, the owner of the eyes will see nothing and the colours will be invisible.

Of what nature are you speaking?

Of that which you term light, I replied.

True, he said.

Noble, then, is the bond which links together [508] sight and visibility, and great beyond other bonds by no small difference of nature; for light is their bond, and light is no ignoble thing?

Nay, he said, the reverse of ignoble.

And which, I said, of the gods in heaven[9] would you say was the lord of this element? Whose is that light which makes the eye to see perfectly and the visible to appear?

You mean the sun, as you and all mankind say.

May not the relation of sight to this deity be described as follows?

How?

Neither sight nor the eye in which sight resides is the sun?

No.

Yet of all the organs of sense the eye is the most like the sun?

By far the most like.

And the power which the eye possesses is a sort of effluence which is dispensed from the sun?[10]

Exactly.

Then the sun is not sight, but the author of sight who is recognised by sight.

True, he said.

And this is he whom I call the child of the good, whom the good begat in his own likeness, to be in the visible world, in relation to sight and the things of sight, what the good is in the intellectual world in relation to mind and the things of mind.

Will you be a little more explicit? he said.

Why, you know, I said, that the eyes, when a person directs them towards objects on which the light of day is no longer shining, but the moon and stars only, see dimly, and are nearly blind; they seem to have no clearness of vision in them?

Very true.

But when they are directed towards objects on which the sun shines, they see clearly and there is sight in them?

Certainly.

And the soul is like the eye: when resting upon that on which truth and being shine, the soul perceives and understands and is radiant with intelligence; but when turned towards the twilight of becoming and perishing, then she has opinion only, and goes blinking about, and is first of one opinion and then of another, and seems to have no intelligence?

Just so.

Now, that which imparts truth to

---

[9] Plato is here speaking of the heavenly bodies as gods.

[10] In *Timaeus* 45 and 67, Plato indicates his theory of vision: (a) there is in the eyeball a fire, like the fire of daylight, which can flow out toward the object seen; (b) daylight itself is a fire flowing from the sun through the air; (c) finally, there is a fire flowing from colored objects. When these streams meet there is the sensation of seeing color.

the known and the power of knowing to the knower is what I would have you term the idea of good, and this you will deem to be the cause of science, and of truth in so far as the latter becomes the subject of knowledge; beautiful too, as are both truth and knowledge, you will be right [509] in esteeming this other nature as more beautiful than either; and, as in the previous instance, light and sight may be truly said to be like the sun, and yet not to be the sun, so in this other sphere, science and truth may be deemed to be like the good, but not the good; the good has a place of honour yet higher.

What a wonder of beauty that must be, he said, which is the author of science and truth, and yet surpasses them in beauty; for you surely cannot mean to say that pleasure is the good?

God forbid, I replied; but may I ask you to consider the image in another point of view?

In what point of view?

You would say, would you not, that the sun is not only the author of visibility in all visible things, but of generation and nourishment and growth, though he himself is not generation?

Certainly.

In like manner the good may be said to be not only the author of knowledge to all things known, but of their being and essence, and yet the good is not essence, but far exceeds essence in dignity and power.

Glaucon said, with a ludicrous earnestness: By the light of heaven, how amazing!

Yes, I said, and the exaggeration may be set down to you; for you made me utter my fancies.

And pray continue to utter them; at any rate let us hear if there is anything more to be said about the similitude of the sun.

Yes, I said, there is a great deal more.

Then omit nothing, however slight.

I will do my best, I said; but I should think that a great deal will have to be omitted.

You have to imagine, then, that there are two ruling powers, and that one of them is set over the intellectual world, the other over the visible. I do not say heaven, lest you should fancy that I am playing upon the name (οὐρανος, ὁρατός). May I suppose that you have this distinction of the visible and intelligible fixed in your mind?

I have.

Now take a line[11] which has been

---

[11]Plato's divided line can be thus illustrated:

	Objects	*Faculties*
INTELLIGIBLE WORLD	Ideas or Forms	Reason
	Mathematical Objects	Understandin
VISIBLE WORLD	Visible things	Faith
	Images	Imagining

Thus, graphically, Plato illustrates four levels of cognition corresponding to the objects known. The lowest level is concerned with mere shadows or images of particular things. The second includes "the animals which we see, and everything that grows or is made." Such knowledge, represented in the two lower levels of the line, is not true knowledge in the full Platonic sense of the word, because it is of the individual, sensible objects cut into two unequal parts, and divide each of them again in the same proportion, and suppose the two main divisions to answer, one to the visible and the other to the intelligible, and then compare the subdivisions in respect of their clearness, and you will find that the first section in the sphere of the visible consists of images. And by images [510] I mean, in the first place, shadows, and in the second place, reflections in water and in solid, smooth and polished bodies and the like: Do you understand?

Yes, I understand.

Imagine, now, the other section, of which this is only the resemblance, to include the animals which we see, and everything that grows or is made.

Very good.

Would you not admit that both the sections of this division have different degrees of truth, and that the copy is to the original as the sphere of opinion is to the sphere of knowledge?

Most undoubtedly.

Next proceed to consider the manner in which the sphere of the intellectual is to be divided.

In what manner?

Thus:—There are two subdivisions, in the lower of which the soul uses the figures given by the former division as images; the enquiry can only be hypothetical, and instead of going upwards to a principle descends to the other end; in the higher of the two, the soul passes out of hypotheses, and goes up to a principle which is above hypotheses, making no use of images as in the former case, but proceeding only in and through the ideas themselves.

I do not quite understand your meaning, he said.

Then I will try again; you will understand me better when I have made some preliminary remarks. You are aware that students of geometry, arithmetic, and the kindred sciences assume the odd and the even and the figures and three kinds of angles and the like in their several branches of science; these are their hypotheses, which they and every body are supposed to know, and therefore they do not design to give any account of them either to themselves or others; but they begin with them, and go on until they arrive at last, and in a consistent manner, at their conclusion?

Yes, he said, I know.

And do you not know also that although they make use of the visible forms and reason about them, they are thinking not of these, but of the ideals which they resemble; not of the figures which they draw, but of the absolute square and the absolute diameter, and so on—the forms which they draw or make, and which have shadows and reflections in water of their own, are converted by them into images, but they are really seeking to behold the things themselves, which can only be seen with the eye of the mind?

That is true [511].

And of this kind I spoke as the intelligible, although in the search after it the soul is compelled to use hypotheses; not ascending to a first principle, because she is unable to rise above the region of hypothesis, but employing the objects of which the shadows below are resemblances in their turn as images, they having

---

which are constantly in a state of flux or becoming. True knowledge for Plato is of the universal, the fixed, the immutable, the truly real. Here, of course, he is referring to the Forms or Ideas.

in relation to the shadows and reflections of them a greater distinctness, and therefore a higher value.

I understand, he said, that you are speaking of the province of geometry and the sister arts.

And when I speak of the other division of the intelligible, you will understand me to speak of that other sort of knowledge which reason herself attains by the power of dialectic, using the hypotheses not as first principles, but only as hypotheses--that is to say, as steps and points of departure into a world which is above hypotheses, in order that she may soar beyond them to the first principle of the whole; and clinging to this and then to that which depends on this, by successive steps she descends again without the aid of any sensible object, from ideas, through ideas, and in ideas she ends.

I understand you, he replied; not perfectly, for you seem to me to be describing a task which is really tremendous; but, at any rate, I understand you to say that knowledge and being, which the science of dialectic contemplates, are clearer than the notions of the arts, as they are termed, which proceed from hypotheses only: these are also contemplated by the understanding, and not by the senses: yet, because they start from hypotheses and do not ascend to a principle, those who contemplate them appear to you not to exercise the higher reason upon them, although when a first principle is added to them they are cognizable by the higher reason. And the habit which is concerned with geometry and the cognate sciences I suppose that you would term understanding and not reason, as being intermediate between opinion and reason.

You have quite conceived my meaning, I said; and now, corresponding to these four divisions, let there be four faculties in the soul—reason answering to the highest, understanding to the second, faith (or conviction) to the third, and perception of shadows to the last—and let there be a scale of them, and let us suppose that the several faculties have clearness in the same degree that their objects have truth.

I understand, he replied, and give my assent, and accept your arrangement.

Book VII

And now, I said, let me show [514] in a figure[12] how far our nature is enlightened or unenlightened:—Behold! human beings living in an underground den, which has a mouth open towards the light and reaching all along the den; here they have been from their childhood, and have their legs and necks chained so that they cannot move, and can only see before them, being prevented by the chains from turning round their heads. Above and behind them a fire is blazing at a distance, and between the fire and the prisoners there is a raised way; and you will

[12]Plato now begins the story or allegory of the cave: as one who sits in darkness and views only shadows or reflections cast on a wall can be brought into daylight to see things directly and even to look upon the sun, the source of illumination, so man can progress from concern with the world of mere appearances and flux to the true knowledge of the immutable and eternal, of Goodness itself.

see, if you look, a low wall built along the way, like the screen which marionette players have in front of them, over which they show the puppets.

I see.

And do you see, I said, men passing along the wall carrying all sorts of vessels, and statues [515] and figures of animals made of wood and stone and various materials, which appear over the wall? Some of them are talking, others silent.

You have shown me a strange image, and they are strange prisoners.

Like ourselves, I replied; and they see only their own shadows, or the shadows of one another, which the fire throws on the opposite wall of the cave?

True, he said; how could they see anything but the shadows if they were never allowed to move their heads?

And of the objects which are being carried in like manner they would only see the shadows?[13]

Yes, he said.

And if they were able to converse with one another, would they not suppose that they were naming what was actually before them?[14]

Very true.

And suppose further that the prison had an echo which came from the other side, would they not be sure to fancy when one of the passers-by spoke that the voice which they heard came from the passing shadow?

No question, he replied.

To them, I said, the truth would be literally nothing but the shadows of the images.

That is certain.

And now look again, and see what will naturally follow if the prisoners are released and disabused of their error. At first, when any of them is liberated and compelled suddenly to stand up and turn his neck round and walk and look towards the light, he will suffer sharp pains; the glare will distress him, and he will be unable to see the realities of which in his former state he had seen the shadows; and then conceive some one saying to him, that what he saw before was an illusion, but that now, when he is approaching nearer to being and his eye is turned towards more real existence, he has a clearer vision,—what will be his reply? And you may further imagine that his instructor is pointing to the objects as they pass and requiring him to name them,—will he not be perplexed?[15] Will he not fancy that the shadows which he formerly saw are truer than the objects which are now shown to him?

Far truer.

And if he is compelled to look straight at the light, will he not have a pain in his eyes which will make him turn away to take refuge in the objects of vision which he can see, and which he will conceive to be in reality clearer than the things which are now being shown to him?

True, he said.

And suppose once more, that he

[13]Were Plato writing today he might have used a movie film and movie theatre to illustrate his position.

[14]Thus, living in and knowing nothing other than these shadows or reflections, they figure that these are the only realities.

[15]In the Platonic dialogue, the engendering of confusion or perplexity is one of the first means used to open a man's mind to new truths or to the realization that his own position is not accurate or clear.

is reluctantly dragged up a steep and rugged ascent, and held fast until he is forced into the presence of the sun himself, is he not likely to be pained [516] and irritated? When he approaches the light his eyes will be dazzled, and he will not be able to see anything at all of what are now called realities.

Not all in a moment, he said.

He will require to grow accustomed to the sight of the upper world. And first he will see the shadows best, next the reflections of men and other objects in the water, and then the objects themselves; then he will gaze upon the light of the moon and the stars and the spangled heaven; and he will see the sky and the stars by night better than the sun or the light of the sun by day?

Certainly.

Last of all[16] he will be able to see the sun, and not mere reflections of him in the water, but he will see him in his own proper place, and not in another; and he will contemplate him as he is.

Certainly.

He will then proceed to argue that this is he who gives the season and the years, and is the guardian of all that is in the visible world, and in a certain way the cause of all things which he and his fellows have been accustomed to behold?

Clearly, he said, he would first see the sun and then reason about him.

[16]Here and in the previous lines, Plato hints at his position that true philosophic knowledge is come by laboriously and very slowly. Actually, he requires many years of mathematical study before approaching moral ideas and contemplation of the Good.

And when he remembered his old habitation, and the wisdom of the den and his fellow-prisoners, do you not suppose that he would facilitate himself on the change, and pity them?

Certainly, he would.

And if they were in the habit of conferring honours among themselves on those who were quickest to observe the passing shadows and to remark which of them went before, and which followed after, and which were together; and who were therefore best able to draw conclusions as to the future, do you think that he would care for such honours and glories, or envy the possessors of them? Would he not say with Homer,

"Better to be the poor servant of a poor master," and to endure anything, rather than think as they do and live after this manner?

Yes, he said, I think that he would rather suffer anything than entertain these false notions and live in this miserable manner.

Imagine once more, I said, such an one coming suddenly out of the sun to be replaced in his old situation; would he not be certain to have his eyes full of darkness?

To be sure, he said.

And if there were a contest, and he had to compete in measuring the shadows with the prisoners [517] who had never moved out of the den, while his sight was still weak, and before his eyes had become steady (and the time which would be needed to acquire this new habit of sight might be very considerable), would he not be ridiculous? Men would say of him that up he went and down he came without his eyes; and that it was better not even to think of ascending; and if any one tried to loose another and lead him up to the light, let them only catch the offender, and they would put him to death.[17]

No question, he said.

This entire allegory, I said, you may now append, dear Glaucon, to the previous argument; the prison-house is the world of sight, the light of the fire is the sun, and you will not misapprehend me if you interpret the journey upwards to be the ascent of the soul into the intellectual world according to my poor belief, which, at your desire, I have expressed—whether rightly or wrongly God knows. But, whether true or false, my opinion is that in the world of knowledge the idea of good appears last of all, and is seen only with an effort; and, when seen, is also inferred to be the universal author of all things beautiful and right, parent of light and of the lord of light in this visible world, and the immediate source of reason and truth in the intellectual;[18] and that this is the power upon which he who would act rationally either in public or private life must have his eye fixed.

I agree, he said, as far as I am able to understand you.

Moreover, I said, you must not wonder that those who attain to this beatific vision are unwilling to descend to human affairs; for their souls are ever hastening into the upper world where they desire to dwell; which desire of theirs is very natural, if our allegory may be trusted.

Yes, very natural.

And is there anything surprising in one who passes from divine contemplations to the evil state of man, misbehaving himself in a ridiculous manner; if, while his eyes are blinking and before he has become accustomed to the surrounding darkness, he is compelled to fight in courts of law, or in other places, about the images or the shadows of images of justice, and is endeavouring to meet the conception of those who have never yet seen absolute justice?

Anything but surprising, he replied.

Any one who has common sense [518] will remember that the bewilderments of the eyes are of two kinds, and arise from two causes, either from coming out of the light or from going into the light, which is true of the mind's eye, quite as much as of the bodily eye; and he who remembers this when he sees any one whose vision is perplexed and weak, will not be too ready to laugh; he will first ask whether that soul of man has come out of the brighter life, and is unable to see because unaccustomed to the dark, or having turned from darkness to the day is dazzled by excess of light. And he will count the one happy in his condition and state of being, and he will pity the other; or, if he have a mind to laugh at the soul which comes from below into the light, there will be more reason in this than in the laugh which greets him who returns from above out of the light into the den.

That, he said, is a very just distinction.

But then, if I am right, certain professors of education must be wrong when they say that they can put a knowledge into the soul which was not there before, like sight into blind eyes.

---

[17]An obvious reference to the death of Socrates.

[18]Here is the apex of true knowledge and of philosophy.

They undoubtedly say this, he replied.

Whereas, our argument shows that the power and capacity of learning exists in the soul already; and that just as the eye was unable to turn from darkness to light without the whole body, so too the instrument of knowledge can only by the movement of the whole soul be turned from the world of becoming into that of being, and learn by degrees to endure the sight of being, and of the brightest and best of being, or in other words, of the good.[19]

Very true.

And must there not be some art which will effect conversion in the easiest and quickest manner; not implanting the faculty of sight, for that exists already, but has been turned in the wrong direction, and is looking away from the truth?

Yes, he said, such an art may be presumed.

And whereas the other so-calle virtues of the soul seem to be aki to bodily qualities, for even whe they are not originally innate the can be implanted later by habit an exercise, the virtue of wisdom mor than anything else contains a divin element which always remains, an by this conversion is rendered use ful and profitable; or, on the othe hand, hurtful [519] and useless. Di you never observe the narrow intel ligence flashing from the keen ey of a clever rogue—how eager he is how clearly his paltry soul sees th way to his end; he is the reverse o blind, but his keen eye-sight i forced into the service of evil, an he is mischievous in proportion t his cleverness?

Very true, he said.

But what if there had been a cir cumcision of such natures in th days of their youth; and they ha been severed from those sensua pleasures, such as eating and drink ing, which, like leaden weights, wer attached to them at their birth, an which drag them down and turn th vision of their souls upon the thing that are below—if, I say, they ha been released from these impedi ments and turned in the opposite di rection, the very same faculty i them would have seen the truth a keenly as they see what their eye are turned to now.

Very likely.

Yes, I said; and there is anothe thing which is likely, or rather a nec essary inference from what has pre ceded, that neither the uneducate and uninformed of the truth, no yet those who never make an end o their education, will be able minis ters of State; not the former, becaus they have no single aim of duty whic is the rule of all their actions, privat

---

[19] There are two difficulties in connection with this true knowledge of the Forms or of the Absolute as proposed by Plato: (1) He seems to imply some sort of direct intuition of the Absolute, and (2) he speaks as though these ideal Forms, or Universals, are the only truly real beings and as though they exist as fully real "apart from" and somehow parallel to the sense world which we experience. If this is true, and insofar as it is true, Plato may be said to belittle our knowledge of this world and to grant an intuition of the Absolute such as is not true of human experience. However, whether it be true or not, the real contribution of Plato to the theory of knowledge should be kept in mind; He rejected an exaggerated relativism of knowledge and of morality, and he showed that values and ideals are not merely the subjective creations or projections of man's mind, but that these concepts have an objective reference and that these standards are transcendent when compared to the sense-world as such.

as well as public; nor the latter, because they will not act at all except upon compulsion, fancying that they are already dwelling apart in the islands of the blest.

Very true, he replied.

Then, I said, the business of us who are the founders of the State will be to compel the best minds to attain that knowledge which we have already shown to be the greatest of all—they must continue to ascend until they arrive at the good; but when they have ascended and seen enough we must not allow them to do as they do now.

What do you mean?

I mean that they remain in the upper world: but this must not be allowed; they must be made to descend again among the prisoners in the den, and partake of their labours and honours, whether they are worth having or not.

But is not this unjust? he said; ought we to give them a worse life, when they might have a better?

You have again forgotten, my friend, I said, the intention of the legislator, who did not aim at making any one class in the State happy above the rest; the happiness was to be in the whole State, and he held the citizens together by persuasion and necessity, making them benefactors of the State, and therefore benefactors [520] of one another; to this end he created them, not to please themselves, but to be his instruments in binding up the State.

True, he said, I had forgotten.

Observe, Glaucon, that there will be no injustice in compelling our philosophers to have a care and providence of others; we shall explain to them that in other States, men of their class are not obliged to share in the toils of politics: and this is reasonable, for they grow up at their own sweet will, and the government would rather not have them. Being self-taught, they cannot be expected to show any gratitude for a culture which they have never received. But we have brought you into the world to be rulers of the hive, kings of yourselves and of the other citizens, and have educated you far better and more perfectly than they have been educated, and you are better able to share in the double duty. Wherefore each of you, when his turn comes, must go down to the general underground abode, and get the habit of seeing in the dark. When you have acquired the habit, you will see ten thousand times better than the inhabitants of the den, and you will know what the several images are, and what they represent, because you have seen the beautiful and just and good in their truth. And thus our State which is also yours will be a reality, and not a dream only, and will be administered in a spirit unlike that of other States, in which men fight with one another about shadows only and are distracted in the struggle for power, which in their eyes is a great good. Whereas the truth is that the State in which the rulers are most reluctant to govern is always the best and most quietly governed, and the State in which they are most eager, the worse.

Quite true, he replied.

2

Demonstration and the Foundation of Wisdom

Aristotle (384-322 B. C.)

In his works on Logic, and especially in his study of the syllogism, Aristotle gives clear evidence of his originality. No one before him had presented Logic as a separate science, and it was he who discovered and analyzed the syllogism. Although contemporary efforts have shown that Aristotle by no means said the last word in the area of logic or even in the matter of demonstration, this in no way detracts from his originality and from the positive value of his contribution in the area which he did cover.

In the initial selections, taken from the *Posterior Analytics,* Aristotle concentrates on the process of deduction as a valid source of knowledge. He places special emphasis on the characteristics which belong to the premises and also on the primary and immediately known principles, on which the premises must ultimately depend. These principles, which are somehow derived from sense experience and are not the fruit of demonstration, are acquired by some sort of intuition whereby the intellect can grasp the universal in the particular.

experience knows facts

In the next group of selections, taken from the *Metaphysics,* Aristotle approaches the subject of Wisdom, which he considers to be the highest type of human knowledge. He traces the development of the mind from perception, through memory, experience, and art, until he arrives at that intellectual interest which is concerned with first principles and first causes. Thus, lowest on the scale is sensation, which man has in common with all animals. Experience, which results from many memories of the same thing, is higher and is had only by man. Still higher, art recognizes the universal, and sees not just the facts but their causes. True Wisdom arrives at knowledge of the first and most universal causes; it is metaphysics. Aristotle explains this by his description of Wisdom: it is concerned with the universal rather than the particular; its objects are the primary; it is more exact; it is pursued for its own sake; and it governs all knowledge. Finally, this knowledge is most divine, both insofar as it is the most worthy of God, and also insofar as it is knowledge of God, the Cause of all things. So Wisdom is the best and also the least necessary of the sciences.

Continuing still with very general considerations, in the second book of the *Metaphysics*, Aristotle says that the investigation of truth is difficult because our knowledge is so fragmentary; yet it is easy in that we never entirely miss the target. At times, even, the difficulty is that we are dazzled by the very clarity of the self-evident. In such studies, however, we are not entirely alone, and we are indebted to many others, even to those whose views were superficial; for all of them have helped our study. Finally, he notes that Philosophy seeks eternal truth rather than action, and as such it seeks first causes and the principles from which all truth derives.

In Book IV, Aristotle studies "being" as such, and in the fourth chapter he turns to what he considers the first of all principles--the principle of contradiction--establishing its validity by showing the difficulties which follow from its denial. He begins by stating that not everything can be demonstrated, else there would be an infinite regress and nothing would be proved. Then, turning to the law under consideration, he merely asks one who denies it to make some meaningful statement. Any statement will suffice, and once it is made Aristotle feels that he can proceed to show that the principle of contradiction is established by the making of the statement. In the procedure he offers seven negative "proofs."

The reader who is interested in the totality of Aristotle's logical studies will find them in the six treatises which constitute his *Organon*, where he analyzes such topics as: variability of the subject and predicate, the opposition and conversion of propositions, syllogisms, premises and their relation to first principles, the practice of dialectic, and fallacies and their solutions.

Moreover, the *Physics* of Aristotle should be read in connection with the *Metaphysics*, not only because it prepares for and leads into the latter, but also because it contains studies of some questions which today are treated as questions in metaphysics.[1]

---

[1]For help in understanding the selections, cf. Frederick Copleston, S.J., *A History of Philosophy* (Westminster, Md.: The Newman Press, 1948), Vol. I, Chaps. 28-29, pp. 277-319.

ANALYTICA POSTERIORA[2]

(Posterior Analytics)

Book I

1 All instruction given [71a] or received by way of argument proceeds from pre-existent knowledge.[3] This becomes evident upon a survey of all the species of such instruction. The mathematical sciences and all other speculative disciplines are acquired in this way, and so are the two forms of dialectical reasoning, syllogistic and inductive; for each of these latter makes use of old knowledge to impart new, the syllogism assuming an audience that accepts its premisses, induction exhibiting the universal as implicit in the clearly known particular.[4] Again, the persuasion exerted by rhetorical arguments is in principle the same, since they use either example, a kind of induction, or enthymeme, a form of syllogism.

The pre-existent knowledge required is of two kinds. In some cases admission of the fact must be assumed, in others comprehension of the meaning of the term used, and sometimes both assumptions are essential. Thus, we assume that every predicate can be either truly affirmed or truly denied of any subject, and that "triangle" means so and so; as regards "unit" we have to make the double assumption of the meaning of the word and the existence of the thing. The reason is that these several objects are not equally obvious to us. Recognition of a truth may in some cases contain as factors both previous knowledge and also knowledge acquired simultaneously with that recognition--knowledge, this latter, of the particulars actually falling under the universal and therein already virtually known. For example, the student knew beforehand that the angles of every triangle are equal to two right angles; but it was only at the actual moment at which he was being led on to recognize this as true in the instance before him that he came to know "this figure inscribed in the semicircle" to be a

---

[2]Selected from *Analytica Posteriora*, Bk. I, Chaps. 1-2; Bk. II, Chap. 19; as found in *The Works of Aristotle*, translated into English under the editorship of W. D. Ross, M. A. (Oxford, England: Clarendon Press, 1928), Vol. I; by kind permission of the Oxford University Press, New York. These can also be found in *The Basic Works of Aristotle*, ed. Richard McKeon (New York: Random House, Inc., 1941).

[3]Although this sounds like Platonic reminiscence, Aristotle proceeds to make it clear that from knowledge already had one goes on to acquire *new* knowledge. Later in this chapter he insists that learning does not mean either learning *what one already knows* or learning *nothing;* rather, from knowing something in one way, one comes to know it in another way. Thus, one knows *in general* that every pair is even; then one comes to know *in particular* that this or that pair, previously unspecified, is equal.

[4]Although Aristotle does not present any detailed study of induction, this remark does indicate a realist theory of knowledge in that the universals are founded on the particular existents, so that the ontological basis for induction is at least hinted at in these works.

triangle. For some things (viz. the singulars finally reached which are not predicable of anything else as subject) are only learnt in this way; i.e. there is here no recognition through a middle or a minor term as subject to a major. Before he was led on to recognition or before he actually drew a conclusion, we should perhaps say that in a manner he knew, in a manner not.

If he did not in an unqualified sense of the term *know* the existence of this triangle, how could he know without qualification that its angles were equal to two right angles? No: clearly he *knows* not without qualification but only in the sense that he *knows* universally. If this distinction is not drawn, we are faced with the dilemma in the *Meno:* either a man will learn nothing or what he already knows; for we cannot accept the solution which some people offer. A man is asked, "Do you, or do you not, know that every pair is even?" He says he does know it. The questioner then produces a particular pair, of the existence, and so *a fortiori* of the evenness, of which he was unaware. The solution which some people offer is to assert that they do not know that every pair is even, but only that everything which they know to be a pair is even: yet what they know [71b] to be even is that of which they have demonstrated evenness, i.e. what they made the subject of their premiss, viz. not merely every triangle or number which they know to be such, but any and every number or triangle without reservation. For no premiss is ever couched in the form "every number which you know to be such," or "every recitilinear figure which you know to be such": the predicate is always construed as applicable to any and every instance of the thing. On the other hand, I imagine there is nothing to prevent a man in one sense knowing what he is learning, in another not knowing it. The strange thing would be, not if in some sense he knew what he was learning, but if he were to know it in that precise sense and manner in which he was learning it.

2 We suppose ourselves to possess unqualified scientific knowledge of a thing, as opposed to knowing it in the accidental way in which the sophist knows, when we think that we know the cause on which the fact depends, as the cause of that fact and of no other, and, further, that the fact could not be other than it is.[5] Now that scientific knowing is something of this sort is evident--witness both those who falsely claim it and those who actually possess it, since the former merely imagine themselves to be, while the latter are also actually, in the condition described. Consequently the proper object of unqualified scientific knowledge is something which cannot be other than it is.

There may be another manner of knowing as well—that will be discussed later. What I now assert is that at all events we do know by demonstration. By demonstration I mean a syllogism productive of scientific knowledge,[6] a syllogism,

---

[5]Aristotle is referring to deduction, which he considers the highest type of scientific knowledge, whereby from the general or from the cause one comes to know the particular or the conditioned. In the process one grasps the necessary connection between the derived fact and its cause.

[6]The logical works of Aristotle provide a masterful analysis of the syllogism

that is, the grasp of which is *eo ipso* such knowledge. Assuming then that my thesis as to the nature of scientific knowing is correct, the premisses[7] of demonstrated knowledge must be true, primary, immediate, better known than and prior to the conclusion, which is further related to them as effect to cause. Unless these conditions are satisfied, the basic truths will not be "appropriate" to the conclusion. Syllogism there may indeed be without these conditions, but such syllogism, not being productive of scientific knowledge, will not be demonstration. The premisses must be true: for that which is non-existent cannot be known—we cannot know, e.g., that the diagonal of a square is commensurate with its side. The premisses must be primary and indemonstrable; otherwise they will require demonstration in order to be known, since to have knowledge, if it be not accidental knowledge, of things which are demonstrable, means precisely to have a demonstration of them. The premisses must be the causes of the conclusion, better known than it, and prior to it; its causes, since we possess scientific knowledge of a thing only when we know its cause; prior, in order to be causes; antecedently known, this antecedent knowledge being not our mere understanding of the meaning, but knowledge of the fact as well. Now "prior" and "better known" are ambiguous terms, for there is a difference between what is prior and better known in the order of being [72[a]] and what is prior and better known to man. I mean that objects nearer to sense are prior and better known to man; objects without qualification prior and better known are those further from sense. Now the most universal causes are furthest from sense and particular causes are nearest to sense, and they are thus exactly opposed to one another. In saying that the premisses of demonstrated knowledge must be primary, I mean that they must be the "appropriate" basic truths, for I identify primary premiss and basic truth. A "basic truth" in a demonstration is an immediate proposition. An immediate proposition is one which has no other proposition prior to it.[8] A proposition is either part of an enunciation, i.e. it predicates a single attribute of a single subject. If a proposition is dialectical, it assumes either part indifferently; if it is demonstrative, it lays down one part to the definite exclusion of the other because that part is true. The term "enunciation" denotes either part of a contradiction indifferently. A contradiction is an opposition which of its own nature excludes a middle. The part of a con-

as the perfect formulation of the basic types of deductive reasoning.

[7]The ensuing considerations will be concerned with the premises: first, how they are to be characterized; next, what those characteristics mean; and, finally, how the premises are acquired. Considered in themselves, the premises must be true, primary, and immediately known. In relation to the conclusion, they must be prior to, better known than, and the cause of the conclusion.

[8]Aristotle does not mean that premises can never be the result of previous demonstration; what he does mean is that not every principle can or need be demonstrated, else there would be an infinite process. Hence, the point is that ultimately there must be behind demonstration *some* immediately and intuitively known first principle (cf. *Posterior Analytics*, I, 3, 72b).

tradiction which conjoins a predicate with a subject is an affirmation; the part disjoining them is a negation. I call an immediate basic truth of syllogism a "thesis" when, though it is not susceptible of proof by the teacher, yet ignorance of it does not constitute a total bar to progress on the part of the pupil: one which the pupil must know if he is to learn anything whatever is an axiom.[9] I call it an axiom because there are such truths and we give them the name of axioms *par excellence*. If a thesis assumes one part or the other of an enunciation, i.e. asserts either the existence or the non-existence of a subject, it is a hypothesis; if it does not so assert, it is a definition. Definition *is* a "thesis" of a "laying something down," since the arithmetician lays it down that to be a unit is to be quantitatively indivisible; but it is not a hypothesis, for to define what a unit is is not the same as to affirm its existence.

Now since the required ground of our knowledge—i.e. of our conviction—of a fact is the possession of such a syllogism as we call demonstration, and the ground of the syllogism is the facts constituting its premisses, we must not only know the primary premisses—some if not all of them—beforehand, but know them better than the conclusion: for the cause of an attribute's inherence in a subject always itself inheres in the subject more firmly than that attribute; e.g. the cause of our loving anything is dearer to us than the object of our love. So since the primary premisses are the cause of our knowledge—i.e. of our conviction—it follows that we know them better—that is, are more convinced of them—than their consequences, precisely because our knowledge of the latter is the effect of our knowledge of the premisses. Now a man cannot believe in anything more than in the things he knows, unless he has either actual knowledge of it or something better than actual knowledge. But we are faced with this paradox if a student whose belief rests on demonstration has not prior knowledge; a man must believe in some, if not in all, of the basic truths more than in the conclusion. Moreover, if a man sets out to acquire the scientific knowledge that comes through demonstration, he must not only have a better knowledge of the basic truths and a firmer conviction of them than of the connexion [72[b]] which is being demonstrated: more than this, nothing must be more certain or better known to him than these basic truths in their character as contradicting the fundamental premisses which lead to the opposed and erroneous conclusion. For indeed the conviction of pure science must be unshakable.

* * *

Book II

19 As regards syllogism and demonstration, the definition of, and the conditions required to produce each of them, are now clear, and with that also the definition of, and the conditions required to produce, demonstrative knowledge, since it

---

[9]This highest of all principles is for Aristotle the principle of contradiction, which will be considered in the selections from the *Metaphysics*.

is the same as demonstration. As to the basic premisses, how they became known[10] and what is the developed state of knowledge of them is made clear by raising some preliminary problems.

We have already said that scientific knowledge through demonstration is impossible unless a man knows the primary immediate premisses. But there are questions[11] which might be raised in respect of the apprehension of these immediate premisses: one might not only ask whether it is of the same kind as the apprehension of the conclusions, but also whether there is or is not scientific knowledge of both; or scientific knowledge of the latter, and of the former a different kind of knowledge; and, further, whether the developed states of knowledge are not innate but come to be in us, or are innate but at first unnoticed. Now it is strange if we possess them from birth; for it means that we possess apprehensions more accurate than demonstration and fail to notice them. If on the other hand we acquire them and do not previously possess them, how could we apprehend and learn without a basis of pre-existent knowledge? For that is impossible, as we used to find in the case of demonstration. So it emerges that neither can we possess them from birth, nor can they come to be in us if we are without knowledge of them to the extent of having no such developed state at all. Therefore we must possess a capacity of some sort,[12] but not such as to rank higher in accuracy than these developed states. And this at least is an obvious characteristic of all animals, for they possess a congenital discriminative capacity which is called sense-perception. But though sense-perception is innate in all animals, in some the sense-impression comes to persist, in others it does not. So animals in which this persistence does not come to be have either no knowledge at all outside the act of perceiving, or no knowledge of objects of which no impression persists; animals in which it does come into being have perception and can continue to retain the sense-impression in the soul [100[a]]: and when such persistence is frequently repeated a further distinction at once arises between those which out of the persistence of such sense-impressions develop a power of systematizing them and those which do not. So out of sense-perception comes to be what we call memory, and out of frequently repeated memories of the same thing develops experience; for a number of memories constitute a single experience. From experience again—i.e. from the universal now stabilized in its entirety within the soul, the one beside the many which is a single identity within them all—originate the skill of the craftsman and the knowledge of the man of science, skill in the sphere of coming to be and science in the sphere of being.

We conclude that these states of

---

[10]He now turns to consider the acquisition of first principles.

[11]As to the origin of first principles, Aristotle sees these as possibilities: (a) that they are the results of demonstration; (b) that they involve a new kind of knowledge — intuition; (c) that they are innate. He will reject the first and third explanations.

[12]This is the act-potency explanation according to which the capacity to know them is reduced to act because of sense experience.

knowledge are neither innate in a determinate form, nor developed from other higher states of knowledge, but from sense-perception. It is like a rout in battle stopped by first one man making a stand and then another, until the original formation has been restored. The soul is so constituted as to be capable of this process.

Let us now restate the account given already, though with insufficient clearness. When one of a number of logically indiscriminable particulars has made a stand, the earliest universal is present in the soul; for though the act of sense-perception is of the particular, its content is universal [100^b]—is man, for example, not the man Callias. A fresh stand is made among these rudimentary universals, and the process does not cease until the indivisible concepts, the true universals, are established: e.g. such and such a species of animal is a step towards the genus animal, which by the same process is a step towards a further generalization.

Thus it is clear that we must get to know the primary premisses by induction;[13] for the method by which even sense-perception implants the universal is inductive. Now of the thinking states by which we grasp truth, some are unfailingly true, others admit of error—opinion, for instance, and calculation, whereas scientific knowing and intuition are always true: further, no other kind of thought except intuition is more accurate than scientific knowledge, whereas primary premisses are more knowable than demonstrations, and all scientific knowledge is discursive. From these considerations it follows that there will be no scientific knowledge of the primary premisses,[14] and since except intuition nothing can be truer than scientific knowledge, it will be intuition that apprehends the primary premisses—a result which also follows from the fact that demonstration cannot be the originative source of demonstration, nor, consequently, scientific knowledge of scientific knowledge. If, therefore, it is the only other kind of true thinking except scientific knowing, intuition will be the originative source of scientific knowledge. And the originative source of science grasps the original basic premiss, while science as a whole is similarly related as originative source to the whole body of fact.

* * *

[13]Induction is not used in the modern technical sense, for what Aristotle means is that first principles are not acquired through demonstration but are rather somehow intuited by the mind in what is sensibly experienced. There is thus a recognition of the universal in the particular.

[14]That is, principles are the source of, not the fruit of, demonstration.

METAPHYSICA[15]
(Metaphysics)

Book I

1 All men by nature desire to know. An indication [980^a] of this is the delight we take in our senses; for even apart from their usefulness they are loved for themselves; and above all others the sense of sight. For not only with a view to action, but even when we are not going to do anything, we prefer seeing (one might say) to everything else. The reason is that this, most of all the senses, makes us know and brings to light many differences between things.

By nature animals are born with the faculty of sensation, and from sensation memory is produced in some of them, though not in others [980^b]. And therefore the former are more intelligent and apt at learning than those which cannot remember; those which are incapable of hearing sounds are intelligent though they cannot be taught, e.g. the bee, and any other race of animals that may be like it; and those which besides memory have this sense of hearing can be taught.

The animals other than man live by appearances and memories, and have but little of connected experience; but the human race lives also by art and reasonings. Now from memory experience is produced in men; for the several memories of the same thing produce finally the capacity for a single experience. And experience [981^a] seems pretty much like science and art, but really science and art come to men *through* experience; for "experience made art," as Polus says, "but inexperience luck." Now art arises when from many notions gained by experience one universal judgment about a class of objects is produced. For to have a judgment that when Callias was ill of this disease this did him good, and similarly in the case of Socrates and in many individual cases, is a matter of experience; but to judge that it has done good to all persons of a certain constitution, marked off in one class, when they were ill of this disease, e.g. to phlegmatic or bilious people when burning with fever--this is a matter of art.[16]

With a view to action experience seems in no respect inferior to art, and men of experience succeed even better than those who have theory without experience. (The reason is that experience is knowledge of individuals, art of universals, and actions and productions are all concerned with the individual; for the

[15]Selected from *Metaphysica*, Bk. I, Chaps. 1-2; Bk. II, Chap. 1; Bk. IV, Chap. 4; as found in *The Works of Aristotle*, *op. cit.*, by kind permission of the Oxford University Press, New York. These can also be found in: *The Basic Works of Aristotle*, *op. cit.*

[16]Aristotle is preparing to show what he means by Wisdom, and he does so by comparing it with other kinds of knowledge. Thus, on the level of *mere experience*, one may know that a certain medicine has actually cured Callias, Socrates, and others. On the level of *art*, one knows *why* it has cured them, and thus has come to know the universal.

physician does not cure *man*, except in an incidental way, but Callias or Socrates or some other called by some such individual name, who happens to be a man. If, then, a man has the theory without the experience, and recognizes the universal but does not know the individual included in this, he will often fail to cure; for it is the individual that is to be cured.) But yet we think that *knowledge* and *understanding* belong to art rather than to experience, and we suppose artists to be wiser than men of experience (which implies that Wisdom depends in all cases rather on knowledge); and this because the former know the cause, but the latter do not. For men of experience know that the thing is so, but do not know why, while the others know the "why" and the cause. Hence we think also that the master-workers in each craft are more honourable and know in a truer sense and are wiser than the manual workers [981b], because they know the causes of the things that are done (we think the manual workers are like certain lifeless things which act indeed, but act without knowing what they do, as fire burns—but while the lifeless things perform each of their functions by a natural tendency, the labourers perform them through habit); thus we view them as being wiser not in virtue of being able to act, but of having the theory for themselves and knowing the causes. And in general it is a sign of the man who knows and of the man who does not know, that the former can teach, and therefore we think art more truly knowledge than experience is; for artists can teach, and men of mere experience cannot.

Again, we do not regard any of the senses as Wisdom; yet surely these give the most authoritative knowledge of particulars. But they do not tell us the "why" of anything—e.g. why fire is hot; they only say *that* it is hot.

At first he who invented any art whatever that went beyond the common perceptions of man was naturally admired by men, not only because there was something useful in the inventions, but because he was thought wise and superior to the rest. But as more arts were invented, and some were directed to the necessities of life,[17] others to recreation,[18] the inventors of the latter were naturally always regarded as wiser than the inventors of the former, because their branches of knowledge did not aim at utility. Hence when all such inventions were already established, the sciences which do not aim at giving pleasure or at the necessities of life were discovered,[19] and first in the places where men first began to have leisure. This is why the mathematical arts were founded in Egypt; for there the priestly caste was allowed to be at leisure.

We have said in the *Ethics* what the difference is between art and science and the other kindred faculties; but the point of our present discussion is this, that all men suppose what is called Wisdom to deal with the first causes and the principles of things; so that, as has been said before, the man of experience is thought to be wiser than the possessors of any sense-perception whatever, the artist wiser than the men of experience, the master-worker than the mechanic, and the

[17] These may be called "useful arts."
[18] These may refer to the "fine arts."
[19] This third division seems to mean "theoretical arts" or sciences.

theoretical kinds of knowledge to be more of the nature of Wisdom than the productive. Clearly then Wisdom is knowledge [982a] about certain principles and causes.[20]

2 Since we are seeking this knowledge, we must inquire of what kind are the causes and the principles, the knowledge of which is Wisdom.[21] If one were to take the notions we have about the wise man, this might perhaps make the answer more evident. We suppose first,[22] then, that the wise man knows all things, as far as possible, although he has not knowledge of each of them in detail; secondly, that he who can learn things that are difficult, and not easy for man to know, is wise (sense-perception is common to all, and therefore easy and no mark of Wisdom); again, that he who is more exact and more capable of teaching the causes is wiser, in every branch of knowledge; and that of the sciences, also, that which is desirable on its own account and for the sake of knowing it is more of the nature of Wisdom than that which is desirable on account of its results, and the superior science is more of the nature of Wisdom than the ancillary; for the wise man must not be ordered but must order, and he must not obey another, but the less wise must obey *him*.

Such and so many are the notions, then, which we have about Wisdom and the wise. Now of these characteristics that of knowing all things must belong to him who has in the highest degree universal knowledge; for he knows in a sense all the instances that fall under the universal. And these things, the most universal, are on the whole the hardest for men to know; for they are farthest from the senses. And the most exact of the sciences are those which deal most with first principles; for those which involve fewer principles are more exact than those which involve additional principles, e.g. arithmetic than geometry. But the science which investigates causes is also *instructive*, in a higher degree, for the people who instruct us are those who tell the causes of each thing. And understanding and knowledge pursued for their own sake are found most in the knowledge of that which is most knowable (for he who chooses to know for the sake of knowing will choose most readily that which is most truly [982b] knowledge, and such is the knowledge of that which is most knowable); and the first principles and the causes are most knowable; for by reason of these, and from these, all other things come to be known, and not these by means of the things

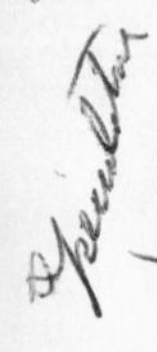

[20] Aristotle has been leading up to this. The note of *utility* characterizes the arts, but the various arts are ranked higher or lower insofar as the element of utility is less or more evident. Hence, the highest sort of knowledge, Wisdom, will not be utilitarian but will seek the knowledge of causes and principles, and will seek this knowledge for its own sake.

[21] Aristotle has already asserted that it is of *first* causes and principles. In this chapter he wants to establish what he has merely asserted thus far.

[22] Here are enumerated the six characteristics of the wise man as people see him: he has (1) universal knowledge; (2) his knowledge is of difficult things, and (3) is exact; he can (4) teach the causes of things; he (5) seeks knowledge for its own sake; and (6) his knowledge is superior and authoritative to other sciences. These are applied to metaphysics in the next paragraph.

subordinate to them. And the science which knows to what end each thing must be done is the most authoritative of the sciences, and more authoritative than any ancillary science; and this end is the good of that thing, and in general the supreme good in the whole of nature. Judged by all the tests we have mentioned, then, the name in question falls to the same science; this must be a science that investigates the first principles and causes; for the good, i.e. the end, is one of the causes.

That it is not a science of production is clear even from the history of the earliest philosophers. For it is owing to their wonder that men both now begin and at first began to philosophize; they wondered originally at the obvious difficulties, then advanced little by little and stated difficulties about the greater matters, e.g. about the phenomena of the moon and those of the sun and of the stars, and about the genesis of the universe. And a man who is puzzled and wonders thinks himself ignorant (whence even the lover of myth is in a sense a lover of Wisdom, for the myth is composed of wonders); therefore since they philosophized in order to escape from ignorance, evidently they were pursuing science in order to know, and not for any utilitarian end. And this is confirmed by the facts; for it was when almost all the necessities of life and the things that make for comfort and recreation had been secured, that such knowledge began to be sought. Evidently then we do not seek it for the sake of any other advantage; but as the man is free, we say, who exists for his own sake and not for another's, so we pursue this as the only free science, for it alone exists for its own sake.

7TH

Hence also the possession of it might be justly regarded as beyond human power; for in many ways human nature is in bondage, so that according to Simonides "God alone can have this privilege," and it is unfitting that man should not be content to seek the knowledge that is suited to him. If, then, there is something in what the poets [983[a]] say, and jealousy is natural to the divine power, it would probably occur in this case above all, and all who excelled in this knowledge would be unfortunate. But the divine power cannot be jealous (nay, according to the proverb, "bards tell many a lie"), nor should any other science be thought more honourable than one of this sort. For the most divine science is also most honourable; and this science alone must be, in two ways, most divine. For the science which it would be most meet for God to have is a divine science, and so is any science that deals with divine objects; and this science alone has both these qualities; for (1) God is thought to be among the causes of all things and to be a first principle, and (2) such a science either God alone can have, or God above all others. All the sciences, indeed, are more necessary than this, but none is better.

Divine

Yet the acquisition of it must in a sense end in something which is opposite of our original inquiries. For all men begin, as we said, by wondering that things are as they are, as they do about self-moving marionettes, or about the solstices or the incommensurability of the diagonal of a square with the side; for it seems wonderful to all who have not yet seen the reason, that there is a thing which cannot be measured even by the smallest unit. But we must end in the contrary and, according to the proverb, the better state, as is the case in these instances too when men learn the cause; for there is nothing which would surprise a geometer so much as if the diagonal turned out to be commensurable.

We have stated, then, what is the nature of the science we are searching for, and what is the mark which our search and our whole investigation must reach.

* * *

Book II

1 The investigation of the truth is in one way hard, in another easy. An indication of this is found in the fact that no one is able to attain the truth adequately, while, on the other hand, we do not collectively fail [993b], but every one says something true about the nature of things, and while individually we contribute little or nothing to the truth, by the union of all a considerable amount is amassed. Therefore, since the truth seems to be like the proverbial door, which no one can fail to hit, in this respect it must be easy, but the fact that we can have a whole truth and not the particular part we aim at shows the difficulty of it.

Perhaps, too, as difficulties are of two kinds, the cause of the present difficulty is not in the facts but in us. For as the eyes of bats are to the blaze of day, so is the reason in our soul to the things which are by nature most evident of all.

It is just that we should be grateful, not only to those with whose views we may agree, but also to those who have expressed more superficial views; for these also contributed something, by developing before us the powers of thought. It is true that if there had been no Timotheus we should have been without much of our lyric poetry; but if there had been no Phrynis there would have been no Timotheus. The same holds good of those who have expressed views about the truth; for from some thinkers we have inherited certain opinions, while the others have been responsible for the appearance of the former.

It is right also that philosophy should be called knowledge of the truth. For the end of theoretical knowledge is truth, while that of practical knowledge is action (for even if they consider how things are, practical men do not study the eternal, but what is relative and in the present). Now we do not know a truth without its cause; and a thing has a quality in a higher degree than other things if in virtue of it the similar quality belongs to the other things as well (e.g. fire is the hottest of things; for it is the cause of the heat of all other things); so that that which causes derivative truths to be true is most true. Hence the principles of eternal things must be always most true (for they are not merely sometimes true, nor is there any cause of their being, but they themselves are the cause of the being of other things), so that as each thing is in respect of being, so is it in respect of truth.

* * *

Book IV

4 There are some who, as we said, both themselves assert that it is possible for the same thing to be and not to be, and say that people can judge this to be the case. And among others [1006[a]] many writers about nature use this language. But we have now posited that it is impossible for anything at the same time to be and not to be, and by this means have shown that this is the most indisputable of all principles. Some indeed demand that even this shall be demonstrated, but this they do through want of education, for not to know of what things one should demand demonstration, and of what one should not, argues want of education. For it is impossible that there should be demonstration of absolutely everything (there would be an infinite regress, so that there would still be no demonstration); but if there are things of which one should not demand demonstration, these persons could not say what principle they maintain to be more self-evident than the present one.

We can, however, demonstrate negatively even that this view is impossible, if our opponent will only say something; and if he says nothing, it is absurd to seek to give an account of our views to one who cannot give an account of anything, in so far as he cannot do so. For such a man, as such, is from the start no better than a vegetable. Now negative demonstration I distinguish from demonstration proper, because in a demonstration one might be thought to be begging the question, but if another person is responsible for the assumption we shall have negative proof, not demonstration. The starting-point for all such arguments is not the demand that our opponent shall say that something either is or is not (for this one might perhaps take to be a begging of the question), but that he shall say something which is *significant* both for himself and for another; for this is necessary, if he really is to say anything. For, if he means nothing, such a man will not be capable of reasoning, either with himself or with another. But if any one grants this, demonstration will be possible;[23] for we shall already have something definite. The person responsible for the proof, however, is not he who demonstrates but he who listens; for while disowning reason he listens to reason. And again he who admits this has admitted that something is true apart from demonstration [so that not everything will be "so and not so"].

First then[24] this at least is obviously true, that the word "be" or "not be" has a definite meaning,[25]

---

[23]The use of the word "demonstration" here can cause some confusion, but the meaning in the context is quite clear: In the strict sense of the word there can be no demonstration or proof for the law of contradiction. It is impossible and unnecessary. The negative "demonstration" which Aristotle admits amounts to showing, by analysis of any meaningful statement, the absurdities which follow from denial of this basic principle.

[24]This first "proof" continues into [1007[b]]. It revolves around the notion that terms must have a determined meaning, that terms essentially refer to something, that all cannot be accidental, but that terms refer basically to substances or essences. These things are essentially what they are, and the principle of contradiction is verified.

[25]Speaking in [1006[a]] of significant statements, Aristotle has insisted that, in general, judgments must have meaning, else nothing is really said and rea-

so that not everything will be "so and not so."—Again, if "man" has one meaning, let this be "two-footed animal"; by having one meaning I understand this:—if "man" means "X," then if *A* is a man "X" will be what "being a man" means for him[26]. (It makes no difference even if one were to say a word has several meanings, if only they are limited [1006^b] in number; for to each definition there might be assigned a different word. For instance, we might say that "man" has not one meaning but several, one of which would have one definition, viz. "two-footed animal," while there might be also several other definitions if only they were limited in number; for a peculiar name might be assigned to each of the definitions. If, however, they were not limited but one were to say that the word has an infinite number of meanings, obviously reasoning would be impossible; for not to have one meaning is to have no meaning, and if words have no meaning our reasoning with one another, and indeed with ourselves, has been annihilated; for it is impossible to think of anything if we do not think of one thing; but if this *is* possible, one name might be assigned to this thing.)

Let it be assumed then, as was said at the beginning, that the name has a meaning and has one meaning; it is impossible, then, that "being a man" should mean precisely "not being a man," if "man" not only signifies something about one subject but also has one significance (for we do not identify "having one significance" with "signifying something about one subject," since on *that* assumption even "musical" and "white" and "man" would have had one significance, so that all things would have been one; for they would all have had the same significance).

And it will not be possible to be and not to be the same thing, except in virtue of an ambiguity, just as if one whom we call "man," others were to call "not-man"; but the point in question is not this, whether the same thing can at the same time be and not be a man in name, but whether it can in fact.—Now if "man" and "not-man" mean nothing different, obviously "not being a man" will mean nothing different from "being a man"; so that "being a man" will be "not being a man"; for they will be one. For being one means this—being related as "raiment" and "dress" are, if their definition is one. And if "being a man" and "being a not-man" are to be one, they must mean one thing. But it was shown earlier that they mean different things.[27]—Therefore, if it is true to say of anything that it is a man, it must be a two-footed animal (for this was what "man" meant); and if this is necessary, it is impossible that the same thing should not at that time be a two-footed animal; for this is what "be-

soning is impossible. Here he points out "that the word 'be' or 'not be' has a definite meaning." He is referring to the "is" or "is not" found in judgments.

[26]Here it is the predicate which is considered, and Aristotle says that it also must have a definite meaning.

[27]The preceding difficult sentences appear to mean that whereas "raiment" and "dress" can be used indifferently to refer to one and the same thing, this does not hold true of "man" and "not-man." These latter are not just two different terms for the same being; rather, they mean objectively *different things*, as was already shown.

ing necessary" means—that it is impossible for the thing not to be. It is, then, impossible that it should be at the same time true to say the same thing is a man and is not a man.

The same account holds good with regard to "not being a man,"[28] for "being a man [1007[a]]" and "being a not-man" mean different things, since even "being white" and "being a man" are different; for the former terms are much more opposed, so that they must *a fortiori* mean different things. And if any one says that *"white"* means one and the same thing as "man," again we shall say the same as what was said before, that it would follow that *all* things are one, and not only opposites. But if this is impossible, then what we have maintained will follow, if our opponent will only answer our question.

And if, when one asks the question simply, he adds the contradictories, he is not answering the question. For there is nothing to prevent the same thing from being both a man and white and countless other things: but still, if one asks whether it is or is not true to say that this is a man, our opponent must give an answer which means one thing, and not add that "it is also white and large." For, besides other reasons, it is impossible to enumerate its accidental attributes, which are infinite in number; let him, then, enumerate either all or none. Similarly, therefore, even if the same thing is a thousand times a man and a not-man, he must not, in answering the question whether this is a man, add that it is also at the same time a not-man, unless he is bound to add also all the other accidents, all that the subject is or is not; and if he does this, he is not observing the rules of argument.

And in general those who say this do away with substance and essence.[29] For they must say that all attributes are accidents, and that there is no such thing as "being essentially a man" or "an animal." For if there is to be any such thing as "being essentially a man" this will not be "being a not-man" or "not being a man" (yet these are negations of it; for there was one thing which it meant, and this was the substance of something. And denoting the substance of a thing means that the essence of the thing is nothing else. But if its being essentially a man is to be the same as either being essentially a not-man or essentially not being a man, then its essence *will* be something else. Therefore our opponents must say that there cannot be such a definition of anything, but that all attributes are accidental; for this is the distinction between substance and accident—"white" is accidental to man, because though he is white, whiteness is not his essence. But if *all* statements are accidental, there will be nothing primary about which they are made, if the accidental always implies predication about a subject. The predication [1007[b]], then, must go on *ad infinitum*. But

[28]Having shown that "being a man" has a definite meaning, he now argues that "not being a man" also has a definite meaning.

[29]Aristotle is pointing out that not all things are accidents, since accidents are predicated of some subject or substance. Thus he completes his proof by clearly insisting on the reality of substances or essences. The term "man" refers to what some being essentially is.

this is impossible; for not even more than two terms can be combined in accidental predication. For (1) an accident is not an accident of an accident, unless it be because both are accidents of the same subject. I mean, for instance, that the white is musical and the latter is white, only because both are accidental to man. But (2) Socrates is musical, not in this sense, that both terms are accidental to something else. Since then some predicates are accidental in this and some in that sense, (*a*) those which are accidental in the latter sense, in which white is accidental to Socrates, cannot form an infinite series in the upward direction; e.g. Socrates the white has not yet another accident; for no unity can be got out of such a sum. Nor again (*b*) will "white" have another term accidental to it, e.g. "musical." For this is no more accidental to that than that is to this; and at the same time we have drawn the distinction, that while some predicates are accidental in this sense, others are so in the sense in which "musical" is accidental to Socrates; and the accident is an accident of an accident not in cases of the latter kind, but only in cases of the other kind, so that not *all* terms will be accidental. There must, then, even so be something which denotes substance. And if this is so, it has been shown that contradictories cannot be predicated at the same time.

Again, if all contradictory statements are true of the same subject at the same time, evidently all things will be one.[30] For the same thing will be a trireme, a wall, and a man, if of everything it is possible either to affirm or to deny anything (and this premiss must be accepted by those who share the views of Protagoras). For if any one thinks that the man is not a trireme, evidently he is not a trireme; so that he also *is* a trireme, if, as they say, contradictory statements are both true. And we thus get the doctrine of Anaxagoras, that all things are mixed together; so that nothing really exists. They seem, then, to be speaking of the indeterminate, and, while fancying themselves to be speaking of being, they are speaking about non-being; for it is that which exists potentially and not in complete reality that is indeterminate. But they *must* predicate of every subject the affirmation or the negation of every attribute. For it is absurd if of each subject its own negation is to be predicable, while the negation of something else which cannot be predicated of it is not to be predicable of it; for instance, if it is true to say of a man that he is not a man, evidently it is also true to say that he is either a trireme or not a trireme. If, then, the affirmative can be predicated, the negative must be predicable too; and if the affirmative is not predicable, the negative [1008[a]], at least, will be more predicable than the negative of the subject itself. If, then, even the latter negative is predicable, the negative of "trireme" will be also predicable; and, if this is predicable, the affirmative will be so too.

---

[30]This is a second "proof" for the law of contradictions; if it is not a law of being, then all things will be one, since the same thing can be affirmed and denied of anything, and it will be true to say that man *is* a trireme and to say man *is not* a trireme.

Those, then, who maintain this view are driven to this conclusion, and to the further conclusion that it is not necessary either to assert or to deny.[31] For if it is true that a thing is a man and a not-man, evidently also it will be neither a man nor a not-man. For to the two assertions there answer two negations, and if the former is treated as a single proposition compounded out of two, the latter also is a single proposition opposite to the former. —Again,[32] either the theory is true in all cases, and a thing is both white and not-white, and existent and non-existent, and all other assertions and negations are similarly compatible, or the theory is true of some statements and not of others. And if not of all, the exceptions will be contradictories of which admittedly only one is true; but if of all, again either the negation will be true wherever the assertion is, and the assertion true wherever the negation is, or the negation will be true where the assertion is, but the assertion not always true where the negation is. And (*a*) in the latter case there will be something which fixedly *is not*, and this will be an indisputable belief; and if non-being is something indisputable and knowable, the opposite assertion will be more knowable. But (*b*) if it is equally possible also to assert all that it is possible to deny, one must either be saying what is true when one separates the predicates (and says, for instance, that a thing is white, and again that it is not-white), or not. And if (i) it is not true to apply the predicates separately, our opponent is not saying what he professes to say, and also nothing at all exists, but how could non-existent things speak or walk, as he does? Also all things would on this view be one, as has been already said, and man and God and trireme and their contradictories will be the same. For if contradictories can be predicated alike of each subject, one thing will in no wise differ from another; for if it differ, this difference will be something true and peculiar to it. And (ii) if one may with truth apply the predicates separately, the above-mentioned result follows none the less, and, further, it follows that all would then be right and all would be in error, and our opponent himself confesses himself to be in error. —And at the same time our discussion with him is evidently about nothing at all; for he says nothing. For he says neither "yes" nor "no," but "yes and no"; and again he denies both of these and says "neither yes nor no"; for otherwise there would already be something definite.

Again,[33] if when the assertion is true, the negation is false, and when this is true, the affirmation is false, it will not be possible to assert and

[31]These few lines may be looked on as a brief third proof, stating that if "a thing is a man and a not-man," then "it will be neither a man nor a not-man." But this denies the principle of excluded middle, so the denial of the principle of contradiction entails the denial of the principle of excluded middle.

[32]A fourth "proof" is begun here, and it proceeds by showing what follows if the law of contradiction is said not to be true merely in some instances, and what follows if it is said never to be true. Ultimately, Aristotle reverts back to the need of having a determined meaning in what is said.

[33]This fifth approach, as Aristotle admits, seems merely to restate the principle in question.

deny the same thing truly at the same time. But perhaps they might say this was the very question at issue [1008^{b}].

Again,[34] is he in error who judges either that the thing is so or that it is not so, and is he right who judges both? If he is right, what can they mean by saying that the nature of existing things is of this kind? And if he is not right, but more right than he who judges in the other way, being will already be of a definite nature, and this will be true, and not at the same time also not true. But if all are alike both wrong and right, one who is in this condition will not be able either to speak or to say anything intelligible; for he says at the same time both "yes" and "no." And if he makes no judgement but "thinks" and "does not think," indifferently, what difference will there be between him and a vegetable?—Thus, then, it is in the highest degree evident that neither any one of those who maintain this view nor any one else is really in this position. For why does a man walk to Megara and not stay at home, when he thinks he ought to be walking there? Why does he not walk early some morning into a well or over a precipice, if one happens to be in his way? Why do we observe him guarding against this, evidently because he does not think that falling in is alike good and not good? Evidently, then, he judges one thing to be better and another worse. And if this is so, he must also judge one thing to be a man and another to be not-a-man, one thing to be sweet and another to be not-sweet. For he does not aim at and judge all things alike, when, thinking it desirable to drink water or to see a man, he proceeds to aim at these things; yet he *ought,* if the same thing were alike a man and not-a-man. But, as was said, there is no one who does not obviously avoid some things and not others. Therefore, as it seems, all men make unqualified judgements, if not about all things, still about what is better and worse. And if this is not knowledge but opinion,[35] they should be all the more anxious about the truth, as a sick man should be more anxious about his health than one who is healthy; for he who has opinions is, in comparison with the man who knows, not in a healthy state as far as the truth is concerned.

Again[36], however much all things may be "so and not so," still there is a more and a less in the nature of things; for we should not say that two and three are equally even, nor is he who thinks four things are five equally wrong with him who thinks they are a thousand. If then they are not equally wrong, obviously one is less wrong and therefore

[34]This sixth analysis seeks to point out that no one really can deny the principle of contradiction — it cannot be a lived denial. This is seen most clearly in practical judgments, especially those concerned with what is "better and worse," for one avoids some things and not others.

[35]That is, if one should claim that he does not really know that some things are better, others worse, but only that he thinks or suspects it, then he should exercise great care in matters of truth.

[36]The final analysis uses the idea that one statement may be more or less wrong, hence also more or less true. If so, there must be some truth to which it is thus related, or at least the extreme view, which allowed no meaning at all, is rejected.

more right. If then that which has more of any quality is nearer the norm, there must be some truth [1009[a]] to which the more true is nearer. And even if there is not, still there is already something better founded and liker the truth, and we shall have got rid of the unqualified doctrine which would prevent us from determining anything in our thought.

3

Abstraction and the Nature of Truth

St. Thomas Aquinas (1225-1274)

Owing to the admitted impact of revelation and of Christian Theology on all his thinking, St. Thomas philosophizes in an intellectual milieu vastly different from that of Aristotle. Yet the influence of the ancient on the medieval thinker is apparent in his every work. St. Thomas' entire philosophy, hence his philosophy of human knowing, is frankly realist and concrete. Like Aristotle, he studies being as being; he starts from the existent world, rather than from ideas of things, and his views on knowledge are intimately linked to his doctrines on the human soul and on the composite unity of man.

The first group of selections indicates his basic doctrine on the process of human knowledge. Man is faced with concrete, singular, material things, and the question is how does he come to know them. St. Thomas replies by showing what type of cognitive power the human intellect is. It is neither limited to an organ, as the senses, nor is it unconnected with the corporeal, as the angelic intellect. So, because the soul is the form of the body, the human intellect relies on sense presentations and finds, by abstraction, its intelligible object in what the senses present. Moreover, in the process the likenesses or *species*, which are thus obtained by abstraction, have a special function to perform: they merely make the object present to the mind; hence, that which is primarily grasped by the mind is the existent object, and only secondarily is the *species* understood.

In the second group of selections, from St. Thomas' work *De Veritate*, he goes into a consideration of truth and falsity. He first establishes that truth is principally in the intellect judging and is only by derivation predicated of things and of human speech. Then, on the characteristics of truth, he points out in what sense it is eternal, how it is immutable, and in what sense it is changeable. Next he discusses how truth may be applied to sensation. Turning to falsity, he considers its verification in things, in sensation, and in intellection.

Further treatment of these topics can be found in the *Summa Theologiae*, I, q. 16, aa. 1, 2, 7, 8; and q. 17, aa. 1, 2, 3.[1]

SUMMA THEOLOGIAE[2]

Question 85

First Article

WHETHER OUR INTELLECT UNDERSTANDS CORPOREAL AND MATERIAL THINGS BY ABSTRACTION FROM PHANTASMS?

We proceed thus to the First Article:—

Objection 1. It would seem that our intellect does not understand corporeal and material things by abstraction from the phantasms.[3] For the intellect is false if it understands a thing otherwise than as it is. Now the forms of material things do not exist in abstraction from the particular things represented by the phantasms. Therefore, if we understand material things by the abstraction of species from phantasms, there will be error in the intellect.

Obj. 2. Further, material things are those natural things which include matter in their definition. But nothing can be understood apart from that which enters into its definition. Therefore material things cannot be understood apart from matter. Now matter is the principle of individuation. Therefore material things cannot be understood by the abstraction of the universal from the particular; and this is to abstract intelligible species from the phantasm.

* * *

On the contrary, The Philosopher says that *things are intelligible in proportion as they are separable from matter.* Therefore material things must needs be understood according as they are abstracted from matter and from material images, namely, phantasms.

I answer that, As stated above, the object of knowledge is proportionate to the power of knowledge.

[1]Cf. Frederick Copleston, S. J., A *History of Philosophy* (Westminster, Md.: The Newman Press, 1950), Vol. II, Chap. 38, pp. 388-397.

[2]The following two selections are from *Summa Theologiae*, I, Q. 85, aa. 1-2, as found in *Basic Writings of Saint Thomas Aquinas*, Anton C. Pegis, ed. (New York: Random House, Inc., 1945). Reprinted by permission.

[3]Abstraction, in general, means the separation of one thing from another. Applied here to human knowledge, it means the separation of a "universal" from the individuating characteristics which concretely determine and limit it to the existing particular and singular objects of experience. The phantasm is a singular, material image sensibly representing the material thing sensed.

Now there are three grades of the cognitive powers. For one cognitive power, namely, the sense, is the act of a corporeal organ. And therefore the object of every sensitive power is a form as existing in corporeal matter; and since such matter is the principle of individuation, therefore every power of the sensitive part can have knowledge only of particulars. There is another grade of cognitive power which is neither the act of a corporeal organ, nor in any way connected with corporeal matter. Such is the angelic intellect, the object of whose cognitive power is therefore a form existing apart from matter; for though angels know material things, yet they do not know them save in something immaterial, namely, either in themselves or in God. But the human intellect holds a middle place; for it is not the act of an organ, and yet it is a power of the soul, which is the form of the body,[4] as is clear from what we have said above. And therefore it is proper to it to know a form existing individually in corporeal matter, but not as existing in this individual matter. But to know what is in individual matter, yet not as existing in such matter, is to abstract the form from individual matter which is represented by the phantasms. Therefore we must needs say that our intellect understands material things by abstracting from phantasms; and that through material things thus considered we acquire some knowledge of immaterial things, just as, on the contrary, angels know material things through the immaterial.

But Plato, considering only the immateriality of the human intellect, and not that it is somehow united to the body, held that the objects of the intellect are separate Ideas, and that we understand, not by abstraction, but rather by participating in abstractions, as was stated above.

Reply Obj. 1. Abstraction may occur in two ways. First, by way of composition and division,[5] and thus we may understand that one thing does not exist in some other, or that it is separate from it. Secondly, by way of a simple and absolute consideration;[6] and thus we understand one thing without considering another. Thus, for the intellect to abstract one from another things which are not really abstract from one another, does, in the first mode of abstraction, imply falsehood. But, in the second mode of abstraction, for the intellect to abstract things which are not really abstract from one another, does not involve falsehood, as clearly appears in the case of the senses. For if we said that color is not in a colored body, or

---

[4]Influencing St. Thomas' theory of knowledge is this fundamental metaphysical position that man is a unity, but a composite unity. Body and soul are not two separate and complete substances, but are *two* only in the sense that they are related as two principles which by their union form one complete being or substance. Hence, man's way of knowing cannot be that of a spirit (an angel), nor is it that of a brute animal; it is, rather, the unique way suitable to a unique being, substantially one, yet composed of an immaterial and of a material principle.

[5]The expression "composition and division" is equivalent to judgment; therefore here he refers to a negative judgment which by denial "separates" the predicate from the subject.

[6]This "absolute consideration" refers to the concept formed by simple apprehension, which apprehends, for example, man or horse without the individuality which each has in any concrete existent.

that it is separate from it, there would be error in what we thought or said. But if we consider color and its properties, without reference to the apple which is colored, or if we express in word what we thus understand, there is no error in such an opinion or assertion; for an apple is not essential to color, and therefore color can be understood independently of the apple. In the same way, the things which belong to the species of a material thing, such as a stone, or a man, or a horse, can be thought without the individual principles which do not belong to the notion of the species. This is what we mean by abstracting the universal from the particular, or the intelligible species from the phantasm; in other words, this is to consider the nature of the species apart from its individual principles represented by the phantasms. If, therefore, the intellect is said to be false when it understands a thing otherwise than as it is, that is so, if the word *otherwise* refers to the thing understood; for the intellect is false when it understands a thing to be otherwise than as it is. Hence, the intellect would be false if it abstracted the species of a stone from its matter in such a way as to think that the species did not exist in matter, as Plato held. But it is not so, if the word *otherwise* be taken as referring to the one who understands. For it is quite true that the mode of understanding, in one who understands, is not the same as the mode of a thing in being; since the thing understood is immaterially[7] in the one who understands, according to the mode of the intellect, and not materially, according to the mode of a material thing.

Reply Obj. 2. Some have thought that the species of a natural thing is a form only, and that matter is not part of the species. If that were so, matter would not enter into the definition of natural things.[8] Therefore we must disagree and say that matter is twofold, common and *signate, or individual*: common, such as flesh and bone; individual, such as this flesh and these bones. The intellect therefore abstracts the species of a natural thing from the individual sensible matter, but not from the common sensible matter. For example, it abstracts the species of *man* from *this flesh and these bones*, which do not belong to the species as such, but to the individual, and need not be considered in the species. But the species of man cannot be abstracted by the intellect from *flesh and bones.*

Mathematical species, however, can be abstracted by the intellect not only from individual sensible matter, but also from common sensible matter. But they cannot be abstracted from common intelligible

---

[7]This presupposes other considerations proving the immateriality of the intellect, which St. Thomas does not offer here, but which can be found, for example, in his *Summa Theologiae*, I, q. 75, a. 2; or in *Q. de Anima*, aa. 1, 14.

[8]Four examples may help to illustrate what St. Thomas has to say in this reply. I can have an idea:

(a) of *this man*, John — this somehow includes the apprehension of what makes him *this individual*, his individual matter, "this flesh and these bones."

(b) of *man* — this includes only what is necessary for a species and is found in *every* individual, common sensible matter, "flesh and bones."

(c) of some *number* or *figure* — this includes quantity and a material subject which is quantified, but omits sensible qualities such as hot or hard or red.

(d) of *being* or *unity* — this excludes all, even intelligible matter, since it can be applied to immaterial beings.

matter, but only from individual intelligible matter. For sensible matter is corporeal matter as subject to sensible qualities, such as being cold or hot, hard or soft, and the like; while intelligible matter is substance as subject to quantity. Now it is manifest that quantity is in substance before sensible qualities are. Hence quantities, such as number, dimension, and figures, which are the terminations of quantity, can be considered apart from sensible qualities, and this is to abstract them from sensible matter. But they cannot be considered without understanding the substance which is subject to the quantity, for that would be to abstract them from common intelligible matter. Yet they can be considered apart from this or that substance, and this is to abstract them from individual intelligible matter.

But some things can be abstracted even from common intelligible matter, such as *being, unity, potency, act,* and the like, all of which can exist without matter, as can be verified in the case of immaterial substances. And because Plato failed to consider the twofold kind of abstraction, as above explained, he held that all those things which we have stated to be abstracted by the intellect, are abstract in reality.

* * *

Second Article

WHETHER THE INTELLIGIBLE SPECIES ABSTRACTED FROM PHANTASMS ARE RELATED TO OUR INTELLECT AS THAT WHICH IS UNDERSTOOD?

We proceed thus to the Second Article:—

Objection 1. It would seem that the intelligible species abstracted from phantasms are related to our intellect as that which is understood. For the understood in act is in the one who understands: since the understood in act is the intellect itself in act. But nothing of what is understood is in the actually understanding intellect save the abstracted intelligible species. Therefore this species is what is actually understood.

Obj. 2. Further, what is actually understood must be in something; or else it would be nothing. But it is not in something outside the soul; for, since what is outside the soul is material, nothing therein can be actually understood. Therefore what is actually understood is in the intellect. Consequently it can be nothing else than the aforesaid intelligible species.

* * *

On the contrary, The intelligible species is to the intellect what the sensible species is to the sense. But the sensible species is not *what* is perceived, but rather that *by which* the sense perceives. Therefore the intelligible species is not what is actually understood, but that by which the intellect understands.

I answer that, Some have asserted that our intellectual powers know only the impressions made on them; as, for example, that sense is cognizant only of the impression made on its own organ. According to this theory, the intellect understands only its own impressions,[9] namely, the intelligible species which it has received.

This is, however, manifestly false for two reasons. First, because the things we understand are also the objects of science. Therefore, if what we understand is merely the intelligible species in the soul, it would follow that every science would be concerned, not with things outside the soul, but only with the intelligible species within the soul; just as, according to the teaching of the Platonists, all the sciences are about Ideas, which they held to be that which is actually understood. Secondly, it is untrue, because it would lead to the opinion of the ancients who maintained that *whatever seems, is true*, and that consequently contradictories are true simultaneously. For if a power knows only its own impressions, it can judge only of them. Now a thing *seems* according to the impression made on the cognitive power. Consequently the cognitive power will always judge of its own impression as such; and so every judgment will be true. For instance, if taste perceived only its own impression, when anyone with a healthy taste perceives that honey is sweet, he would judge truly, and if anyone with a corrupt taste perceives that honey is bitter, this would be equally true; for each would judge according to the impression on his taste. Thus every opinion, in fact, every sort of apprehension, would be equally true.

Therefore it must be said that the intelligible species is related to the intellect as that by which it understands.[10] Which is proved thus. Now action is twofold, as it is said in *Metaph.* ix: one which remains in the agent (for instance, to see and to understand), and another which passes into an external object (for instance, to heat and to cut). Each of these actions proceeds in virtue of some form. And just as the form from which proceeds an act tending to something external is the likeness of the object of the action, as heat in the heater is a likeness of the thing heated, so the form from which proceeds an action remaining in the agent is a likeness of the object. Hence that by which the sight sees is the likeness of the visible thing; and the likeness of the thing understood, that is, the intelligible species, is the form by which the intellect understands. But since the intellect reflects upon itself, by such reflection it understands both its own act of understanding, and the species by which it understands. Thus the intelligible species is sec-

---

[9]Here St. Thomas faces the same basic problem which looms large in the writings of many modern philosophers such as Descartes, Locke, and Berkeley. The problem is one of determining both the immediate object of knowledge, or *what* is known, and the manner in which or *how* it is known. St. Thomas equivalently says that while the *human way* of knowing a material object is through ideas or species, *what* is primarily known is the thing represented by the species or likeness. The moderns start from the knowledge of ideas as objects and then ask whether we can know or how we can know the external object. (Cf. *infra*, Chaps. 4, 7 and 8.)

[10]The unique role of the species is to render the object present to the knower. Hence, it is known as a *formal* sign rather than an *instrumental* sign, since, unlike other signs, it is not itself *first* known. Cf. Reginald F. O'Neill, *Theories of Knowledge* (Englewood Cliffs, N. J.: Prentice-Hall, Inc., 1960), pp. 30-31; also below Chapter XII.

ondarily that which is understood; but that which is primarily understood is the thing, of which the species is the likeness.

This also appears from the opinion of the ancient philosophers, who said that *like is known by like.* For they said that the soul knows the earth outside itself by the earth within itself; and so of the rest. If, therefore, we take the species of the earth instead of the earth, in accord with Aristotle who says *that a stone is not in the soul, but only the likeness of the stone*, it follows that by means of its intelligible species the soul knows the things which are outside it.

Reply Obj. 1. The thing understood is in the knower by its own likeness. It is in this sense that we say that the thing actually understood is the intellect in act, because the likeness of the thing understood is the form of the intellect, just as the likeness of a sensible thing is the form of the sense in act. Hence it does not follow that the abstracted intelligible species is what is actually understood; but rather that it is the likeness thereof.

Reply Obj. 2. In these words *the thing actually understood* there is a double meaning:—the thing which is understood, and the fact that it is understood. In like manner, the words *abstract universal* mean two things, the nature of a thing and its abstraction or universality. Therefore the nature itself which suffers the act of being understood, or the act of being abstracted, or the intention of universality, exists only in individuals; but that it is understood, abstracted or considered as universal is in the intellect. We see something similar to this in the senses. For the sight sees the color of the apple apart from its smell. If therefore it be asked where is the color which is seen apart from the smell, it is quite clear that the color which is seen is only in the apple; but that it be perceived apart from the smell, this is owing to the sight, inasmuch as sight receives the likeness of color and not of smell. In like manner, the humanity which is understood exists only in this or that man; but that humanity be apprehended without the conditions of individuality, that is, that it be abstracted and consequently considered as universal, befalls humanity inasmuch as it is perceived by the intellect, in which there is a likeness of the specific nature, but not of the individual principles.

DE VERITATE[11]

Question 1

Article II

IN THE SECOND ARTICLE WE ASK: IS TRUTH FOUND PRINCIPALLY IN THE INTELLECT OR IN THINGS?

1'. The Philosopher says: "The true and the false are not in things but in the mind."

2'. Truth is "the conformity of things and intellect." But since this conformity can be only in the intellect, truth is only in the intellect.

REPLY:

When a predicate is used primarily and secondarily of many things, it is not necessary that that which is the cause of the others receive the primary predication of the common term, but rather that in which the meaning of the common term is first fully verified. For example, *healthy* is primarily predicated of an animal, for it is in an animal that the nature of health is first found in its fullest sense. But inasmuch as medicine causes health, it is also said to be healthy. Therefore, since truth is predicated of many things[12] in a primary and a secondary sense, it ought to be primarily predicated of that in which its full meaning is primarily found.

Now, the fulfillment of any motion is found in the term of the motion; and, since the term of the motion of a cognitive power is the soul, the known must be in the knower after the manner of the knower. But the motion of an appetitive power terminates in things. For this reason the Philosopher speaks of a sort of circle formed by the acts of the soul: for a thing outside the soul moves the intellect, and the thing known moves the appetite, which tends to reach the things from which the motion originally started. Since good, as mentioned previously, expresses a relation to appetite, and true, a relation to the intellect, the Philosopher says that good and evil are in things, but true and false are in the mind. A thing is not called true, however, unless it conforms to an intellect. The true, therefore, is found secondarily in things and primarily in intellect.[13]

Note, however, that a thing is referred differently to the practical intellect than it is to the speculative intellect. Since the practical intellect causes things, it is a measure of what it causes. But, since the speculative intellect is receptive in regard to things, it is, in a certain sense, moved by things and conse-

[11]The following selections are from *De Veritate*, Q. 1, aa. 2-3, 5-6, 9-12, as found in St. Thomas Aquinas, *Truth*, trans. by Robert W. Mulligan, S. J. (Chicago, Ill.: Henry Regnery Co., 1952). Reprinted by permission.

[12]Thus we predicate truth of words, as "he is telling the truth"; of things, as "that is true gold"; and also of our judgments.

[13]This is the point of the article. The thing outside moves the intellect, the term of the motion is in the soul, so here only is found that conformity which "truth" always requires. In the mind, then, truth is had primarily; and only secondarily is it said of things.

quently measured by them. It is clear, therefore, that, as is said in the *Metaphysics*, natural things from which our intellect gets its scientific knowledge measure our intellect. Yet these things are themselves measured by the divine intellect, in which are all created things—just as all works of art find their origin in the intellect of an artist. The divine intellect, therefore, measures and is not measured; a natural thing both measures and is measured; but our intellect is measured, and measures only artifacts, not natural things.

A natural thing, therefore, being placed between two intellects is called *true* in so far as it conforms to either. It is said to be true with respect to its conformity with the divine intellect in so far as it fulfills the end to which it was ordained by the divine intellect. This is clear from the writings of Anselm and Augustine, as well as from the definition of Avicenna, previously cited: "The truth of anything is a property of the act of being which has been established for it." With respect to its conformity with a human intellect, a thing is said to be true in so far as it is such as to cause a true estimate about itself; and a thing is said to be false if, as Aristotle says, "by nature it is such that it seems to be what it is not, or seems to possess qualities which it does not possess."

In a natural thing, truth is found especially in the first, rather than in the second, sense; for its reference to the divine intellect comes before its reference to a human intellect. Even if there were no human intellects, things could be said to be true because of their relation to the divine intellect. But if, by an impossible supposition, intellect did not exist and things did continue to exist, then the essentials of truth would in no way remain.

* * *

Article III

IN THE THIRD ARTICLE WE ASK: IS TRUTH ONLY IN THE INTELLECT JOINING AND SEPARATING?

1'. In the *Metaphysics*[14] we read: "The true and the false are not in things but in the mind. In regard to simple natures and quiddities, however, it is not in the mind."

2'. In *The Soul*[14] the statement is made that the true and the false are not to be found in simple apprehension.

REPLY:

Just as the true is found primarily in the intellect rather than in things, so also is it found primarily in an act of the intellect joining and separating, rather than in an act by which it forms the quiddities of things. For the nature of the true consists in a conformity of thing and intellect. Nothing becomes conformed with itself, but conformity requires distinct terms. Consequently, the nature of truth is first found in the intellect when the intellect begins to possess something proper to itself, not possessed by the thing outside the soul, yet cor-

[14]From these two works of Aristotle, St. Thomas indicates his own doctrine that truth is had only in the judgment, "joining and separating," and not in the order of simple apprehension or of concepts, where are had the "quiddities of things."

responding to it, so that between the two—intellect and thing—a conformity may be found.[15] In forming the quiddities of things, the intellect merely has a likeness of a thing existing outside the soul, as a sense has a likeness when it receives the species of a sensible thing. But when the intellect begins to judge about the thing it has apprehended, then its judgment is something proper to itself—not something found outside in the thing. And the judgment is said to be true when it conforms to the external reality. Moreover, the intellect judges about the thing it has apprehended at the moment when it says that something is or is not. This is the role of "the intellect composing and dividing."

For these reasons, the Philosopher says that composition and division are in the intellect, and not in things. Moreover, this is why truth is found primarily in the joining and separating by the intellect, and only secondarily in its formation of the quiddities of things or definitions, for a definition is called true or false because of a true or false combination. For it may happen that a definition will be applied to something to which it does not belong, as when the definition of a circle is assigned to a triangle. Sometimes, too, the parts of a definition cannot be reconciled, as happens when one defines a thing as "an animal entirely without the power of sensing." The judgment implied in such a definition—"some animal is incapable of sensing"—is false. Consequently, a definition is said to be true or false only because of its relation to a judgment, as a thing is said to be true because of its relation to intellect.

From our discussion, then, it is clear that the true is predicated, first of all, of joining and separating by the intellect; second, of the definitions of things in so far as they imply a true or a false judgment. Third, the true may be predicated of things in so far as they are conformed with the divine intellect or in so far as, by their very nature, they can be conformed with human intellects. Fourth, true or false may be predicated of man in so far as he chooses to express truth, or in so far as he gives a true or false impression of himself or of others by his words and actions; for truth can be predicated of words in the same way as it can be predicated of the ideas which they convey.

* * *

Article V

IN THE FIFTH ARTICLE WE ASK: IS SOME TRUTH BESIDES THE FIRST TRUTH ETERNAL?

1'. No creature is eternal, and every truth, except the first, is created. Therefore, only the first truth is eternal.

2'. Being and the true are interchangeable. But only one being is eternal. Therefore, only one truth is eternal.

[15] Truth is essentially this relation of conformity, hence the two terms of the relation are needed — not that both need to be now existing, since I can know something which existed or will exist. Moreover, this relation is not reciprocal: it is a real relation only in one of the terms. The relation from knower to known is real, for knowers really know. The relation from known to knower is only conceptual or logical, for to be known does not really add anything to that which is.

REPLY:

As mentioned previously, truth means a proportion and commensuration. Hence, something is said to be true just as something is said to be commensurate. A body, however, is measured both by an intrinsic measure, such as a line, surface, or depth, and by an extrinsic measure, such as happens when a located body is measured by place, or when motion is measured by time, or a piece of cloth by an elbow length. Similarly, a thing can receive the name *true* in two ways: by its inherent truth or by an extrinsic truth. In this latter way, all things receive the name *true* from the first truth; and since truth in the intellect is measured by things themselves, it follows that not only the truth of things, but also the truth of the intellect or of a proposition signifying what is understood, gets its name from the first truth.

In this commensuration or conformity of intellect and thing it is not necessary that each of the two actually exist. Our intellect can be in conformity with things that, although not existing now, will exist in the future. Otherwise, it would not be true to say that "the Antichrist will be born." Hence, a proposition is said to be true because of the truth that is in the intellect alone even when the thing stated does not exist. Similarly, the divine intellect can be in conformity with things that did not exist externally but were created in time; thus, those in time can be said to be true from eternity because of the eternal truth.

If we take truth, therefore, as meaning the inherent truth of true created things—the truth we find in things and in a created intellect—then truth is not eternal whether it be that of things or that of propositions; for neither the things themselves nor the intellect in which these truths inhere exists from all eternity. On the other hand, if we take it to mean the truth of true created things, by which all are said to be true—their extrinsic measure, as it were, which is the first truth—then the truth of everything—of things, propositions, and intellects—is eternal. Both Augustine and Anselm search for an eternal truth of this sort; the latter writes: "You can understand how I have proved in my *Monologion* that the highest truth does not have a beginning or end from the truth that is in speech."

This first truth must be one for all things. For in our intellect truth is multiplied in only two ways: first, by the multiplicity of the things known, for this results in a multiplicity of conceptions upon which there follows a multiplicity of truths in our soul; second, by the multiplicity of our ways of knowing, for even though Socrates' running is one thing, the soul understands time along with it by joining and separating- as it is said in *The Soul*. Consequently, the soul knows his running as present, as past, and as future—each in a different way. Accordingly, it forms separate conceptions in which separate truths are found. In divine knowledge, however, neither of these two kinds of diversity can be found. For God does not have separate acts of knowing for separate things, but by one act He knows all, since He knows all by a single principle, that is, by His essence, as Dionysius points out, and He does not direct His act of knowing toward things one by one. Similarly, too, His own act of knowng does not involve time, since it s measured by eternity, which abstracts from all time inasmuch as t embraces all. It remains, therefore, that there are not many truths rom eternity, but one alone.

* * *

Article VI

IN THE SIXTH ARTICLE WE ASK: IS CREATED TRUTH IMMUTABLE?

Effects are changed when their causes are changed. But things, which cause the truth of a proposition, undergo changes. Therefore, the truth of propositions changes.

REPLY:

A thing is said to be changed in two ways. First, because it is the subject of a change, as when we say that a body is changeable. In this meaning, no form is said to be changeable. Consequently, a form is said to be something steadfast in an unchanging essence; since truth consists in a form, the present question is not whether truth is mutable in this sense. Second, a thing is said to be changed because something else changes according to it, as when we say that whiteness is changed because a body is changed in its whiteness. It is in this sense that we ask whether or not the truth is changeable.

To clarify this point, we should note that the thing according to which there is a change is sometimes said to be changed and sometimes not. For, when it is inhering in a thing which is affected in its respect, then it is said to be changed itself—as whiteness or quantity is said to be changed when something is changed in their respect because they succeed each other in a subject. When, however, that according to which the change occurs is extrinsic, the thing itself is not changed but remains unaffected throughout the whole change. For example, a place is not said to be moved when a thing moves with respect to it. For this reason, it is said in the *Physics* that place is "the unchangeable boundary of the container," because local motion does not mean a succession of loci in regard to one located body, but a succession of many located bodies in one place.

Now, there are two ways in which inhering forms are said to be changed with respect to a change of their subject; for general forms are said to be changed in one way and special forms in another. After a change, a special form does not remain the same either according to its act of existing or according to its intelligible character. For example, when a qualitative change has been made, whiteness does not remain at all. But, after a change has been made, a general form retains the same intelligible character, though not the same act of existing. For example, after a change from white to black has taken place, color, according to the general character of color, remains unchanged; but the same species of color does not remain.

It was noted previously, however, that a thing is said to be true by the first truth as by an extrinsic measure; but it is said to be true by an inherent truth as by an intrinsic measure. Consequently, created things change in their participation of the first truth, yet the first truth itself, according to which they are said to be true, does not change in any way. This is what Augustine says: "Our minds sometimes see more, sometimes less, of truth itself; but truth itself remains, and neither increases nor decreases."

If we take truth as inherent in things, however, then truth is said to be changed inasmuch as some things are said to be changed with respect to truth. For, as pointed out previously, truth in creatures is found in two different subjects: in things themselves and in intellect. The truth of an action is included in the truth of a thing, and the truth of a proposition is included in the truth of the understanding which it signifies. A thing, however, is said to be true by its relation to intellect, divine and human.

Consequently, if the truth of a thing is considered according to its reference to the divine intellect, then, indeed, the truth of a changeable thing is changed into another truth, but not into falsity. For truth is a most general form because the true and being are interchangeable. Hence, just as, even after any change has been made, a thing nevertheless remains a being, although it is other as a result of the other form by which it has existence; so, also, a thing always remains true — but by another truth; for, no matter what form or what privation[16] it acquires through the change, it is conformed in that respect to the divine intellect, which knows it as it is, whatever may be its state.

If, however, the truth of a thing is considered in its reference to a human intellect, or conversely, then sometimes there is a change from truth into falsity, sometimes from one truth to another. For truth is "an equation of thing and intellect"; and, if equal amounts are taken from things that are equal, these things remain equal, although the equality is not the same. Hence, when intellect and thing are similarly changed, truth remains; but it is another truth. For example, when Socrates sits, what is understood is that Socrates is sitting. Afterwards, when he does not sit, what is understood is that he is not sitting. But, if something is taken from one of two equal things, and nothing from the other, or if unequal amounts are taken from each, then inequality must result; and this corresponds to falsity, just as equality corresponds to truth.

Consequently, if an intellect is true, and it is not changed when a thing is changed, or vice versa, or if each is changed but not similarly, falsity results, and there will be a change from truth to falsity. For example, if, when Socrates is white, he is understood to be white, the intellect is true. If, however, the intellect later understands him to be black, although Socrates still is white; or if, conversely, he is still understood to be white, although he has turned black; or if, when he has turned pale, he is understood to be reddish—then there will be falsity in the intellect. Accordingly, it is clear how truth changes and how it does not.[17]

* * *

[16]Form may be looked on in general as any perfection, on whatever level of being it may be; privation means lack of a perfection.

[17]From the context, it is clear that when St. Thomas speaks of truth chang-

Article IX

IN THE NINTH ARTICLE WE ASK: IS TRUTH IN SENSE?

Difficulties:

It seems that it is not, for

1. Anselm says: "Truth is a correctness perceivable only by the mind." But sense does not have the same nature as the mind. Hence, truth is not in sense.

2. Augustine proves that truth is not known by the bodily senses, and his reasons were set down above. Hence, truth is not in sense.

To the Contrary:

Augustine says: "Truth manifests that which is." But that which is, is manifested not only to the intellect, but also to sense. Therefore.

REPLY:

Truth is both in intellect and in sense, but not in the same way. It is in intellect as a consequence of the act of the intellect and as known by the intellect. Truth follows the operation of the intellect inasmuch as it belongs to the intellect to judge about a thing as it is. And truth is known by the intellect in view of the fact that the intellect reflects upon its own act—not merely as knowing its own act, but as knowing the proportion of its act to the thing. Now, this proportion cannot be known without knowing the nature of the act; and the nature of the act cannot be known without knowing the nature of the active principle, that is, the intellect itself, to whose nature it belongs to be conformed to things. Consequently, it is because the intellect reflects upon itself that it knows truth.

Truth is in sense also as a consequence of its act, for sense judges of things as they are. Truth is not in sense, however, as something known by sense; for, although sense judges truly about things, it does not know the truth by which it truly judges. Although sense knows that it senses, it does not know its own nature; consequently, it knows neither the nature of its act nor the proportion of this act to things.[18] As a result, it does not know its truth.

The reason for this is that the most perfect beings, such as, for example, intellectual substances return to their essence with a complete return: knowing something external to themselves, in a certain sense they go outside of themselves; but by knowing that they know, they are already beginning to return to themselves, because the act of cognition mediates between the knower and the thing known. That return is completed inasmuch as they know their own essences. Hence, it is said in *The Causes*: "A being which is such as to know its own essence

ing, he is worlds removed from the Relativism found in contemporary philosophers. For St. Thomas, while things may and do change, and our knowledge of them must change accordingly, still in every instance truth consists in conformity to *what is*, and is not wholly dependent on the knower. Cf. *Theories of Knowledge*, Chaps. 4, 17.

[18]This is a fundamental difference between sense knowledge and intellectual knowledge. The latter involves full self-consciousness, whereby it knows itself as a knowing nature; the former cannot arrive at such self-awareness because of its material limitations. Cf. Theories of Knowledge, Chap. 2.

returns to it by a complete return."

Since sense is closer to an intellectual substance than other things are, it begins to return to its essence; it not only knows the sensible, but it also knows that it senses. Its return, however, is not complete, since it does not know its own essence. Avicenna has given the reason for this by pointing out that the sense knows nothing except through a bodily organ, and a bodily organ cannot be a medium between a sensing power and itself. But powers without any ability to sense cannot return to themselves in any way, for they do not know that they are acting. For example, fire does not know that it is heating.

From this discussion the solutions to the difficulties are clear.

Article X

IN THE TENTH ARTICLE WE ASK: IS THERE ANY FALSE THING?

Difficulties:

It seems not, for

1. According to Augustine: "The true is that which is." Hence, the false is that which is not. Now, what is not is not a thing. Therefore, no thing is false.

2. It was said that the true is a differentia of being; consequently, the false, like the true, is that which is.—On the contrary, no dividing differentia is interchangeable with that whose differentia it is. Now, as was said, the true is interchangeable with being. Consequently, the true is not a dividing differentia of being, for this would make it possible to call some thing false.

3. Truth is a conformity of thing and intellect. Now, all things are conformed to the divine intellect, since in itself nothing can be other than it is known to be by the divine intellect. Hence, all things are true, and nothing is false.

4. All things possess truth from their forms. For example, one is said to be a true man if he has the true form of a man. But there is nothing which does not have some form, for every act of existing comes from form. Hence, everything is true, and there is no thing which is false.

5. Good and evil are related as true and false are related. Now, since evil is found in things, it has concrete reality only in something good as Dionysius and Augustine say. Therefore, if falseness is found in things, it can have reality only in what is true. But this does not seem possible, for then the same thing would be both true and false; but this is impossible. This would mean, for example, that man and white are the same because whiteness is made real in a man.

6. Augustine proposes the following difficulty. If a thing is called false, it is either because it is similar or because it is dissimilar. "If because it is dissimilar, there is nothing that cannot be called false, for there is nothing that is not unlike something else. If because it is similar, all things loudly protest, for they are true because they are similar." Therefore, falsity cannot be found in things in any way.

To the Contrary:

1'. Augustine defines the false as follows: "The false is that which approaches the likeness of something else without being that whose likeness it bears." But every creature bears the likeness of God. Therefore, since no creature is identical with God Himself, it seems that every creature is false.

2'. Augustine says that "Every body is a true body and a false unity." Now, a body is said to be false because it imitates unity, yet is not a unity. Therefore, since every creature, in so far as it is perfect, imitates the divine perfection, and, nevertheless, in any perfection which it has, remains infinitely distant from it, it seems that every creature is false.

3'. The good, like the true, is interchangeable with being. But the interchangeability of the good and being does not stand in the way of a thing's being evil. Therefore, the fact that the true is interchangeable with being does not stand in the way of a thing's being false.

4'. Anselm says that there are two kinds of truth in propositions. "The first type occurs when the proposition has the meaning which was given to it." For example, this proposition, "Socrates sits," means that Socrates is sitting, whether he is actually sitting or not. "The second type of truth occurs when the proposition signifies that for which it was formed"—and it has been formed to signify that something is when it is. In this respect, a proposition is properly said to be true. In the same way, a thing may be called true when it fulfills its purpose, and false when it does not do so. But everything which falls short of its end does not fulfill its purpose; and, since there are many things of this sort, it seems that many things are false.

REPLY:

Just as truth consists in an equation of thing and intellect, so falsity consists in an inequality between them. Now, as was said, a thing is related to divine and human intellects. In regard to everything that is positively predicated of things or found in them, it is related to the divine in one way as the measured to its measure; for all such things come from the divine intellect's art. A thing is related in another way to the divine intellect: as a thing known is related to the knower. In this way even negations and defects are equated to the divine intellect, since God knows all these even though He does not cause them. It is clear, then, that a thing is conformed to the divine intellect in whatever way it exists, under any form whatsoever or even under a privation or a defect. Consequently, it is clear that everything is true in its relation to the divine intellect. Hence, Anselm says: "There is, then, truth in the essence of all things which are, for they are what they are in the highest truth." Therefore, in its relation to the divine intellect, nothing can be false.

In its relation to a human intellect, however, an inequality of thing with intellect, caused in some way by the thing, is occasionally found; for a thing makes itself known in the soul by its exterior appearance, since our cognition takes its beginning from sense, whose direct object is sensible qualities. For this reason it is said in *The Soul*: "Accidents greatly contribute to our knowledge of the quiddity." Consequently, when there are manifested in any object sensible qualities indicating a nature which does not actually underlie them, that thing is said to be false.

Hence, the Philosopher says that those things are called false "which are such as to seem to be what they are not, or of a kind which they are not." For example, that is called "false" gold which has in its external appearance the color and other accidents of genuine gold, whereas the nature of gold does not interiorly underlie them. But a thing is not to be the cause of falsity in the soul in the sense that it necessarily causes falsity; for truth and falsity exist principally in the soul's judgment; and the soul, inasmuch as it judges about things, is not acted upon by things, but rather, in a sense, acts upon them. Hence, a thing is not said to be false because it always of itself causes a false apprehension, but rather because its natural appearance is likely to cause a false apprehension.

As was pointed out previously, however, the relation to the divine intellect is essential to a thing; and in this respect a thing is said to be true in itself. Its relation to the human intellect is accidental to it; and in this respect a thing is not true, absolutely speaking but, as it were, in some respect and in potency. Therefore, all things are true absolutely speaking, and nothing is false. But in a certain respect, that is, with reference to our intellect, some things are said to be false. Hence, it is necessary to answer the arguments of both sides.

Answers to Difficulties:

1. The definition, "The true is that which is," does not perfectly express the intelligible character of truth. It expresses it, as it were, only materially, unless *is* here signifies the affirmation of a proposition, and means that a thing is said to be true when it is said to be or to be understood as it is in reality. Taken in this sense, the false may be said to be that which does not exist; it is not as it is said or understood to be. And this type of falsity can be found in things.

2. Properly speaking, the true cannot be a differentia of being, for being does not have any differentia, as is proved in the *Metaphysics*. But in some sense the true, as well as the good, is related to being in the manner of a differentia, since it expresses something about being which is not expressed by the noun *being;* and in this sense the meaning of being is indeterminate with respect to the meaning of the true. Consequently, the meaning of the true is compared to the notion of being somewhat as a differentia is compared to its genus.

3. That argument must be conceded, since it treats a thing in its relation to the divine intellect.

4. All things have some form, yet not everything has that form whose characteristics are externally manifested by sensible qualities; and it is in regard to these that a thing is said to be false if it is naturally apt to produce a false estimation about itself.

5. As is clear from what has been said, something outside the soul is said to be false if it is naturally such as to give a false impression of itself. But what is nothing is not capable of making any impression, since it does not move a knowing power. What is said to be false, therefore, must be a being; and since every being, in so far as it is a being, is true, falsity must exist in things and be based upon some truth. For this reason Augustine says that a tragedian representing true persons in dramas would not be false

without being a true tragedian. Similarly, a painting of a horse would not be a false horse were it not a true picture. It does not follow, however, that contradictories are true, because the affirmation and the negation in expressing the true and the false do not refer to the same reality.

6. A thing is said to be false in so far as, by its nature, it is likely to deceive. When I say *deceive*, however, I mean an action that brings on some defect; for nothing can act except to the extent that it is being, and every defect is non-being. Moreover, everything has some likeness to the true to the extent that it is a being; and in so far as it does not exist it departs from this likeness. Consequently, this *deceiving* as implying action arises from likeness; but the defect it implies (and in which the intelligible character of falsity formally consists) arises from unlikeness. Hence, Augustine says that falsity arises from unlikeness.

Answers to Contrary Difficulties:

1'. The soul is not so constituted as to be deceived by any likeness whatsoever, but only by a considerable resemblance which makes it difficult to discover the unlikeness. Hence, the soul is deceived by similarities, more or less great, according to the varying degrees of its acuteness in discovering unlikenesses. A thing, however, should not be said to be absolutely false because it leads into error, however much it may do that, but only because it is such as to deceive many or highly intelligent men. Now, although creatures bear some resemblance to God in themselves, so great is the dissimilarity between the two that only because of great stupidity could it happen that a mind would be deceived by such similarity. Hence, from the similarity and dissimilarity between creatures and God, it does not follow that all creatures should be called false.

2'. Some have thought that God is a body; and, since He is the unity by which all things are one, they consequently thought that body was unity itself, because of its likeness to unity. Therefore, a body is called a false unity for this reason, that it has led or could lead some into the error of believing it to be unity.

3'. There are two kinds of perfection, first and second. First perfection is the form of each thing, and that by which it has its act of existing. Nothing is without it while it continues in existence. Second perfection is operation, which is the end of a thing or the means by which a thing reaches its end; and a thing is sometimes deprived of this perfection. The note of truth in things results from first perfection; for it is because a thing has a form that it imitates the art of the divine intellect and produces knowledge of itself in the soul. But the note of goodness in things results from its second perfection, for this goodness arises from the end. Consequently, evil, but not falsity, is found in things absolutely.

4'. According to the Philosopher, the true itself is the good of the intellect, for an operation of intellect is perfect because its concept is true. And since a proposition is a sign of what is understood, truth is its end. But this is not the case with other things, and so there is no similarity.

Article XI

IN THE ELEVENTH ARTICLE WE ASK:
IS FALSITY IN SENSE?

Difficulties:

It seems that it is not, for

1. As is said in *The Soul:* "The intellect is always correct." Now, since the intellect is the superior part of man, his other parts must also pursue correctness - just as the disposition of lower bodies in the universe depends on the motion of the higher bodies. Therefore, sense, which is the inferior part of the soul, will also always be correct; there is, then, no falsity in it.

2. Augustine says: "Our eyes do not deceive us: they can report to the mind only their own modification. And if all the bodily senses report as they are affected, I do not know what more we can require of them." Hence, there is no falsity in the senses.

3. Anselm says: "It seems to me that truth or falsity is not in the sense but in opinion." This confirms our thesis.

To the Contrary:

1'. Anselm says: "Truth is, indeed, in our senses, but not always; for they sometimes deceive us."

2'. According to Augustine: "A thing is called false because it is far from being a likeness of the true, even though it does in some way imitate the true." Now, a sense has at times a likeness of certain things other than they are in reality. For example, when the eye is pressed, one thing is sometimes seen as two. Consequently, there is falsity in sense.

3'. The answer was given that sense is not deceived with regard to proper sensibles, but only with regard to common sensibles.—On the contrary, whenever something is apprehended about a thing other than it is, the apprehension is false. Now, when a white body is seen through a green glass, the sense apprehends it other than it is, for it sees it as green and judges accordingly—unless a higher judgment is present, detecting the falsity. Therefore, sense is deceived even with regard to proper sensibles.

REPLY:

Our knowledge, taking its start from things, proceeds in this order. First, it begins in sense; second, it is completed in the intellect. As a consequence, sense is found to be in some way an intermediary between the intellect and things; for with reference to things, it is, as it were, an intellect, and with reference to intellect, it is, as it were, a thing. Hence, truth or falsity is said to be in sense in two respects. The first is in the relation of sense to intellect. In this respect, the sense is said to be true or false as a thing is, namely, in so far as it causes a true or false judgment in the intellect. The second respect is in the relation of sense to things. In this, truth and falsity are said to be in sense as they are said to be in the intellect, namely, in so far as the sense judges that what is, is or is not.

Hence, if we speak of a sense in the first meaning, in a way there is falsity in sense, and in a way there is not. For sense, in itself, is a thing; and it also passes judgment on other things. If, in its relation to the intellect, it is considered as a thing, then there is no falsity in sense; for a sense reveals its state to the intellect exactly as it is affected. Hence, Augustine says, in the passage referred to: "The senses can report to the mind only how they are affected." On the other hand, if sense is considered in its relation to the intellect as representing some other thing, it may be called false in view of the fact that it sometimes represents a thing to the intellect other than it actually is. For, in that case, as we said about things, it is such as to cause a false judgment in the intellect—but not necessarily, since the intellect judges on what is presented by sense just as it judges about things. Thus, in its relation to the intellect, sense always produces a true judgment in the intellect with respect to its own condition, but not always with respect to the condition of things.

If sense is considered in its relation to things, however, then there are truth and falsity in sense in the manner in which these are in the intellect. For truth and falsity are found primarily and principally in the judgment of the intellect as it associates and dissociates, and in the formation of quiddities, only in their relation to the judgment following upon this formation. Hence, truth and falsity are properly said to be in sense inasmuch as it judges about sensible objects, but inasmuch as it apprehends a sensible object, there is not properly truth or falsity, except in the relation of this apprehension to the judgment, in so far as a judgment of this or that sort naturally follows upon a particular apprehension.

The judgment of sense about certain things—for example, proper sensibles—takes place spontaneously. About other things, however, it takes place by means of a certain comparison, made in man by the cogitative power, a sense power, whose place in animals is taken by a spontaneous estimation. This sensitive power judges about common sensibles and accidental sensibles. However, the spontaneous action of a thing always takes place in one way, unless by accident it is impeded intrinsically by some defect or extrinsically by some impediment. Consequently, the judgment of sense about proper sensibles is always true unless there is an impediment in the organ or in the medium; but its judgment about common or accidental sensibles is sometimes wrong. Thus, it is clear how there can be falsity in the judgment of sense.

As regards the apprehension of the senses, it must be noted that there is one type of apprehensive power, for example, a proper sense, which apprehends a sensible species in the presence of a sensible thing; but there is also a second type, the imagination, for example, which apprehends a sensible species when the thing is absent. So, even though the sense always apprehends a thing as it is, unless there is an impediment in the organ or in the medium, the imagination usually apprehends a thing as it is not, since it apprehends it as present though it is absent. Consequently, the Philosopher says: "Imagination, not sense, is the master of falsity."

Answers to Difficulties:

1. In the macrocosm the higher bodies do not receive anything from the lower. Just the opposite occurs. In man, the microcosm, the intellect, which is superior, does receive

something from sense. Hence, no parallel can be made.

2-3. Our previous discussion will easily answer the other difficulties.

Article XII

IN THE TWELFTH ARTICLE WE ASK: IS FALSITY IN INTELLECT?

Difficulties:

It seems not, for

1. The intellect has two operations. By one it forms quiddities, and, as the Philosopher says, the false is not in this. By the other it joins and separates, and the false is not in this either, as is clear from Augustine's saying: "No one has intellectual knowledge of false things." Consequently, falsity is not in the intellect.

2. According to Augustine: "Whoever is deceived does not understand that in which he is deceived." The intellect is always true, therefore, and there can be no falsity in it.

3. Algazel says: "Either we understand something as it is or we do not understand." But whoever understands a thing as it is truly understands it. Therefore, the intellect is always true, and there is no falsity in it.

To the Contrary:

The Philosopher says: "Where there is a joining of concepts, there the true and the false begin to be." Hence, falsity is found in the intellect.

REPLY:

The name *intellect* arises from the intellect's ability to know the most profound elements of a thing; for to understand *(intelligere)* means to read what is inside a thing *(intus legere)*. Sense and imagination know only external accidents, but the intellect alone penetrates to the interior and to the essence of a thing. But even beyond this, the intellect, having perceived essences, operates in different ways by reasoning and inquiring. Hence, *intellect* can be taken in two senses.

First, it can be taken merely according to its relation to that from which it first received its name. We are said to understand, properly speaking, when we apprehend the quiddity of things or when we understand those truths that are immediately known by the intellect, once it knows the quiddities of things. For example, first principles are immediately known when we know their terms, and for this reason intellect or understanding is called "a habit of principles." The proper object of the intellect, however, is the quiddity of a thing. Hence, just as the sensing of proper sensibles is always true, so the intellect is always true in knowing *what a thing is*, as is said in *The Soul*. By accident, however, falsity can occur in this knowing of quiddities, if the intellect falsely joins and separates. This happens in two ways: when it attributes the definition of one thing to another, as would happen were it to conceive that "mortal rational animal" were the definition of an ass; or when it joins together parts of definitions that cannot be joined, as would happen were it to conceive that "irrational, immortal animal" were the definition of an ass. For it is false to say that some irrational animal is immortal. So it is clear that a definition cannot be false except to the extent that it implies a false affirmation. (This twofold mode of falsity is touched upon in the *Metaphysics*.) Similarly, the intellect is not deceived in any way with respect to first principles. It is plain, then, that if intellect is taken in the first sense—according to that action from which it receives the name *intellect*—falsity is not in the intellect.

Intellect can also be taken in a second sense—in general, that is, as extending to all its operations, including opinion and reasoning. In that case, there is falsity in the intellect. But it never occurs if a reduction to first principles is made correctly.

From this discussion, the answers to the difficulties are clear.

THE CLASSICAL MODERN PERIOD

Part II

The outstanding feature of this period is its almost exclusive preoccupation with the nature and extent of human knowledge. Descartes' reflections on his ideas eventually led him to introduce a duality of being into human nature because of his position that mind and body are two independent and radically distinct substances. This duality expressed itself in the subsequent lines of philosophical development. Thus, Rationalism stressed the superiority of mind, its independence of sense experience, and its ability to develop *a priori* systems of explanation; whereas Empiricism stressed the limitations of knowledge to the particular, contingent content of actual experiences, and not only despised systems but even hesitated to admit the validity of general ideas and propositions. Again, Idealism emphasized the active, dynamic, even creative role of the mind in knowing, while Realism insisted on the mind's passivity and receptivity. Eventually, Materialism, in the face of the Cartesian dichotomy, ignored or rejected the existence of mind in any sense of "spirit" and contented itself with the material and its powers. Immaterialism, on the other hand, denied the reality of matter and affirmed the existence of spirit alone.

The seeds of all these "isms" and of others are contained in the philosophy of Descartes, and the selections offered for this period, which has now acquired the status of being classical, will illustrate many of them. Thus, the development of ideas introduced by Descartes may be seen as they unfold with a certain logical inevitability in the history of thought.

4

Thought Versus Matter

René Descartes (1596-1650)

Descartes, who has become known as the father of modern philosophy, has to a great extent set the tone and determined the problems which have characterized philosophical investigation for the past three centuries. Distressed by the Scepticism, Atheism, and Materialism of his day and by the sorry state in which philosophy found itself, he attempted a one-man revolution for the avowed purpose of reinstating metaphysics in a secure position of prominence. This, he felt, would be at least well started if he could find irrefutable and convincing proofs for the immateriality of the human soul, for the existence of God, and for the existence of a material world.

The novelty of his approach to philosophy is manifested by his concentrated reflections on ideas, making them the immediate object of knowledge, and by his analyses of them to discover what they had to offer by way of indubitable truths. His studies did awaken new interest in metaphysics. They emphasized anew the active role of the knowing subject, the dynamic character of knowledge, and the importance of method in approaching philosophy.

An outstanding feature of Descartes' reflections is his effort to find and employ some one homogeneous method which would be applicable in every field of scientific knowledge. Impressed as he was by the probative power and certainty of mathematics, he decided that his new method must lie in that direction, and so he aimed at developing a *mathesis universalis*. By omitting the quantitative aspects and by emphasizing the aspects of order and measure in our knowledge of beings of all sorts, he felt that his new method could achieve universal application. Others have also sought some such oneness of method, only to run up against the ever-recurring difficulty that there are various levels of being and different levels of penetration and explanation open to the human mind.

The selections that follow indicate his progress, by the technique of general doubt, to the establishment of his own existence, the existence of God, and the existence of the world.

Serious reflection on Descartes' philosophy will show that the use of the technique of universal doubt cannot logically yield positive fruit; that his ontological proof for the existence of God, bound up in his analyses of the idea of God, smuggles in a leap from the ideal to the existential order; and that his indirect route (from the self to God) to the material world is a tortuous and unnecessary road to travel. All in all, we find in Descartes the rationalistic mode of transit from the order of ideas to the order of existence, and this is open to the age-old objections offered against that procedure.

A DISCOURSE ON METHOD[1]

Part I

Good Sense is, of all things among men, the most equally distributed; for every one thinks himself so abundantly provided with it, that those even who are the most difficult to satisfy in everything else, do not usually desire a larger measure of this quality than they already possess. And in this it is not likely that all are mistaken: the conviction is rather to be held as testifying that the power of judging aright and of distinguishing Truth from Error, which is properly what is called Good Sense or Reason, is by nature equal in all men; and that the diversity of our opinions, consequently, does not arise from some being endowed with a larger share of Reason than others, but solely from this, that we conduct our thoughts along different ways, and do not fix our attention on the same objects. For to be possessed of a vigorous mind is not enough; the prime requisite is rightly to apply it. The greatest minds, as they are capable of the highest excellencies, are open likewise to the greatest aberrations; and those who travel very slowly may yet make far greater progress, provided they keep always to the straight road, than those who, while they run, forsake it.

For myself, I have never fancied my mind to be in any respect more perfect than those of the generality; on the contrary, I have often wished that I were equal to some others in promptitude of thought, or in clearness and distinctness of imagination, or in fulness and readiness of memory. And besides these, I know

[1]Selected from René Descartes, *A Discourse on Method* (1637), Trans. by John Veitch (La Salle, Ill.: Open Court Publishing Co., 1946).

of no other qualities that contribute to the perfection of the mind; for as to the Reason or Sense, inasmuch as it is that alone which constitutes us men, and distinguishes us from the brutes, I am disposed to believe that it is to be found complete in each individual; and on this point to adopt the common opinion of philosophers, who say that the difference of greater and less holds only among the *accidents*, and not among the *forms* or *natures* of *individuals* of the same *species*.

I will not hesitate, however, to avow my belief that it has been my singular good fortune to have very early in life fallen in with certain tracks which have conducted me to considerations and maxims, of which I have formed a Method that gives me the means, as I think, of gradually augmenting my knowledge, and of raising it by little and little to the highest point which the mediocrity of my talents and the brief duration of my life will permit me to reach. For I have already reaped from it such fruits that, although I have been accustomed to think lowly enough of myself, and although when I look with the eye of a philosopher at the varied courses and pursuits of mankind at large, I find scarcely one which does not appear vain and useless, I nevertheless derive the highest satisfaction from the progress I conceive myself to have already made in the search after truth, and cannot help entertaining such expectations of the future as to believe that if, among occupations of men as men, there is any one really excellent and important, it is that which I have chosen.

After all, it is possible I may be mistaken; and it is but a little copper and glass, perhaps, that I take for gold and diamonds. I know how very liable we are to delusion in what relates to ourselves, and also how much the judgments of our friends are to be suspected when given in our favour. But I shall endeavour in this Discourse to describe the paths I have followed, and to delineate my life as in a picture, in order that each one may be able to judge of them for himself, and that in the general opinion entertained of them, as gathered from current report, I myself may have a new help towards instruction to be added to those I have been in the habit of employing.

My present design, then, is not to teach the Method which each ought to follow for the right conduct of his reason, but solely to describe the way in which I have endeavoured to conduct my own. They who set themselves to give percepts must of course regard themselves as possessed of greater skill than those to whom they prescribe; and if they err in the slightest particular, they subject themselves to censure. But as this Tract is put forth merely as a history, or, if you will, as a tale, in which, amid some examples worthy of imitation, there will be found, perhaps, as many more which it were advisable not to follow, I hope it will prove useful to some without being hurtful to any, and that my openness will find some favour with all.

* * *

Part II

I cannot in any degree approve of those restless and busy meddlers who, called neither by birth nor fortune to take part in the management of public affairs, are yet always projecting reforms; and if I thought that this Tract contained aught which might justify the suspicion that I was a victim of such folly, I would by no means permit its publication. I have never contemplated anything higher than the reformation of my own opinions, and basing them on a foundation wholly my own. And although my own satisfaction with my work has led me to present here a draft of it, I do not by any means therefore recommend to every one else to make a similar attempt. Those whom God has endowed with a larger measure of genius will entertain, perhaps, designs still more exalted; but for the many I am much afraid lest even the present undertaking be more than they can safely venture to imitate. The single design to strip one's self of all past beliefs is one that ought not to be taken by every one. The majority of men is composed of two classes, for neither of which would this be at all a befitting resolution: in the *first* place, of those who with more than a due confidence in their own powers, are precipitate in their judgments and want the patience requisite for orderly and circumspect thinking; whence it happens, that if men of this class once take the liberty to doubt of their accustomed opinions, and quit the beaten highway, they will never be able to thread the byeway that would lead them by a shorter course, and will lose themselves and continue to wander for life; in the *second* place, of those who, possessed of sufficient sense or modesty to determine that there are others who excel them in the power of discriminating between truth and error, and by whom they may be instructed, ought rather to content themselves with the opinions of such than trust for more correct to their own Reason.

For my own part, I should doubtless have belonged to the latter class, had I received instruction from but one master, or had never known the diversities of opinion that from time immemorial have prevailed among men of the greatest learning. But I had become aware even so early as during my college life, that no opinion, however absurd and incredible, can be imagined, which has not been maintained by some one of the philosophers; and afterwards in the course of my travels I remarked that all those whose opinions are decidedly repugnant to ours are not on that account barbarians and savages, but on the contrary that many of these nations make an equally good, if not a better, use of their Reason than we do. I took into account also the very different character which a person brought up from infancy in France or Germany exhibits, from that which, with the same mind originally, this individual would have possessed had he lived always among the Chinese or with savages; and the circumstance that in dress itself the fashion which pleased us ten years ago, and which may again, perhaps, be received into favour before ten years have gone, appears to us at this moment extravagant and ridiculous. I was thus led to infer that the ground of our opinions is far more custom and example than any certain knowledge. And, finally, although such be the ground of our opinions, I remarked that a plurality of suffrages is no guarantee of truth where it is at all of difficult discovery, as in such cases it is much more likely that it will be found by one than by many. I could, however, select from the crowd no one whose opinions seemed worthy of preference, and thus I found myself constrained, as it were, to use my own Reason in the conduct of my life.

But like one walking alone and in the dark, I resolved to proceed so slowly and with such circumspection, that if I did not advance far, I would at least guard against falling. I did not even choose to dismiss summarily any of the opinions that had crept into my belief without having been introduced by Reason, but first of all took sufficient time carefully to satisfy myself of the general nature of the task I was setting myself, and ascertain the true Method by which to arrive at the knowledge of whatever lay within the compass of my powers.

Among the branches of Philosophy, I had, at an earlier period, given some attention to Logic, and among those of the Mathematics to Geometrical Analysis and Algebra—three arts or Sciences which ought, as I conceived, to contribute something to my design. But, on examination, I found that, as for Logic, its syllogisms and the majority of its other precepts are of avail rather in the communication of what we already know, or even as the Art of Lully, in speaking without judgment of things of which we are ignorant, than in the investigation of the unknown; and although this Science contains indeed a number of correct and very excellent precepts, there are, nevertheless, so many others, and these either injurious or superfluous, mingled with the former, that it is almost quite as difficult to effect a severance of the true from the false as it is to extract a Diana or a Minerva from a rough block of marble. Then as to the Analysis of the ancients and the Algebra of the moderns, besides that they embrace only matters highly abstract, and, to appearance, of no use, the former is so exclusively restricted to the consideration of figures, that it can exercise the Understanding only on condition of greatly fatiguing the Imagination; and, in the latter, there is so complete a subjection to certain rules and formulas, that there results an art full of confusion and obscurity calculated to embarrass, instead of a science fitted to cultivate the mind. By these considerations I was induced to seek some other Method which would comprise the advantages of the three and be exempt from their defects. And as a multitude of laws often only hampers justice, so that a state is best governed when, with few laws, these are rigidly administered; in like manner, instead of the great number of precepts of which Logic is composed, I believed that the four following would prove perfectly sufficient for me, provided I took the firm and unwavering resolution never in a single instance to fail in observing them.[2]

[2]These rules *verbally* express nothing but an honest and sincere desire to be careful, objective, and accurate. As such, they not only reflect the influence on Descartes of previous logicians, but

The *first* was never to accept anything for true which I did not clearly know to be such; that is to say, carefully to avoid precipitancy and prejudice, and to comprise nothing more in my judgment than what was presented to my mind so clearly and distinctly as to exclude all ground of doubt.

The *second*, to divide each of the difficulties under examination into as many parts as possible, and as might be necessary for its adequate solution.

The *third*, to conduct my thoughts in such order that, by commencing with objects the simplest and easiest to know, I might ascend by little and little, and, as it were, step by step, to the knowledge of the more complex; assigning in thought a certain order even to those objects which in their own nature do not stand in a relation of antecedence and sequence.

And the *last*, in every case to make enumerations so complete, and reviews so general, that I might be assured that nothing was omitted.

The long chains of simple and easy reasonings by means of which geometers are accustomed to reach the conclusions of their most difficult demonstrations, had led me to imagine that all things, to the knowledge of which man is competent, are mutually connected in the same way, and that there is nothing so far removed from us as to be beyond our reach, or so hidden that we cannot discover it, provided only we abstain from accepting the false for the true, and always preserve in our thoughts the order necessary for the deduction of one truth from another. And I had little difficulty in determining the objects with which it was necessary to commence, for I was already persuaded that it must be with the simplest and easiest to know, and, considering that of all those who have hitherto sought truth in the Sciences, the mathematicians alone have been able to find any demonstrations, that is, any certain and evident reasons, I did not doubt but that such must have been the rule of their investigations. I resolved to commence, therefore, with the examination of the simplest objects, not anticipating, however, from this any other advantage than that to be found in accustoming my mind to the love and nourishment of truth, and to a distaste for all such reasonings as were unsound. But I had no intention on that account of attempting to master all the particular Sciences commonly denominated Mathematics: but observing that, however different their objects, they all agree in considering only the various relations or proportions subsisting among those objects, I thought it best for my purpose to consider these proportions in the most general form possible, without referring them to

---

also recommend themselves to the serious searcher after truth. However, better acquaintance with Descartes, and with the manner in which he concretely applies these rules, shows that (1) the first rule functions only through Cartesian methodic doubt and involves his desire to argue from the ideal to the real order; (2) the second rule calls for a resolutive analysis, difficult or impossible of realization, and much stressed by Descartes; (3) the third rule implies the acceptance of a chain of truths going from the self to God and then to the material world; and (4) the final rule aims at a homogeneous body of wisdom, through a single intuitive habit of mind. Thus in each there is a definite Cartesian twist.

any objects in particular, except such as would most facilitate the knowledge of them, and without by any means restricting them to these, that afterwards I might thus be the better able to apply them to every other class of objects to which they are legitimately applicable. Perceiving further, that in order to understand these relations I should sometimes have to consider them one by one, and sometimes only to bear them in mind, or embrace them in the aggregate, I thought that, in order the better to consider them individually, I should view them as subsisting between straight lines, than which I could find no objects more simple, or capable of being more distinctly represented to my imagination and senses; and on the other hand, that in order to retain them in the memory, or embrace an aggregate of many, I should express them by certain characters the briefest possible. In this way I believed that I could borrow all that was best both in Geometrical Analysis and in Algebra, and correct all the defects of the one by help of the other.

* * *

Part IV

I am in doubt as to the propriety of making my first meditations ... matter of discourse; for these are so metaphysical, and so uncommon, as not, perhaps, to be acceptable to every one. And yet, that it may be determined whether the foundations that I have laid are sufficiently secure, I find myself in a measure constrained to advert to them. I had long before remarked that, in relation to practice, it is sometimes necessary to adopt, as if above doubt, opinions which we discern to be highly uncertain, as has been already said; but as I then desired to give my attention solely to the search after truth, I thought that a procedure exactly the opposite was called for, and that I ought to reject as absolutely false all opinions in regard to which I could suppose the least ground for doubt,[3] in order to ascertain whether after that there remained aught in my belief that was wholly indubitable. Accordingly, seeing that our senses sometimes deceive us, I was willing to suppose that there existed nothing really such as they presented to us; and because some men err in reasoning, and fall into paralogisms, even on the simplest matters of Geometry, I, convinced that I was as open to error as any other, rejected as false all the reasonings I had hitherto taken for demonstrations; and finally, when I considered that the very same thoughts (presentations) which we experience when awake may also be experienced when we are asleep, while there is at that time not one of them true, I supposed that all the objects (presentations) that had ever entered into my mind when awake, had in them no more truth than the illusions of my dreams. But immediately upon that I observed that, whilst I thus wished to think that all was false, it was absolutely

[3]This deliberate treatment of the *doubtful* as *false* is a basic trait in Cartesian method. Even on face value it does not appear a reasonable way in which to treat the doubtful.

necessary that I, who thus thought, should be somewhat; and as I observed that this truth, *I think, hence I am,* was so certain and of such evidence, that no ground of doubt, however extravagant, could be alleged by the Sceptics capable of shaking it, I concluded that I might, without scruple, accept it as the first principle of the Philosophy of which I was in search.[4]

In the next place, I attentively examined what I was, and as I observed that I could suppose that I had no body, and that there was no world nor any place in which I might be; but that I could not therefore suppose that I was not; and that, on the contrary, from the very circumstance that I thought to doubt of the truth of other things, it most clearly and certainly followed that I was; while, on the other hand, if I had only ceased to think, although all the other objects which I had ever imagined had been in reality existent, I would have had no reason to believe that I existed; I thence concluded that I was a substance whose whole essence or nature consists only in thinking, and which, that it may exist, has need of no place, nor is dependent on any material thing; so that "I," that is to say, the mind by which I am what I am, is wholly distinct from the body, and is even more easily known than the latter, and is such, that although the latter were not, it would still continue to be all that it is.

After this I inquired in general into what is essential to the truth and certainty of a proposition; for since I had discovered one which I knew to be true, I thought that I must likewise be able to discover the ground of this certitude. And as I observed that in the words *I think, hence I am,* there is nothing at all which gives me assurance of their truth beyond this, that I see very clearly that in order to think it is necessary to exist, I concluded that I might take, as a general rule, the principle, that all the things which we very clearly and distinctly conceive are true, only observing, however, that there is some difficulty in rightly determining the objects which we distinctly conceive.[5]

In the next place, from reflecting on the circumstance that I doubted, and that consequently my being was not wholly perfect, (for I clearly saw that it was a greater perfection to know than to doubt,) I was led to inquire whence I had learned to think of something more perfect

[4]The preceding has always been the subject of much comment, since it lies in fact at the very heart of Descartes' philosophy. No detailed study can be made here, but the following remarks can be offered for consideration: (1) The wholesale rejection of sensation, reasoning, and of all objects would seem to necessitate the rejection, as false, of many things which are experienced as evidently as one's own existence. (2) The subsequent history of this approach has shown that one's own existence, in the Cartesian sense, is not satisfactory as *the* first noetic principle. (3) Descartes' *cogito* concretely means a sort of Mentalism with the concomitant false problem of how one gets from the ideal order to the order of existence. (4) In what immediately follows on the nature of the self as a "substance whose whole essence or nature consists only in thinking," and on the self as a "mind" which is more easily known than the body, there is good reason, based on experience, to disagree sharply with Descartes.

[5]This is the Cartesian criterion of clear and distinct ideas, a criterion with a strongly subjective bias, and one which at least in principle divorces itself from the regulation and control of being.

than myself; and I clearly recognised that I must hold this notion from some Nature which in reality was more perfect. As for the thoughts of many other objects external to me, as of the sky, the earth, light, heat, and a thousand more, I was less at a loss to know whence these came; for since I remarked in them nothing which seemed to render them superior to myself, I could believe that, if these were true, they were dependencies on my own nature, in so far as it possessed a certain perfection, and, if they were false, that I held them from nothing, that is to say, that they were in me because of a certain imperfection of my nature. But this could not be the case with the idea of a Nature more perfect than myself; for to receive it from nothing was a thing manifestly impossible; and, because it is not less repugnant that the more perfect should be an effect of, and dependence on the less perfect, than that something should proceed from nothing, it was equally impossible that I could hold it from myself; accordingly, it but remained that it had been placed in me by a Nature which was in reality more perfect than mine, and which even possessed within itself all the perfections of which I could form any idea; that is to say, in a single word, which was God.[6] And to this I added that, since I knew some perfections which I did not possess, I was not the only being in existence, (I will here, with your permission, freely use the terms of the schools); but, on the contrary, that there was of necessity some other more perfect Being upon whom I was dependent, and from whom I had received all that I possessed; for if I had existed alone, and independently of every other being, so as to have had from myself all the perfection, however little, which I actually possessed, I should have been able, for the same reason, to have had from myself the whole remainder of perfection, of the want of which I was conscious, and thus could of myself have become infinite, eternal, immutable, omniscient, all-powerful, and, in fine, have possessed all the perfections which I could recognise in God. For in order to know the nature of God, (whose existence has been established by the preceding reasonings,) as far as my own nature permitted, I had only to consider in reference to all the properties of which I found in my mind some idea, whether their possession was a mark of perfection; and I was assured that no one which indicated any imperfection was in him, and that none of the rest was wanting. Thus I perceived that doubt, inconstancy, sadness, and such like, could not be found in God, since I myself would have been happy to be free from them. Besides, I had ideas of many sensible and corporeal things; for although I might suppose that I was dreaming, and that all which I saw or imagined was false, I could not, nevertheless, deny that the ideas were in reality in my thoughts. But, because I had already very clearly recognised in myself that the intelligent nature is distinct from the corporeal, and as I observed that all composition is

---

[6]This is but a summary presentation of the proof for God's existence which receives more detailed treatment in the *Meditations*. Basically, the argument proceeds from the *idea* to the *existent* and is open to all the objections brought to bear against any such procedure.

an evidence of dependency, and that a state of dependency is manifestly a state of imperfection, I therefore determined that it could not be a perfection in God to be compounded of these two natures, and that consequently he was not so compounded; but that if there were any bodies in the world, or even any intelligences, or other natures that were not wholly perfect, their existence depended on his power in such a way that they could not subsist without him for a single moment.

I was disposed straightway to search for other truths; and when I had represented to myself the object of the geometers, which I conceived to be a continuous body, or a space indefinitely extended in length, breadth, and height or depth, divisible into divers parts which admit of different figures and sizes, and of being moved or transposed in all manner of ways, (for all this the geometers suppose to be in the object they contemplate,) I went over some of their simplest demonstrations. And, in the first place, I observed, that the great certitude which by common consent is accorded to these demonstrations, is founded solely upon this, that they are clearly conceived in accordance with the rules I have already laid down. In the next place, I perceived that there was nothing at all in these demonstrations which could assure me of the existence of their object: thus, for example, supposing a triangle to be given, I distinctly perceived that its three angles were necessarily equal to two right angles, but I did not on that account perceive anything which could assure me that any triangle existed: while, on the contrary, recurring to the examination of the idea of a Perfect Being, I found that the existence of the Being was comprised in the idea in the same way that the equality of its three angles to two right angles is comprised in the idea of a triangle, or as in the idea of a sphere, the equidistance of all points on its surface from the centre, or even still more clearly; and that consequently it is at least as certain that God, who is this Perfect Being, is, or exists, as any demonstration of Geometry can be.

But the reason which leads many to persuade themselves that there is a difficulty in knowing this truth, and even also in knowing what their mind really is, is that they never raise their thoughts above sensible objects, and are so accustomed to consider nothing except by way of imagination, which is a mode of thinking limited to material objects, that all that is not imaginable seems to them not intelligible. The truth of this is sufficiently manifest from the single circumstance, that the philosophers of the Schools accept as a maxim that there is nothing in the Understanding which was not previously in the Senses, in which however it is certain that the ideas of God and of the soul have never been; and it appears to me that they who make use of their imagination to comprehend these ideas do exactly the same thing as if, in order to hear sounds or smell odours, they strove to avail themselves of their eyes;[7] unless indeed that there

[7]Descartes here makes a good point to the effect that human knowledge is not limited to the imaginable; hence, to deny the existence of God or of the soul because they are not sensible or imaginable is about as reasonable as to demand

s this difference, that the sense of ight does not afford us an inferior .ssurance to those of smell or .earing; in place of which, neither ur imagination nor our senses can ;ive us assurance of anything un- ess our Understanding intervene.

Finally, if there be still persons vho are not sufficiently persuaded f the existence of God and of the oul, by the reasons I have adduced, am desirous that they should know hat all the other propositions, of he truth of which they deem them- elves perhaps more assured, as hat we have a body, and that there xist stars and an earth, and such ike, are less certain; for, although ve have a moral assurance of these hings, which is so strong that there s an appearance of extravagance in loubting of their existence, yet at he same time no one, unless his ntellect is impaired, can deny, when he question relates to a metaphysi- :al certitude, that there is suffi- :ient reason to exclude entire as- urance, in the observation that vhen asleep we can in the same vay imagine ourselves possessed f another body and that we see ther stars and another earth, when here is nothing of the kind. For ow do we know that the thoughts vhich occur in dreaming are false ather than those other which we xperience when awake, since the ormer are often not less vivid and distinct than the latter? And though men of the highest genius study this question as long as they please, I do not believe that they will be able to give any reason which can be suf- ficient to remove this doubt, unless they presuppose the existence of God. For, in the first place, even the principle which I have already taken as a rule, viz., that all the things which we clearly and dis- tinctly conceive are true, is certain only because God is or exists, and because he is a Perfect Being, and because all that we possess is de- rived from him: whence it follows that our ideas or notions, which to the extent of their clearness and distinctness are real, and proceed from God, must to that extent be true. Accordingly, whereas we not unfrequently have ideas or notions in which some falsity is contained, this can only be the case with such as are to some extent confused and obscure, and in this proceed from nothing, (participate of negation,) that is, exist in us thus confused because we are not wholly perfect. And it is evident that it is not less repugnant that falsity or imperfec- tion, in so far as it is imperfection, should proceed from God, than that truth or perfection should proceed from nothing. But if we did not know that all which we possess of real and true proceeds from a Perfect and Infinite Being, however clear and distinct our ideas might be, we should have no ground on that ac- count for the assurance that they possessed the perfection of being true.

But after the knowledge of God and of the soul has rendered us cer- tain of this rule, we can easily understand that the truth of the thoughts we experience when awake,

hat the eye hear sounds or smell odors. till, it should be recalled that when "the hilosophers of the Schools" proposed heir maxim that all knowledge depends n sensation, they by no means meant hat everything known was formally ensed or imagined or that knowledge id not penetrate to the truly intelligible spects of the sensed and, by analogy, go ven beyond to some knowledge of spir- tual reality.

ought not in the slightest degree to be called in question on account of the illusions of our dreams. For if it happened that an individual, even when asleep, had some very distinct idea, as, for example, if a geometer should discover some new demonstration, the circumstance of his being asleep would not militate against its truth; and as for the most ordinary error of our dreams, which consists in their representing various objects in the same way as our external senses, this is not prejudicial, since it leads us very properly to suspect the truth of the ideas of sense; for we are not unfrequently deceived in the same manner when awake; as when persons in the jaundice see all objects yellow, or when the stars or bodies at a great distance appear to us much smaller than they are. For, in fine, whether awake or asleep, we ought never to allow ourselves to be persuaded of the truth of anything unless on the evidence of our Reason. And it must be noted that I say of our *Reason,* and not of our imagination or of our senses: thus, for example, although we very clearly see the sun, we ought not therefore to determine that it is only of the size which our sense of sight presents; and we may very distinctly imagine the head of a lion joined to the body of a goat, without being therefore shut up to the conclusion that a chimæra exists; for it is not a dictate of Reason that what we thus see or imagine is in reality existent; but it plainly tells us that all our ideas or notions contain in them some truth; for otherwise it could not be that God, who is wholly perfect and veracious, should have placed them in us. And because our reasonings are never so clear or so complete during sleep as when we are awake, although sometimes the acts of our imagination are then as lively and distinct, if not more so than in our waking moments, Reason further dictates that, since all our thoughts cannot be true because of our partial imperfection, those possessing truth must infallibly be found in the experience of our waking moments rather than in that of our dreams.

THE MEDITATIONS ON THE FIRST PHILOSOPHY[8]

Meditation II

OF THE NATURE OF THE HUMAN MIND: AND THAT IT IS MORE EASILY KNOWN THAN THE BODY.

The Meditation of yesterday[9] has filled my mind with so many doubts, that it is no longer in my power to forget them. Nor do I see, meanwhile, any principle on which they can be resolved; and, just as if I had fallen all of a sudden into very deep water, I am so greatly disconcerted as to be unable either to plant my feet firmly on the bottom or sustain myself by swimming on the surface. I will, nevertheless, make an effort, and try anew the same path on which I had entered yesterday, that is, proceed by casting aside all that admits of the slightest doubt, not less than if I had discovered it to be absolutely false; and I will continue always in this track until I shall find something that is certain, or at least, if I can do nothing more, until I shall know with certainty that there is nothing certain. Archimedes, that he might transport the entire globe from the place it occupied to another, demanded only a point that was firm and immoveable; so also, I shall be entitled to entertain the highest expectations, if I am fortunate enough to discover only one thing that is certain and indubitable.

I suppose, accordingly, that all the things which I see are false (fictitious); I believe that none of those objects which my fallacious memory represents ever existed; I suppose that I possess no senses; I believe that body, figure, extension, motion, and place are merely fictions of my mind. What is there, then, that can be esteemed true? Perhaps this only, that there is absolutely nothing certain.

But how do I know that there is not something different altogether from the objects I have now enumerated, of which it is impossible to entertain the slightest doubt? Is there not a God, or some being, by whatever name I may designate him, who causes these thoughts to arise in my mind? But why suppose such a being, for it may be I myself am capable of producing them? Am I, then, at least not something? But I before denied that I possessed senses or a body; I hesitate, however, for what follows from that? Am I so dependent on the body and the senses that without these I cannot exist? But I had the persuasion that there was absolutely nothing in the world, that there was no sky and no earth, neither minds nor bodies; was I not, therefore, at the same time, persuaded that I did not exist? Far from it; I assuredly existed, since I was persuaded. But there is I know not what being, who is possessed at once of the

---

[8]The following selections are from *The Meditations on the First Philosophy* (1641), as found in René Descartes, *Meditations and Selections from the Principles of Philosophy*, trans. by John Veitch (La Salle, Ill.: The Open Court Publishing Co., 1959).

[9]Descartes is referring to the First Meditation, where he has built up his reasons for doubting and indicated the extent of his doubt.

highest power and the deepest cunning, who is constantly employing all his ingenuity in deceiving me. Doubtless, then, I exist, since I am deceived; and, let him deceive me as he may, he can never bring it about that I am nothing, so long as I shall be conscious that I am something. So that it must, in fine, be maintained, all things being maturely and carefully considered, that this proposition (*pronounciatum*) I am, I exist, is necessarily true each time it is expressed by me, or conceived in my mind.[10]

But I do not yet know with sufficient clearness what I am, though assured that I am; and hence, in the next place, I must take care, lest perchance I inconsiderately substitute some other object in room of what is properly myself, and thus wander from truth, even in that knowledge (cognition) which I hold to be of all others the most certain and evident. For this reason, I will now consider anew what I formerly believed myself to be, before I entered on the present train of thought; and of my previous opinion I will retrench all that can in the least be invalidated by the grounds of doubt I have adduced, in order that there may at length remain nothing but what is certain and indubitable. What then did I formerly think I was? Undoubtedly I judged that I was a man. But what is a man? Shall I say a rational animal? Assuredly not; for it would be necessary forthwith to inquire into what is meant by animal, and what by rational, and thus, from a single question, I should insensibly glide into others, and these more difficult than the first; nor do I now possess enough of leisure to warrant me in wasting my time amid subtleties of this sort. I prefer here to attend to the thoughts that sprung up of themselves in my mind, and were inspired by my own nature alone, when I applied myself to the consideration of what I was. In the first place, then, I thought that I possessed a countenance, hands, arms, and all the fabric of members that appears in a corpse, and which I called by the name of body. It further occurred to me that I was nourished, that I walked, perceived, and thought, and all those actions I referred to the soul; but what the soul itself was I either did not stay to consider, or, if I did, I imagined that it was something extremely rare and subtile, like wind, or flame, or ether, spread through my grosser parts. As regarded the body, I did not even doubt of its nature, but thought I distinctly knew it, and if I had wished to describe it according to the notions I then entertained, I should have explained myself in this manner: By body I understand all that can be terminated by a certain figure; that can be comprised in a certain place, and so fill a certain space as therefrom to exclude every other body; that can be perceived either by touch, sight, hearing, taste, or smell; that can be moved in different ways, not indeed of itself, but by something foreign to it by which it is touched [and from which it receives the impression];[11] for the power of self-motion, as likewise that of perceiving and thinking, I held as by no means pertaining to

[10] Cf. footnote 4.

[11] Brackets denote additions to the original text of the revised French translation.

the nature of body; on the contrary, I was somewhat astonished to find such faculties existing in some bodies.

But [as to myself, what can I now say that I am], since I suppose there exists an extremely powerful, and, if I may so speak, malignant being, whose whole endeavours are directed towards deceiving me? Can I affirm that I possess any one of all those attributes of which I have lately spoken as belonging to the nature of body? After attentively considering them in my own mind, I find none of them that can properly be said to belong to myself.[12] To recount them were idle and tedious. Let us pass, then, to the attributes of the soul. The first mentioned were the powers of nutrition and walking; but, if it be true that I have no body, it is true likewise that I am capable neither of walking nor of being nourished. Perception is another attribute of the soul; but perception too is impossible without the body: besides, I have frequently, during sleep, believed that I perceived objects which I afterwards observed I did not in reality perceive. Thinking is another attribute of the soul; and here I discover what properly belongs to myself. This alone is inseparable from me. I am—I exist: this is certain; but how often? As often as I think; for perhaps it would even happen, if I should wholly cease to think, that I should at the same time altogether cease to be. I now admit nothing that is not necessarily true: I am therefore, precisely speaking, only a thinking thing, that is, a mind (*mens sive animus*), understanding, or reason,[13]—terms whose signification was before unknown to me. I am, however, a real thing, and really existent; but what thing? The answer was, a thinking thing. The question now arises, am I aught besides? I will stimulate my imagination with a view to discover whether I am not still something more than a thinking being. Now it is plain I am not the assemblage of members called the human body; I am not a thin and penetrating air diffused through all these members, or wind, or flame, or vapour, or breath, or any of all the things I can imagine; for I supposed that all these were not, and, without changing the supposition, I find that I still feel assured of my existence.

But it is true, perhaps, that those very things which I suppose to be non-existent, because they are unknown to me, are not in truth different from myself whom I know. This is a point I cannot determine, and do not now enter into any dis-

[12]To such a point Descartes is led by his exaggerated and hyperbolic methodic doubt. His expressed intention was to doubt whatever and whenever there was good reason for doubting. This intention, as so expressed, is reasonable. However, whether Descartes had *good reasons* for doubting some of the things which he actually professed to doubt can be questioned or even denied.

[13]That the existing self is concretely known in any conscious activity, such as thinking or willing, can readily be admitted. However, much depends on just what is meant. From the sequel, it becomes clear that for methodological reasons Descartes concluded that the *self* is a substance whose essence is to think. Is this the truly human experience of the self? One emphasis of current Existentialism (as well as of Scholasticism) is the insistence that the "incarnational" or the corporeal aspects of the self are concretely and immediately experienced.

pute regarding it. I can only judge of things that are known to me: I am conscious that I exist, and I who know that I exist inquire into what I am. It is, however, perfectly certain that the knowledge of my existence, thus precisely taken, is not dependent on things, the existence of which is as yet unknown to me: and consequently it is not dependent on any of the things I can feign in imagination. Moreover, the phrase itself, I frame an image (*effingo*), reminds me of my error; for I should in truth frame one if I were to imagine myself to be anything, since to imagine is nothing more than to contemplate the figure or image of a corporeal thing; but I already know that I exist, and that it is possible at the same time that all those images, and in general all that relates to the nature of body, are merely dreams [or chimeras]. From this I discover that it is not more reasonable to say, I will excite my imagination that I may know more distinctly what I am, than to express myself as follows: I am now awake, and perceive something real; but because my perception is not sufficiently clear, I will of express purpose go to sleep that my dreams may represent to me the object of my perception with more truth and clearness. And, therefore, I know that nothing of all that I can embrace in imagination belongs to the knowledge which I have of myself, and that there is need to recall with the utmost care the mind from this mode of thinking, that it may be able to know its own nature with perfect distinctness.

But what, then, am I? A thinking thing, it has been said. But what is a thinking thing? It is a thing that doubts, understands, [conceives], affirms, denies, wills, refuses, that imagines also, and perceives. Assuredly it is not little, if all these properties belong to my nature. But why should they not belong to it? Am I not that very being who now doubts of almost everything; who, for all that, understands and conceives certain things; who affirms one alone as true, and denies the others; who desires to know more of them, and does not wish to be deceived; who imagines many things, sometimes even despite his will; and is likewise percipient of many, as if through the medium of the senses. Is there nothing of all this as true as that I am, even although I should be always dreaming, and although he who gave me being employed all his ingenuity to deceive me? Is there also any one of these attributes that can be properly distinguished from my thought, or that can be said to be separate from myself? For it is of itself so evident that it is I who doubt, I who understand, and I who desire, that it is here unnecessary to add anything by way of rendering it more clear. And I am as certainly the same being who imagines; for, although it may be (as I before supposed) that nothing I imagine is true, still the power of imagination does not cease really to exist in me and to form part of my thought. In fine, I am the same being who perceives, that is, who apprehends certain objects as by the organs of sense, since, in truth, I see light, hear a noise, and feel heat. But it will be said that these presentations are false, and that I am dreaming. Let it be so. At all events it is certain that I seem to see light, hear a noise, and feel heat; this cannot be false, and this is what in me is properly called perceiving (*sentire*), which is nothing else than thinking. From this I begin to know what I am with somewhat greater clearness and distinctness than heretofore.

But, nevertheless, it still seems to me, and I cannot help believing, that corporeal things, whose images are formed by thought, [which fall under the senses], and are examined by the same, are known with much greater distinctness than that I know not what part of myself which is not imaginable; although, in truth, it may seem strange to say that I know and comprehend with greater distinctness things whose existence appears to me doubtful, that are unknown, and do not belong to me, than others of whose reality I am persuaded, that are known to me, and appertain to my proper nature; in a word, than myself. But I see clearly what is the state of the case. My mind is apt to wander, and will not yet submit to be restrained within the limits of truth. Let us therefore leave the mind to itself once more, and, according to it every kind of liberty, [permit it to consider the objects that appear to it from without], in order that, having afterwards withdrawn it from these gently and opportunely, [and fixed it on the consideration of its being and the properties it finds in itself], it may then be the more easily controlled.

Let us now accordingly consider the objects that are commonly thought to be [the most easily, and likewise] the most distinctly known, viz., the bodies we touch and see; not, indeed, bodies in general, for these general notions are usually somewhat more confused, but one body in particular. Take, for example, this piece of wax;[14] it is quite fresh, having been but recently taken from the bee-hive; it has not yet lost the sweetness of the honey it contained; it still retains somewhat of the odour of the flowers from which it was gathered; its colour, figure, size, are apparent (to the sight); it is hard, cold, easily handled; and sounds when struck upon with the finger. In fine, all that contributes to make a body as distinctly known as possible, is found in the one before us. But, while I am speaking, let it be placed near the fire—what remained of the taste exhales, the smell evaporates, the colour changes, its figure is destroyed, its size increases, it becomes liquid, it grows hot, it can hardly be handled, and, although struck upon, it emits no sound. Does the same wax still remain after this change? It must be admitted that it does remain; no one doubts it, or judges otherwise. What, then, was it I knew with so much distinctness in the piece of wax? Assuredly, it could be nothing of all that I observed by means of the senses, since all the things that fell under taste, smell, sight, touch, and hearing are changed, and yet the same wax remains. It was perhaps

[14]These famous observations concerning a piece of wax propose a position which has received wide acceptance — namely, that secondary qualities are not really qualities of corporeal beings but are subjective reactions. This position received great impetus from John Locke's writings. Whatever one may ultimately hold on this question, Descartes' present reflections on the changing qualities of a piece of wax is far from cogent proof for his position. In fact, in recording the variable and varying qualities, he is actually relying on what he senses. Moreover, implicit in his analysis is a reification of accidents.

what I now think, viz., that this wax was neither the sweetness of honey, the pleasant odour of flowers, the whiteness, the figure, nor the sound, but only a body that a little before appeared to me conspicuous under these forms, and which is now perceived under others. But, to speak precisely, what is it that I imagine when I think of it in this way? Let it be attentively considered, and, retrenching all that does not belong to the wax, let us see what remains. There certainly remains nothing, except something extended, flexible, and movable. But what is meant by flexible and movable? Is it not that I imagine that the piece of wax, being round, is capable of becoming square, or of passing from a square into a triangular figure? Assuredly such is not the case, because I conceive that it admits of an infinity of similar changes; and I am, moreover, unable to compass this infinity by imagination, and consequently this conception which I have of the wax is not the product of the faculty of imagination. But what now is this extension? Is it not also unknown? for it becomes greater when the wax is melted, greater when it is boiled, and greater still when the heat increases; and I should not conceive [clearly and] according to truth, the wax as it is, if I did not suppose that the piece we are considering admitted even of a wider variety of extension than I ever imagined. I must, therefore, admit that I cannot even comprehend by imagination what the piece of wax is, and that it is the mind alone (*mens*, Lat., *entendement*, F.) which perceives it. I speak of one piece in particular; for, as to wax in general, this is still more evident. But what is the piece of wax that can be perceived only by the [understanding or] mind? It is certainly the same which I see, touch, imagine; and, in fine, it is the same which, from the beginning, I believed it to be. But (and this it is of moment to observe) the perception of it is neither an act of sight, of touch, nor of imagination, and never was either of these, though it might formerly seem so, but is simply an intuition (*inspectio*) of the mind, which may be imperfect and confused, as it formerly was, or very clear and distinct, as it is at present, according as the attention is more or less directed to the elements which it contains, and of which it is composed.

But, meanwhile, I feel greatly astonished when I observe [the weakness of my mind, and] its proneness to error. For although, without at all giving expression to what I think, I consider all this in my own mind, words yet occasionally impede my progress, and I am almost led into error by the terms of ordinary language. We say, for example, that we see the same wax when it is before us, and not that we judge it to be the same from its retaining the same colour and figure: whence I should forthwith be disposed to conclude that the wax is known by the act of sight, and not by the intuition of the mind alone, were it not for the analogous instance of human beings passing on in the street below, as observed from a window. In this case I do not fail to say that I see the men themselves, just as I say that I see the wax;[15] and yet what do I see from

[15]This "analogy" between external clothing and the "accidents" of wax illustrates what has just been called the reification of accidents, and it shows a mentality which became much more articulate in the British empiricists. This

the window beyond hats and cloaks that might cover artificial machines, whose motions might be determined by springs? But I judge that there are human beings from these appearances, and thus I comprehend, by the faculty of judgment alone which is in the mind, what I believed I saw with my eyes.

The man who makes it his aim to rise to knowledge superior to the common, ought to be ashamed to seek occasions of doubting from the vulgar forms of speech: instead, therefore, of doing this, I shall proceed with the matter in hand, and inquire whether I had a clearer and more perfect perception of the piece of wax when I first saw it, and when I thought I knew it by means of the external sense itself, or, at all events, by the common sense (*sensus communis*), as it is called, that is, by the imaginative faculty; or whether I rather apprehend it more clearly at present, after having examined with greater care, both what it is, and in what way it can be known. It would certainly be ridiculous to entertain any doubt on this point. For what, in that first perception, was there distinct? What did I perceive which any animal might not have perceived? But when I distinguish the wax from its exterior forms, and when, as if I had stripped it of its vestments, I consider it quite naked, it is certain, although some error may still be found in my judgment, that I cannot, nevertheless, thus apprehend it without possessing a human mind.

But, finally, what shall I say of the mind itself, that is, of myself? for as yet I do not admit that I am anything but mind. What, then! I who seem to possess so distinct an apprehension of the piece of wax,—do I not know myself, both with greater truth and certitude, and also much more distinctly and clearly? For it I judge that the wax exists because I see it, it assuredly follows, much more evidently, that I myself am or exist, for the same reason: for it is possible that what I see may not in truth be wax, and that I do not even possess eyes with which to see anything; but it cannot be that when I see, or, which comes to the same thing, when I think I see, I myself who think am nothing. So likewise, if I judge that the wax exists because I touch it, it will still also follow that I am; and if I determine that my imagination, or any other cause, whatever it be, persuades me of the existence of the wax, I will still draw the same conclusion. And what is here remarked of the piece of wax, is applicable to all the other things that are external to me. And further, if the [notion or] perception of wax appeared to me more precise and distinct, after that not only sight and touch, but many other causes besides, rendered it manifest to my apprehension, with how much greater distinctness must I now know myself, since all the reasons that contribute to the knowledge of the nature of wax, or of any body whatever, manifest still better the nature of my mind? And there are besides so many other things in the mind itself that contribute to the illustration of its nature, that those dependent on the body, to which I have here referred, scarcely merit to be taken into account.

But, in conclusion, I find I have

---

view looks on qualities or accidents as constituting an exterior shell or cover, apparently composed of a bundle of beings which effectively conceal the "hidden substance."

insensibly reverted to the point I desired; for, since it is now manifest to me that bodies themselves are not properly perceived by the senses nor by the faculty of imagination, but by the intellect alone; and since they are not perceived because they are seen and touched, but only because they are understood [or rightly comprehended by thought], I readily discover that there is nothing more easily or clearly apprehended than my own mind. But because it is difficult to rid one's self so promptly of an opinion to which one has been long accustomed, it will be desirable to tarry for some time at this stage, that, by long continued meditation, I may more deeply impress upon my memory this new knowledge.

* * *

Meditation VI

OF THE EXISTENCE OF MATERIAL THINGS, AND OF THE REAL DISTINCTION BETWEEN THE MIND AND BODY OF MAN.

There now only remains the inquiry as to whether material things exist.[16] With regard to this question, I at least know with certainty that such things may exist, in as far as they constitute the object of the pure mathematics, since, regarding them in this aspect, I can conceive them clearly and distinctly. For there can be no doubt that God possesses the power of producing all the objects I am able distinctly to conceive, and I never considered anything impossible to him, unless when I experienced a contradiction in the attempt to conceive it aright. Further, the faculty of imagination which I possess, and of which I am conscious that I make use when I apply myself to the consideration of material things, is sufficient to persuade me of their existence: for, when I attentively consider what imagination is, I find that it is simply a certain application of the cognitive faculty (*facultas cognoscitiva*) to a body which is immediately present to it, and which therefore exists.

And to render this quite clear, I remark, in the first place, the difference that subsists between imagination and pure intellection [or conception]. For example, when I imagine a triangle I not only conceive (*intelligo*) that it is a figure comprehended by three lines, but at the same time also I look upon (*intueor*) these three lines as present by the power and internal application of my mind (*acie mentis*), and this is what I call imagining. But if I desire to think of a chiliogon, I indeed rightly conceive that it is

[16]Descartes, having deliberately expounded his doubts as to the existence of material things, now finds himself compelled to *prove* their existence. However, this is an unrewarding expenditure of energy, because if the existence of material things is an *evidence* and the very basis of all knowledge and proof, then no proof is required; if, on the other hand, they are not evident but are hidden from our gaze, then no proof is possible. What really needs to be done in an analysis of human knowledge is to face the fact that material things do present themselves as objects for knowledge, that they do exist, and then the question is not "do they exist" but rather "*how* are they known."

figure composed of a thousand ides, as easily as I conceive that triangle is a figure composed of nly three sides; but I cannot imgine the thousand sides of a chiligon as I do the three sides of a riangle, nor, so to speak, view nem as present [with the eyes of ny mind]. And although, in acordance with the habit I have of lways imagining something when think of corporeal things, it may appen that, in conceiving a chilogon, I confusedly represent some igure to myself, yet it is quite vident that this is not a chiliogon, ince it in no wise differs from nat which I would represent to myelf, if I were to think of a myrigon, or any other figure of many ides; nor would this representaion be of any use in discovering nd unfolding the properties that onstitute the difference between a hiliogon and other polygons. But the question turns on a pentagon, is quite true that I can conceive s figure, as well as that of a hiliogon, without the aid of imagnation; but I can likewise imagine by applying the attention of my nind to its five sides, and at the ame time to the area which they ontain. Thus I observe that a speial effort of mind is necessary to he act of imagination, which is not equired to conceiving or undertanding (*ad intelligendum*); and this pecial exertion of mind clearly hows the difference between imagnation and pure intellection (*imagnatio et intellectio pura*). I remark, esides, that this power of imaginaion which I possess, in as far as it liffers from the power of conceivng, is in no way necessary to my nature or] essence, that is, to the ssence of my mind; for although I did not possess it, I should still remain the same that I now am, from which it seems we may conclude that it depends on something different from the mind. And I easily understand that, if some body exists, with which my mind is so conjoined and united as to be able, as it were, to consider it when it chooses, it may thus imagine corporeal objects; so that this mode of thinking differs from pure intellection only in this respect, that the mind in conceiving turns in some way upon itself, and considers some one of the ideas it possesses within itself; but in imagining it turns towards the body, and contemplates in it some object conformed to the idea which it either of itself conceived or apprehended by sense. I easily understand, I say, that imagination may be thus formed, if it is true that there are bodies; and because I find no other obvious mode of explaining it, I thence, with probability, conjecture that they exist, but only with probability; and although I carefully examine all things, nevertheless I do not find that, from the distinct idea of corporeal nature I have in my imagination, I can necessarily infer the existence of any body.

But I am accustomed to imagine many other objects besides that corporeal nature which is the object of the pure mathematics, as, for example, colours, sounds, tastes, pain, and the like, although with less distinctness; and, inasmuch as I perceive these objects much better by the senses, through the medium of which and of memory, they seem to have reached the imagination, I believe that, in order the more advantageously to examine them, it is proper I should at the same time examine what sense-perception is, and inquire whether from those ideas that are apprehended by this mode of thinking (consciousness), I cannot obtain a certain proof of the existence of corporeal objects.

And, in the first place, I will recall to my mind the things I have hitherto held as true, because perceived by the senses, and the foundations upon which my belief in their truth rested; I will, in the second place, examine the reasons that afterwards constrained me to doubt of them; and, finally, I will consider what of them I ought now to believe.

Firstly, then, I perceived that I had a head, hand, feet, and other members composing that body which I considered as part, or perhaps even as a whole, of myself. I perceived further, that that body was placed among many others, by which it was capable of being affected in diverse ways, both beneficial and hurtful; and what was beneficial I remarked by a certain sensation of pleasure, and what was hurtful by a sensation of pain. And, besides this pleasure and pain, I was likewise conscious of hunger, thirst, and other appetites, as well as certain corporeal inclinations towards joy, sadness, anger, and similar passions. And, out of myself, besides the extension, figure, and motions of bodies, I likewise perceived in them hardness, heat, and the other tactile qualities, and, in addition, light, colours, odours, tastes, and sounds, the variety of which gave me the means of distinguishing the sky, the earth, the sea, and generally all the other bodies, from one another. And certainly, considering the ideas of all these qualities, which were presented to my mind, and which alone I properly and immediately perceived, it was not without reason that I thought I perceived certain objects wholly different from my thought, namely, bodies from which those ideas proceeded; for I was conscious that the ideas were presented to me without my consent being required, so that I could not perceive any object, however desirous I might be, unless it were present to the organ of sense; and it was wholly out of my power not to perceive it when it was thus present. And because the ideas I perceived by the senses were much more lively and clear, and even, in their own way, more distinct than any of those I could of myself frame by meditation, or which I found impressed on my memory, it seemed that they could not have proceeded from myself, and must therefore have been caused in me by some other objects; and as of those objects I had no knowledge beyond what the ideas themselves gave me, nothing was so likely to occur to my mind as the supposition that the objects were similar to the ideas which they caused. And because I recollected also that I had formerly trusted to the senses rather than to reason, and that the ideas which I myself formed were not so clear as those I perceived by sense, and that they were even for the most part composed of parts of the latter, I was readily persuaded that I had no idea in my intellect which had not formerly passed through the senses. Nor was I altogether wrong in likewise believing that that body which, by special right, I called my own pertained to me more properly and strictly than any of the others; for in truth, I could never be separate from it as from other bodies: I felt in it and on account of it all my appetites and affections, and in fine I was affected in its parts by pain and the titillation of pleasure, and not in the parts of the other bodies that were separated from it. But when I inquired into the reason why, from this I know not what sensation of pain, sadness of mind should follow, and why from the sensation of pleasure joy should arise, or why this indescribable twitching of the stomach, which I call hunger, should put me in mind of taking food, and the parchedness of the throat of drink, and so in other cases, I was unable to give any explanation, unless that I was so taught by nature; for there is assuredly no affinity, at least none that I am able to comprehend, between this irritation of the stomach and the desire of food, any more than between the perception of an object that causes pain and the consciousness of sadness which springs from the perception. And in the same way it seemed to me that all he other judgments I had formed egarding the objects of sense, vere dictates of nature; because I emarked that those judgments vere formed in me, before I had eisure to weigh and consider the easons that might constrain me to orm them.

But, afterwards, a wide experince by degrees sapped the faith I ad reposed in my senses;[17] for I frequently observed that towers, which at a distance seemed round, appeared square when more closely viewed, and that colossal figures, raised on the summits of these towers, looked like small statues, when viewed from the bottom of them; and, in other instances without number, I also discovered error in judgments founded on the external senses; and not only in those founded on the external, but even in those that rested on the internal senses; for is there aught more internal than pain? and yet I have sometimes been informed by parties whose arm or leg had been amputated, that they still occasionally seemed to feel pain in that part of the body which they had lost,—a circumstance that led me to think that I could not be quite certain even that any one of my members was affected when I felt pain in it. And to these grounds of doubt I shortly afterwards also added two others of very wide generality: the first of them was that I believed I never perceived anything when awake which I could not occasionally think I also perceived when asleep, and as I do not believe that the ideas I seem to perceive in my sleep proceed from objects external to me, I did not any more observe any ground for believing this of such as I seem to perceive when awake; the second was that since I was as yet ignorant of the author of my being, or at least supposed myself to be

[17]Descartes' criticism of the senses re and elsewhere indicates an impaence with the natural and necessary nitations which are inevitable in mateal faculties. The senses are highly ecialized and extremely limited in nge; hence, the wholesale rejection of ir reliability simply because too much is expected of them would not seem to be warranted. A more balanced approach would be to examine specific instances and determine the area of competence for each sense. This, however, is not easily done, and, furthermore, it does not fit in with the rationalistic approach of Descartes.

so, I saw nothing to prevent my having been so constituted by nature as that I should be deceived even in matters that appeared to me to possess the greatest truth. And, with respect to the grounds on which I had before been persuaded of the existence of sensible objects, I had no great difficulty in finding suitable answers to them; for as nature seemed to incline me to many things from which reason made me averse, I thought that I ought not to confide much in its teachings. And although the perceptions of the senses were not dependent on my will, I did not think that I ought on that ground to conclude that they proceeded from things different from myself, since perhaps there might be found in me some faculty, though hitherto unknown to me, which produced them.

But now that I begin to know myself better, and to discover more clearly the author of my being, I do not, indeed, think that I ought rashly to admit all which the senses seem to teach, nor, on the other hand, is it my conviction that I ought to doubt in general of their teachings.

And, firstly, because I know that all which I clearly and distinctly conceive can be produced by God exactly as I conceive it, it is sufficient that I am able clearly and distinctly to conceive one thing apart from another, in order to be certain that the one is different from the other, seeing they may at least be made to exist separately, by the omnipotence of God; and it matters not by what power this separation is made, in order to be compelled to judge them different; and, therefore, merely because I know with certitude that I exist, and because, in the meantime, I do not observe that aught necessarily belongs to my nature or essence beyond my being a thinking thing, I rightly conclude that my essence consists only in my being a thinking thing, [or a substance whose whole essence or nature is merely thinking]. And although I may, or rather, as I will shortly say, although I certainly do possess a body with which I am very closely conjoined; nevertheless, because, on the one hand, I have a clear and distinct idea of myself, in as far as I am only a thinking and unextended thing, and as, on the other hand, I possess a distinct idea of body, in as far as it is only an extended and unthinking thing, it is certain that I, [that is, my mind, by which I am what I am], is entirely and truly distinct from my body, and may exist without it.[18]

Moreover, I find in myself diverse faculties of thinking that have each their special mode: for example, I find I possess the faculties of imagining and perceiving, without which I can indeed clearly and distinctly conceive myself as entire, but I cannot reciprocally conceive them without conceiving myself, that is to say, without an intelligent substance in which they reside, for [in

---

[18]By this distinction between mind and body, Descartes means that each of them is a complete substance, so that the individual "man" is a combination of two beings — the one material, the other immaterial. This view gives rise to great difficulties relative to the *unity* of man and these difficulties Descartes did not and could not satisfactorily solve. For if man is made up of two such beings then their union must be an accidenta one, and there can be no more unity i the human composite than in any othe juxtaposition of two beings. This basi split introduced into man's nature ha had its repercussions in the whole mod ern history of the so-called "mind-bod problem."

the notion we have of them, or to use the terms of the schools] in their formal concept, they comprise some sort of intellection; whence I perceive that they are distinct from myself as modes are from things. I remark likewise certain other faculties, as the power of changing place, of assuming diverse figures, and the like, that cannot be conceived and cannot therefore exist, any more than the preceding, apart from a substance in which they inhere. It is very evident, however, that these faculties, if they really exist, must belong to some corporeal or extended substance, since in their clear and distinct concept there is contained some sort of extension, but no intellection at all. Farther, I cannot doubt but that there is in me a certain passive faculty of perception, that is, of receiving and taking knowledge of the ideas of sensible things; but this would be useless to me, if there did not also exist in me, or in some other thing, another active faculty capable of forming and producing those ideas. But this active faculty cannot be in me [in as far as I am but a thinking thing], seeing that it does not presuppose thought, and also that those ideas are frequently produced in my mind without my contributing to it in any way, and even frequently contrary to my will. This faculty must therefore exist in some substance different from me, in which all the objective reality of the ideas that are produced by this faculty, is contained formally or eminently, as I before remarked; and this substance is either a body, that is to say, a corporeal nature in which is contained formally [and in effect] all that is objectively [and by representation] in those ideas; or it is God himself, or some other creature, of a rank superior to body, in which the same is contained eminently. But as God is no deceiver, it is manifest that he does not of himself and immediately communicate those ideas to me, nor even by the intervention of any creature in which their objective reality is not formally, but only eminently, contained. For as he has given me no faculty whereby I can discover this to be the case, but, on the contrary, a very strong inclination to believe that those ideas arise from corporeal objects, I do not see how he could be vindicated from the charge of deceit, if in truth they proceeded from any other source, or were produced by other causes than corporeal things: and accordingly it must be concluded, that corporeal objects exist.[19] Nevertheless they are not perhaps exactly such as we perceive by the senses, for their comprehension by the senses is, in many instances, very obscure and confused; but it is at least necessary to admit that all which I clearly and distinctly conceive as in them, that is, generally speaking, all that is comprehended in the object of speculative geometry, really exists external to me.

But with respect to other things which are either only particular, as, for example, that the sun is of such a size and figure, etc., or are conceived with less clearness and distinctness, as light, sound, pain, and the like, although they are highly dubious and uncertain, never-

[19]By this process Descartes returns to the admission of the existence of corporeal beings. Cf. footnote 16.

theless on the ground alone that God is no deceiver, and that consequently he has permitted no falsity in my opinions which he has not likewise given me a faculty of correcting, I think I may with safety conclude that I possess in myself the means of arriving at the truth. And, in the first place, it cannot be doubted that in each of the dictates of nature there is some truth: for by nature, considered in general, I now understand nothing more than God himself, or the order and disposition established by God in created things; and by my nature in particular I understand the assemblage of all that God has given me.

But there is nothing which that nature teaches me more expressly [or more sensibly] than that I have a body which is ill affected when I feel pain, and stands in need of food and drink when I experience the sensations of hunger and thirst, etc. And therefore I ought not to doubt but that there is some truth in these informations.

Nature likewise teaches me by these sensations of pain, hunger, thirst, etc., that I am not only lodged in my body as a pilot in a vessel, but that I am besides so intimately conjoined, and as it were intermixed with it, that my mind and body compose a certain unity. For if this were not the case, I should not feel pain when my body is hurt, seeing I am merely a thinking thing, but should perceive the wound by the understanding alone, just as a pilot perceives by sight when any part of his vessel is damaged: and when my body has need of food or drink, I should have a clear knowledge of this, and not be made aware of it by the confused sensations of hunger and thirst: for, in truth, all these sensations of hunger, thirst, pain, etc., are nothing more than certain confused modes of thinking, arising from the union and apparent fusion of mind and body.

Besides this, nature teaches me that my own body is surrounded by many other bodies, some of which I have to seek after, and others to shun. And indeed, as I perceive different sorts of colours, sounds, odours, tastes, heat, hardness, etc., I safely conclude that there are in the bodies from which the diverse perceptions of the senses proceed, certain varieties corresponding to them, although, perhaps, not in reality like them; and since, among these diverse perceptions of the senses, some are agreeable, and others disagreeable, there can be no doubt that my body, or rather my entire self, in as far as I am composed of body and mind, may be variously affected, both beneficially and hurtfully, by surrounding bodies.

But there are many other beliefs which, though seemingly the teaching of nature, are not in reality so, but which obtained a place in my mind through a habit of judging inconsiderately of things. It may thus easily happen that such judgments shall contain error: thus, for example, the opinion I have that all space in which there is nothing to affect [or make an impression on] my senses is void; that in a hot body there is something in every respect similar to the idea of heat in my mind; that in a white or green body there is the same whiteness or greenness which I perceive; that in a bitter or sweet body there is the same taste, and so in other instances; that the stars, towers, and all distant bodies, are of the same size and figure as they appear to our eyes, etc. But that I may avoid everything like indistinctness of conception, I must accurately define what I properly understand by being taught by nature. For nature is here taken in a narrower sense than when it signifies the sum of all the things which God has given me; seeing that in that meaning the notion comprehends much that belongs only to the mind [to which I am not here to be understood as referring when I use the term nature]; as, for example, the notion I have of the truth, that what is done cannot be undone, and all the other truths I discern by the natural light [without the aid of the body]; and seeing that it comprehends likewise much besides that belongs only to body, and is not here any more contained under the name nature, as the quality of heaviness, and the like, of which I do not speak,—the term being reserved exclusively to designate the things which God has given to me as a being composed of mind and body. But nature, taking the term in the sense explained, teaches me to shun what causes in me the sensation of pain, and to pursue what affords me the sensation of pleasure, and other things of this sort; but I do not discover that it teaches me, in addition to this, from these diverse perceptions of the senses, to draw any conclusions respecting external objects without a previous [careful and mature] consideration of them by the mind; for it is, as appears to me, the office of the mind alone, and not of the composite whole of mind and body, to discern the truth in those matters. Thus, although the impression a star makes on my eye is not larger than that from the flame of a candle, I do not, nevertheless, experience any real or positive impulse determining me to believe that the star is not greater than the flame; the true account of the matter being merely that I have so judged from my youth without any rational ground. And, though on approaching the fire I feel heat, and even pain on approaching it too closely, I have, however, from this no ground for holding that something resembling the heat I feel is in the fire, any more than that there is something similar to the pain; all that I have ground for believing is, that there is something in it, whatever it may be, which excites in me those sensations of heat or pain. So also, although there are spaces in which I find nothing to excite and affect my senses, I must not therefore conclude that those spaces contain in them no body; for I see that in this, as in many other similar matters, I have been accustomed to pervert the order of nature, because these perceptions of the senses, although given me by nature merely to signify to my mind what things are beneficial and hurtful to the composite whole of which it is a part, and being sufficiently clear and distinct for that purpose, are nevertheless used by me as infallible rules by which to determine immediately the essence of the bodies that exist out of me, of which they can of course afford me only the most obscure and confused knowledge.

5

Knowledge as Virtue

Benedict de Spinoza (1632-1677)

Spinoza, having meditated on the sad state of philosophy and the turn it had taken in the studies of Descartes, decided that the fundamental difficulty was the general failure on the part of philosophers to recognize the true nature of the mind and of human knowledge, to see the metaphysical source of the mind's limitations, and to remedy the situation by forthright action.

The true nature of the mind, he taught, is grasped in recognizing that it is part of the divine Mind. This must be so, since there is but one Substance—infinite, perfect, eternal, immense, and omnipotent. All other "beings" are and can be only "modes," existing in, by, and through this one Substance. Hence, each human mind is but a limited "mode" or finite expression of the divine attribute of thought. Moreover, since the human mind is but a part of the divine Mind, since it is influenced by imagination, and since it can get lost in "abstractions," it can and does err.

According to Spinoza, the remedy for this situation is the full recognition of our true nature as "modes" of the one Substance, God. We will thus be raised to the divine standpoint where all is viewed *sub specie aeternitatis*, where all is seen as part of God, where we will know all things in their intimate essence, and thus, through the right sort of knowledge, we will be made perfect and arrive at supreme happiness.

The first selection follows Spinoza as he seeks to establish the correct way in which true knowledge should proceed—that is, by recognizing God as the first in being from Whom all else proceeds, and by recognizing the idea of God as the first true idea from which all other ideas can be deduced. Here is the supreme rationalistic attitude, which unduly stresses the power of the mind and unduly belittles the role of sensation in the acquisition of knowledge. Surely knowledge is not limited to the sense level, but equally surely human knowledge is dependent on and takes its start in sensation.

The second selection illustrates Spinoza's procedure in the *Ethics*. This is his major philosophical work. There, by "proving" proposition after proposition, he seeks to lead the reader from a consideration of what constitutes true knowledge to the recognition of the intellectual love of God as the true power, liberty, happiness, and salvation of man. Ultimately, it means accepting oneself as a mode of the divine Substance, fully predetermined by God.[1]

ON THE IMPROVEMENT OF THE UNDERSTANDING[2]

After experience had taught me that all the usual surroundings of social life are vain and futile; seeing that none of the objects of my fears contained in themselves anything either good or bad, except in so far as the mind is affected by them, I finally resolved to inquire whether there might be some real good having power to communicate itself, which would affect the mind singly, to the exclusion of all else; whether, in fact, there might be anything of which the discovery and attainment would enable me to enjoy continuous, supreme, and unending happiness.[3] I say "I *finally* resolved," for at first sight it seemed unwise willingly to lose hold on what was sure for the sake of something then uncertain. I could see the benefits which are acquired through fame and riches, and that I should be obliged to abandon the quest of such objects, if I seriously devoted myself to the search for something different and new. I perceived that if true happiness chanced to be placed in the former I should necessarily miss it; while if, on the other hand, it were not so placed, and I gave them my whole attention, I should equally fail.

I therefore debated whether it would not be possible to arrive at the new principle, or at any rate at a certainty concerning its existence, without changing the conduct and usual plan of my life; with this end

---

[1]Interpreters of Spinoza's philosophy have generally underscored its Monism and Pantheism. That such evaluations have much justification in the works of Spinoza may be seen by a reading of Parts I, II, and V of his *Ethics* — especially in Part I, Props. XIV, XV, XXI, XXV, and in Part II, Props. I, II, X and corollary, XI corollary.

[2]Selected from *On the Improvement of the Understanding* (1677), as found in Benedict de Spinoza, *Philosophy of Benedict de Spinoza*, trans. by R. Elwes (New York: Tudor Publishing Company, 1936), pp. 1-14, 23-26.

[3]This indicates the *moral* tone of all Spinoza's works. In the present essay he studies knowledge, and this is done because he feels that only the highest sort of knowledge enables us to pursue the highest good and thus arrive at the supreme source of happiness.

in view I made many efforts, but in vain. For the ordinary surroundings of life which are esteemed by men (as their actions testify) to be the highest good, may be classed under the three heads—Riches, Fame, and Pleasures of Sense: with these three the mind is so absorbed that it has little power to reflect on any different good. By sensual pleasure the mind is enthralled to the extent of quiescence, as if the supreme good were actually attained, so that it is quite incapable of thinking of any other object; when such pleasure has been gratified it is followed by extreme melancholy, whereby the mind, though not enthralled, is disturbed and dulled.

The pursuit of honors and riches is likewise very absorbing, especially if such objects be sought simply for their own sake, inasmuch as they are then supposed to constitute the highest good. In the case of fame the mind is still more absorbed, for fame is conceived as always good for its own sake, and as the ultimate end to which all actions are directed. Further, the attainment of riches and fame is not followed as in the case of sensual pleasures by repentance, but, the more we acquire, the greater is our delight, and, consequently, the more we are incited to increase both the one and the other; on the other hand, if our hopes happen to be frustrated we are plunged into the deepest sadness. Fame has the further drawback that it compels its votaries to order their lives according to the opinions of their fellow-men, shunning what they usually shun, and seeking what they usually seek.

When I saw that all these ordinary objects of desire would be obstacles in the way of a search for something different and new—nay, that they were so opposed thereto, that either they or it would have to be abandoned, I was forced to inquire which would prove the most useful to me: for, as I say, I seemed to be willingly losing hold on a sure good for the sake of something uncertain. However, after I had reflected on the matter, I came in the first place to the conclusion that by abandoning the ordinary objects of pursuit, and betaking myself to a new quest, I should be leaving a good, uncertain by reason of its own nature, as may be gathered from what has been said, for the sake of a good not uncertain in its nature (for I sought for a fixed good), but only in the possibility of its attainment.

Further reflection convinced me, that if I could really get to the root of the matter, I should be leaving certain evils for a certain good. I thus perceived that I was in a state of great peril, and I compelled myself to seek with all my strength for a remedy, however uncertain it might be; as a sick man struggling with a deadly disease, when he sees that death will surely be upon him unless a remedy be found, is compelled to seek such a remedy with all his strength, inasmuch as his whole hope lies therein. All the objects pursued by the multitude, not only bring no remedy that tends to preserve our being, but even act as hindrances, causing the death not seldom of those who possess them, and always of those who are possessed by them.

* * *

I will here only briefly state what I mean by true good, and also what is the nature of the highest good. In order that this may be rightly understood, we must bear in mind that the terms good and evil are only applied relatively, so that the same thing may be called both good and bad, according to the relations in view, in the same way as it may be called perfect or imperfect. Nothing regarded in its own nature can be called perfect or imperfect; especially when we are aware that all things which come to pass, come to pass according to the eternal order and fixed laws of nature. However, human weakness cannot attain to this order in its own thoughts, but meanwhile man conceives a human character much more stable than his own, and sees that there is no reason why he should not himself acquire such a character. Thus he is led to seek for means which will bring him to this pitch of perfection, and calls everything which will serve as such means a true good. The chief good is that he should arrive, together with other individuals if possible, at the possession of the aforesaid character. What that character is we shall show in due time, namely, that it is the knowledge of the union existing between the mind and the whole of nature.[4] This, then, is the end for which I strive, to attain to such a character myself, and to endeavor that many should attain to it with me. In other words, it is part of my happiness to lend a helping hand, that many others may understand even as I do, so that their understanding and desire may entirely agree with my own. In order to bring this about, it is necessary to understand as much of nature as will enable us to attain to the aforesaid character, and also to form a social order such as is most conducive to the attainment of this character by the greatest number with the least difficulty and danger. We must seek the assistance of Moral Philosophy and the Theory of Education; further, as health is no insignificant means for attaining our end, we must also include the whole science of Medicine, and, as many difficult things are by contrivance rendered easy, and we can in this way gain much time and convenience, the science of Mechanics must in no way be despised. But, before all things, a means must be devised for improving the understanding and purifying it, as far as may be at the outset, so that it may apprehend things without error, and in the best possible way.

* * *

I will now betake myself to the first and most important task, namely, the amendment of the understanding,[5] and the rendering it capable of understanding things in the

[4]This brief statement implies the entire philosophy of Spinoza. The union here mentioned is that between a mode (mind) and the unique substance (God or nature), and at this point he merely postulates that the recognition of this union is the goal of knowledge. Later this assumption regulates his method, and his method is used to justify the assumption. Hence, there is a circularity in his procedure.

[5]The *improving* or *purifying* or *amendment* of the understanding is really a *healing*, since Spinoza feels that the understanding has really been injured by straying from the truth. Spinoza develops his method so that by thinking right the mind may be healed and pursue its true happiness.

manner necessary for attaining our end.

In order to bring this about, the natural order demands that I should here recapitulate all the modes of perception, which I have hitherto employed for affirming or denying anything with certainty, so that I may choose the best, and at the same time begin to know my own powers and the nature which I wish to perfect.

Reflection shows that all modes of perception or knowledge may be reduced to four:

I. Perception arising from hearsay or from some sign which everyone may name as he pleases.

II. Perception arising from mere experience—that is, from experience not yet classified by the intellect, and only so called because the given event has happened to take place, and we have no contradictory fact to set against it, so that it therefore remains unassailed in our mind.

III. Perception arising when the essence of one thing is inferred from another thing, but not adequately; this comes when from some effect we gather its cause, or when it is inferred from some general proposition that some property is always present.

IV. Lastly, there is the perception arising when a thing is perceived solely through its essence, or through the knowledge of its proximate cause.

All these kinds of perception I will illustrate by examples. By hearsay I know the day of my birth, my parentage, and other matters about which I have never felt any doubt. By mere experience I know that I shall die, for this I can affirm from having seen that others like myself have died, though all did not live for the same period, or die by the same disease. I know by mere experience that oil has the property of feeding fire, and water of extinguishing it. In the same way I know that a dog is a barking animal, man a rational animal, and in fact nearly all the practical knowledge of life.

We deduce one thing from another as follows: when we clearly perceive that we feel a certain body and no other, we thence clearly infer that the mind is united to the body, and that their union is the cause of the given sensation; but we cannot thence absolutely understand the nature of the sensation and the union. Or, after I have become acquainted with the nature of vision, and know that it has the property of making one and the same thing appear smaller when far off than when near, I can infer that the sun is larger than it appears, and can draw other conclusions of the same kind.

Lastly, a thing may be perceived solely through its essence;[6] when, from the fact of knowing something, I know what it is to know that thing, or when, from knowing the essence of the mind, I know that it is united to the body. By the same kind of knowledge we know that two and three make five, or that two lines each parallel to a third, are parallel to one another, etc. The things which I have been able to know by this kind of knowledge are as yet very few.

* * *

[6]This intuition of essences, which will mean an insight into the whole of reality, is proposed as possible and even necessary for man. This concretely means overcoming human limits and elevation to the divine standpoint. Such a view indicates the Rationalism of Spinoza.

In order that from these modes of perception the best may be selected, it is well that we should briefly enumerate the means necessary for attaining our end.

I. To have an exact knowledge of our nature which we desire to perfect, and to know as much as is needful of nature in general.

II. To collect in this way the differences, the agreements, and the oppositions of things.

III. To learn thus exactly how far they can or cannot be modified.

IV. To compare this result with the nature and power of man. We shall thus discern the highest degree of perfection to which man is capable of attaining. We shall then be in a position to see which mode of perception we ought to choose.

As to the first mode, it is evident that from hearsay our knowledge must always be uncertain, and, moreover, can give us no insight into the essence of a thing, as is manifest in our illustration; now one can only arrive at knowledge of a thing through knowledge of its essence, as will hereafter appear. We may, therefore, clearly conclude that the certainty arising from hearsay cannot be scientific in its character. For simple hearsay cannot affect anyone whose understanding does not, so to speak, meet it half way.

The second mode of perception cannot be said to give us the idea of the proportion of which we are in search. Moreover its results are very uncertain and indefinite, for we shall never discover anything in natural phenomena by its means, except accidental properties, which are never clearly understood, unless the essence of the things in question be known first. Wherefore this mode also must be rejected.

Of the third mode of perception we may say in a manner that it gives us the idea of the thing sought, and that it enables us to draw conclusions without risk of error; yet it is not by itself sufficient to put us in possession of the perfection we aim at.

The fourth mode alone apprehends the adequate essence of a thing without danger of error. This mode, therefore, must be the one which we chiefly employ. How, then, should we avail ourselves of it so as to gain the fourth kind of knowledge with the least delay concerning things previously unknown? I will proceed to explain.

Now that we know what kind of knowledge is necessary for us, we must indicate the way and the method whereby we may gain the said knowledge concerning the things needful to be known. In order to accomplish this, we must first take care not to commit ourselves to a search, going back to infinity—that is, in order to discover the best method for finding out the truth, there is no need of another method to discover such method; nor of a third method for discovering the second, and so on to infinity. By such proceedings, we should never arrive at the knowledge of the truth, or, indeed, at any knowledge at all. The matter stands on the same footing as the making of material tools, which might be argued about in a similar way. For, in order to work iron, a hammer is needed, and the hammer cannot be forthcoming unless it has been made; but, in order to make it, there was need of another hammer and other tools, and so on to infinity. We might thus vainly endeavor to prove that men have no power of working iron. But as men at first made use of the instruments supplied by nature to accomplish very easy pieces of workmanship, laboriously and imperfectly, and then, when these were finished, wrought other things more difficult with less labor and greater perfection; and so gradually mounted from the simplest operations to the making of tools, and from the making of tools to the making of more complex tools, and fresh feats of workmanship, till they arrived at making, with small expenditure of labor, the vast number of complicated mechanisms which they now possess. So, in like manner, the intellect, by its native strength, makes for itself intellectual instruments, whereby it acquires strength for performing other intellectual operations, and from these operations gets again fresh instruments, or the power of pushing its investigations further, and thus gradually proceeds till it reaches the summit of wisdom.

That this is the path pursued by the understanding may be readily seen, when we understand the nature of the method for finding out the truth, and of the natural instruments so necessary for the construction of more complex instruments, and for the progress of investigation. I thus proceed with my demonstration.

A true idea (for we possess a true idea) is something different from its correlate *(ideatum)*; thus a circle is different from the idea of a circle. The idea of a circle is not something having a circumference and a centre, as a circle has; nor is the idea of a body that body itself. Now, as it is something different from its correlate, it is capable of being understood through itself; in other words, the idea, in so far as its actual essence *(essentia formalis)* is concerned, may be the subject of another subjective essence *(essentia objectiva)*.[7] And, again, this second subjective essence will, regarded in itself, be something real, and capable of being understood; and so on, indefinitely. For instance, the man Peter is something real, the true idea of Peter is the reality of Peter represented subjectively, and is in itself something real, and quite distinct from the actual Peter. Now, as this true idea of Peter is in itself something real, and has its own individual existence, it will also be capable of being understood—that is, of being the subject of another idea, which will contain by representation *(objective)* all that the idea of Peter contains actually *(formaliter)*. And, again, this idea of the idea of Peter has its own individuality, which may become the subject of yet another idea; and so on, indefinitely. This every one may make trial of for himself, by reflecting that he knows what Peter is, and also knows that he knows, and further knows that he knows that he knows, etc. Hence it is plain that, in order to understand the actual Peter, it is not necessary first to understand the idea of Peter, and still less the idea of the idea of Peter. This is the same as saying that, in order to know, there is no need to know that we know, much less to know that we know that we know. This is no more necessary than to know the nature of a circle before knowing the nature of a triangle. But, with these ideas, the contrary is the case:

[7]Spinoza here uses Cartesian terminology, and the formal essence is the actual nature of the thing known, whereas the representative or objective essence is the idea of the thing in the mind.

for, in order to know that I know, I must first know. Hence it is clear that certainty is nothing else than the subjective essence of a thing: in other words, the mode in which we perceive an actual reality is certainty. Further, it is also evident that, for the certitude of truth, no further sign is necessary beyond the possession of a true idea:[8] for, as I have shown, it is not necessary to know that we know that we know. Hence, again, it is clear that no one can know the nature of the highest certainty, unless he possesses an adequate idea, or the subjective essence of a thing: for certainty is identical with such subjective essence. Thus, as the truth needs no sign—it being sufficient to possess the subjective essence of things, or, in other words, the ideas of them, in order that all doubts may be removed—it follows that the true method does not consist in seeking for the signs of truth after the acquisition of the idea, but that the true method teaches us the order in which we should seek for truth itself, or the subjective essences of things, or ideas, for all these expressions are synonymous. Again, method must necessarily be concerned with reasoning or understanding—I mean, method is not identical with reasoning in the search for causes, still less is it the comprehension of the causes of things: it is the discernment of a true idea, by distinguishing it from other perceptions and by investigating its nature in order that we may thus know our power of understanding, and may so train our mind that it may, by a given standard, comprehend whatsoever is intelligible, by laying down certain rules as aids, and by avoiding useless mental exertion.

Whence we may gather that method is nothing else than reflective knowledge, or the idea of an idea; and that as there can be no idea of an idea—unless an idea exists previously,—there can be no method without a pre-existent idea. Therefore, that will be a good method which shows us how the mind should be directed, according to the standard of the given true idea.

Again, seeing that the ratio existing between two ideas is the same as the ratio between the actual realities corresponding to those ideas,[9] it follows that the reflective knowledge which has for its object the most perfect being is more excellent than reflective knowledge concerning other objects—in other words, that method will be most perfect which affords the standard of the given idea of the most perfect being whereby we may direct our mind.

[8]In fact, ideas must be their own guarantee, since there can be no regulation by existent finite things. According to Spinoza, ideas are not drawn from things but come from the native power of the mind, and so we are again faced with a belittling of the noetic role of sensation and with a doctrine that presents a rigorous dualism of body and mind.

[9]Although not derived from things, ideas do conform to them. Even more, the order of ideas is, in this view, exactly the same as the order of being. Thus, just as things ontologically proceed from God, Spinoza asserts that we can begin with the idea of God and derive all our ideas from this all-perfect idea. This is an expression of supreme Rationalism — that the order of knowing is identical with the order of being. Unfortunately, this is not our human experience, nor is it possible for man, since our knowledge actually has far humbler beginnings and more limited methods of procedure.

We thus easily understand how, in proportion as it acquires new ideas, the mind simultaneously acquires fresh instruments for pursuing its inquiries further. For we may gather from what has been said, that a true idea must necessarily first of all exist in us as a natural instrument; and that when this idea is apprehended by the mind, it enables us to understand the difference existing between itself and all other perceptions. In this, one part of the method consists.

Now it is clear that the mind apprehends itself better in proportion as it understands a greater number of natural objects; it follows, therefore, that this portion of the method will be more perfect in proportion as the mind attains to the comprehension of a greater number of objects, and that it will be absolutely perfect when the mind gains a knowledge of the absolutely perfect being or becomes conscious thereof. Again, the more things the mind knows, the better does it understand its own strength and the order of nature; by increased self-knowledge it can direct itself more easily, and lay down rules for its own guidance; and, by increased knowledge of nature, it can more easily avoid what is useless.

And this is the sum total of method, as we have already stated. We may add that the idea in the world of thought is in the same case as its correlate in the world of reality. If, therefore, there be anything in nature which is without connection with any other thing, and if we assign to it a subjective essence, which would in every way correspond to the objective reality, the subjective essence would have no connection with any other ideas—in other words, we could not draw any conclusion with regard to it. On the other hand, those things which are connected with others—as all things that exist in nature—will be understood by the mind, and their subjective essences will maintain the same mutual relations as their objective realities—that is to say, we shall infer from these ideas other ideas, which will in turn be connected with others, and thus our instruments for proceeding with our investigation will increase. This is what we are endeavoring to prove. Further, from what has just been said—namely, that an idea must, in all respects, correspond to its correlate in the world of reality—it is evident that, in order to reproduce in every respect the faithful image of nature, our mind must deduce all its ideas from the idea which represents the origin and source of the whole of nature,[10] so that it may itself become the source of other ideas.

It may, perhaps, provoke astonishment that, after having said that the good method is that which teaches us to direct our mind according to the standard of the given true idea, we should prove our point by reasoning, which would seem to indicate that it is not self-evident. We may, therefore, be questioned as to the validity of our reasoning. If our reasoning be sound, we must take as a starting point a true idea. Now, to be certain that our starting point is really a

[10]The grasp of this idea of God, and the deduction of all other ideas in their proper order, constitutes for Spinoza the real healing of our intellect; this is true virtue and power. We need only add that this is one of the extreme positions which can arise once the unity of man is broken and emphasis is placed on mind to the exclusion of man's concrete situation.

true idea, we need a proof. This first course of reasoning must be supported by a second, the second by a third, and so on to infinity. To this I make answer that, if by some happy chance anyone had adopted this method in his investigations of nature—that is, if he had acquired new ideas in the proper order, according to the standard of the original true idea, he would never have doubted of the truth of his knowledge, inasmuch as truth, as we have shown, makes itself manifest, and all things would flow, as it were, spontaneously toward him. But as this never, or rarely, happens, I have been forced so to arrange my proceedings, that we may acquire by reflection and forethought what we cannot acquire by chance, and that it may at the same time appear that, for proving the truth, and for valid reasoning, we need no other means than the truth and valid reasoning themselves: for by valid reasoning I have established valid reasoning, and, in like measure, I seek still to establish it. Moreover, this is the order of thinking adopted by men in their inward meditations. The reasons for its rare employment in investigations of nature are to be found in current misconceptions, whereof we shall examine the causes hereafter in our philosophy. Moreover, it demands, as we shall show, a keen and accurate discernment. Lastly, it is hindered by the conditions of human life, which are, as we have already pointed out, extremely changeable. There are also other obstacles, which we will not here inquire into.[11]

[11]Spinoza makes these concessions, because even the supreme rationalist must at times admit that there are concrete human limitations in knowledge.

If any one asks why I have not at the starting point set forth all the truths of nature in their due order, inasmuch as truth is self-evident, I reply by warning him not to reject as false any paradoxes he may find here, but to take the trouble to reflect on the chain of reasoning by which they are supported; he will then be no longer in doubt that we have attained to the truth. This is why I have begun as above.

If there yet remains some sceptic, who doubts of our primary truth, and of all deductions we make, taking such truth as our standard, he must either be arguing in bad faith, or we must confess that there are men in complete mental blindness either innate or due to misconceptions—that is, to some external influence.

* * *

As regards that which constitutes the reality of truth, it is certain that a true idea is distinguished from a false one, not so much by its extrinsic object as by its intrinsic nature. If an architect conceives a building properly constructed, though such a building may never have existed, and may never exist, nevertheless the idea is true; and the idea remains the same, whether it be put into execution or not. On the other hand, if any one asserts, for instance, that Peter exists, without knowing whether Peter really exists or not, the assertion, as far as its asserter is concerned, is false, or not true, even though Peter actually does exist. The assertion that Peter exists is true only with regard to him who knows for certain that Peter does exist.[12] Whence it follows that there is in ideas something real, whereby the true are distinguished from the false. This reality must be inquired into, if we are to find the best standard of truth (we have said that we ought to determine our thoughts by the given standard of a true idea, and that method is reflective knowledge), and to know the properties of our understanding. Neither must we say that the difference between true and false arises from the fact that true knowledge consists in knowing things through their primary causes, wherein it is totally different from false knowledge, as I have just explained it: for thought is said to be true, if it involves subjectively the essence of any principle which has no cause, and is known through itself and in itself. Wherefore the reality *(forma)* of true thought must exist in the thought itself, without reference to other thoughts; it does not acknowledge the object as its cause, but must depend on the actual power and nature of the understanding. For, if we suppose that the understanding has perceived some new entity which has never existed, as some conceive the understanding of God before He created things (a perception which certainly could not arise from any object), and has legitimately deduced other thoughts from the said perception, all such thoughts would be true, without being determined by any external object; they would depend solely on the power and nature of the understanding. Thus, that which constitutes the reality of a true thought must be sought in the thought itself and deduced from the nature of the understanding. In order to pursue our investigation, let us confront ourselves with some TRUE idea, whose object we know for certain to be dependent on our power of thinking, and to have nothing corresponding to it in nature. With an idea of this kind before us, we shall, as appears from what has just been said, be more easily able to carry on the research we have in view. For instance, in order to form the conception of a sphere, I invent a cause at my pleasure—namely, a semi-circle revolving around its centre, and thus producing a sphere. This is indisputably a true idea; and, although we know that no sphere in nature has ever actually been so formed, the perception remains true, and is the easiest manner of conceiving a sphere. We must observe that this perception asserts the rotation of a semicircle—which assertion would be false, if it were not associated with the conception of a sphere, or of a cause determining a motion of the kind, or absolutely, if the assertion were isolated. The mind would then only tend to the affirmation of the sole motion of a semicircle which is not contained in the conception of a semicircle, and does not arise from the conception of any cause capable of producing such motion.

Thus FALSITY consists only in this, that something is affirmed of a thing, which is not contained in the conception we have formed of that thing, as motion or rest of a semicircle. Whence it follows that simple ideas cannot be other than TRUE—*e.g.*, the simple idea of a semicircle, of motion, of rest, of quantity, etc.

---

[12]While reading this section, the distinction between logical truth (in the judgment), moral truth (in the assertion), and ontological truth (in things) should be kept in mind.

Whatsoever affirmation such ideas contain is equal to the concept formed, and does not extend further. Wherefore we may form as many simple ideas as we please, without any fear of error. It only remains for us to inquire by what power our mind can form true ideas, and how far such power extends. It is certain that such power cannot extend itself infinitely. For when we affirm somewhat of a thing, which is not contained in the concept we have formed of that thing, such an affirmation shows a defect of our perception, or that we have formed fragmentary or mutilated ideas. Thus we have seen that the motion of a semicircle is false when it is isolated in the mind, but true when it is associated with the concept of a sphere, or of some cause determining such a motion. But if it be the nature of a thinking being, as seems, *prima facie*, to be the case, to form true or adequate thoughts, it is plain that inadequate ideas arise in us only because we are parts of a thinking being, whose thoughts—some in their entirety, others in fragments only—constitute our mind.[13]

But there is another point to be considered, which was not worth raising in the case of fiction, but which gives rise to complete deception—namely, that certain things presented to the imagination also exist in the understanding—in other words, are conceived clearly and distinctly. Hence, so long as we do not separate that which is distinct from that which is confused, certainty, or the true idea, becomes mixed with indistinct ideas. For instance, certain Stoics heard, perhaps, the term "soul," and also that the soul is immortal, yet imagined it only confusedly; they imagined, also, and understood that very subtle bodies penetrate all others, and are penetrated by none. By combining these ideas, and being at the same time certain of the truth of the axiom, they forthwith became convinced that the mind consists of very subtle bodies; that these very subtle bodies cannot be divided, etc. But we are freed from mistakes of this kind, so long as we endeavor to examine all our perceptions by the standard of the given true idea. We must take care, as has been said, to separate such perceptions from all those which arise from hearsay or unclassified experience.

Moreover, such mistakes arise from things being conceived too much in the abstract; for it is sufficiently self-evident that what I conceive as in its true object I cannot apply to anything else. Lastly, they

[13]Here and in the following Spinoza lists the causes of error as (1) the fact that our minds are partial; that is, they are only parts of the divine Substance and, hence, they give fragmentary knowledge; (2) the influence of the imagination which can give rise to confused knowledge; (3) the unfortunate influence of abstraction; and (4) the failure to begin with the primary, with the source and origin of nature.

These reasons imply Spinoza's Pantheism — his view that there is but one unique substance, that we are all parts of God, and that the mind is a mode under the divine attribute of thought. However, the question remains how such aberrations can arise in a Monism of divine Substance; how we can so thoroughly forget our partial nature; and why so many people have to get their knowledge of God from lowly beginnings in experience. In actual fact, there is a vast difference between the order of our knowledge and the order of being, and it is difficult to reconcile this experienced difference with Spinoza's views on knowledge.

arise from a want of understanding of the primary elements of nature as a whole; whence we proceed without due order, and confound nature with abstract rules, which, although they be true enough in their sphere, yet, when misapplied, confound themselves, and pervert the order of nature. However, if we proceed with as little abstraction as possible, and begin from primary elements—that is, from the source and origin of nature, as far back as we can reach,--we need not fear any deceptions of this kind. As far as the knowledge of the origin of nature is concerned, there is no danger of our confounding it with abstractions. For when a thing is conceived in the abstract, as are all universal notions, the said universal notions are always more extensive in the mind than the number of individuals forming their contents really existing in nature.

Again, there are many things in nature, the difference between which is so slight as to be hardly perceptible to the understanding; so that it may readily happen that such things are confounded together, if they be conceived abstractedly. But since the first principle of nature cannot (as we shall see hereafter) be conceived abstractedly or universally, and cannot extend further in the understanding than it does in reality, and has no likeness to mutable things, no confusion need be feared in respect to the idea of it, provided (as before shown) that we possess a standard of truth. This is, in fact, a being single and infinite; in other words, it is the sum total of being, beyond which there is no being found.

ETHICS[14]

Part II

In order not to omit anything necessary to be known, I will briefly set down the causes, whence are derived the terms styled TRANSCENDENTAL, such as Being, Thing, Something. These terms arose from the fact, that the human body, being limited, is only capable of distinctly forming a certain number of images within itself at the same time; if this number be exceeded the images will begin to be confused; if this number of images which the body is capable of forming distinctly within itself, be largely exceeded, all will become entirely confused one with another. This being so, it is evident that the human mind can distinctly imagine as many things simultaneously, as its body can form images simultaneously. When the images become quite confused in the body, the mind also imagines all bodies confusedly without any distinction, and will comprehend them, as it were, under one attribute, namely, under the attri-

[14]Selected from *Ethics Demonstrated According to the Geometrical Order* (1677), as found in *Philosophy of Benedict de Spinoza, op. cit.*, pp. 109–115, 267–273.

bute of Being, Thing, etc. The same conclusion can be drawn from the fact that images are not always equally vivid, and from other analogous causes, which there is no need to explain here; for the purpose which we have in view it is sufficient for us to consider one only. All may be reduced to this, that these terms represent ideas in the highest degree confused. From similar causes arise those notions, which we call GENERAL, such as man, horse, dog, etc. They arise, to wit, from the fact that so many images, for instance, of men, are formed simultaneously in the human mind, that the powers of imagination break down, not indeed utterly, but to the extent of the mind losing count of small differences between individuals (*e.g.*, color, size, etc.) and their definite number, and only distinctly imagining that, in which all the individuals, in so far as the body is affected by them, agree; for that is the point, in which each of the said individuals chiefly affected the body; this the mind expresses by the name man, and this it predicates of an infinite number of particular individuals. For, as we have said, it is unable to imagine the definite number of individuals.[15] We must, however, bear in mind, that these general notions are not formed by all men in the same way, but vary in each individual according as the point varies, whereby the body has been most often affected and which the mind most easily imagines or remembers. For instance, those who have most often regarded with admiration the stature of man, will by the name of man understand an animal of erect stature; those who have been accustomed to regard some other attribute, will form a different general image of man, for instance, that man is a laughing animal, a two-footed animal without feathers, a rational animal, and thus, in other cases, everyone will form general images of things according to the habit of his body.

It is thus not to be wondered at, that among philosophers, who seek to explain things in nature merely by the images formed of them, so many controversies should have arisen.

Note II.—From all that has been said above it is clear, that we, in many cases, perceive and form our general notions: (1) From particular things represented to our intellect fragmentarily, confusedly, and without order through our senses. I have settled to call such perceptions by the name of knowledge from the mere suggestions of experience. (2) From symbols, *e.g.*, from the fact of having read or heard certain words we remember things and form certain ideas concerning them, similar to those through which we imagine things. I shall call both these ways of regarding things KNOWLEDGE OF THE FIRST KIND, OPINION, OR IMAGINATION. (3) From the fact that we have notions common to all men, and adequate ideas of the properties of things; this I call REASON and KNOWLEDGE OF THE SECOND KIND. Besides these two kinds of knowledge, there is, as I will hereafter show, a third kind

---

[15]This account of the formation of general ideas is required by Spinoza's view that there is no causal influence between mind and body, but only a sort of parallelism. Hence there can be no true abstraction; there are only images, and as these become confused there will be, so Spinoza feels, corresponding confused or general ideas in the mind.

of knowledge, which we will call intuition. This kind of knowledge proceeds from an adequate idea of the absolute essence of certain attributes of God to the adequate knowledge of the essence of things.[16] I will illustrate all three kinds of knowledge by a single example. Three numbers are given for finding a fourth, which shall be to the third as the second is to the first. Tradesmen without hesitation multiply the second by the third, and divide the product by the first; either because they have not forgotten the rule which they received from a master without any proof, or because they have often made trial of it with simple numbers, or by virtue of the proof of the nineteenth proposition of the seventh book of Euclid, namely, in virtue of the general property of proportionals.

But with very simple numbers there is no need of this. For instance, one, two, three, being given, everyone can see that the fourth proportional is six; and this is much clearer, because we infer the fourth number from an intuitive grasping of the ratio, which the first bears to the second.

Prop. XLI. Knowledge of the first kind is the only source of falsity, knowledge of the second and third kinds is necessarily true.[17]

Proof.—To knowledge of the first kind we have (in the foregoing note) assigned all those ideas, which are inadequate and confused; therefore this kind of knowledge is the only source of falsity. Furthermore, we assigned to the second and third kinds of knowledge those ideas which are adequate; therefore these kinds are necessarily true. Q.E.D.

Prop. XLII. Knowledge of the second and third kinds, not knowledge of the first kind, teaches us to distinguish the true from the false.

Proof.—This proposition is self-evident. He, who knows how to distinguish between true and false, must have an adequate idea of true and false. That is, he must know the true and the false by the second or third kind of knowledge.

Prop. XLIII. He, who has a true idea, simultaneously knows that he has a true idea, and cannot doubt of the truth of the thing perceived.

Proof.—A true idea in us is an idea which is adequate in God, in so far as he is displayed through the nature of the human mind. Let us suppose that there is in God, in so far as he is displayed through the human mind, an adequate idea, A. The idea of this idea must also necessarily be in God, and be referred to him in the same way as the idea A. But the idea A is supposed to be referred to God, in so far as he is displayed through the human mind; therefore the idea of the idea A must be referred to God in the same manner; that is, the adequate idea of the idea A will be in the mind, which has the adequate idea A; therefore,

---

[16]These three kinds of knowledge are the same as the four kinds presented in the previous selection. Here, however, he combines two kinds under the name of opinion or imagination.

In this part Spinoza explicitly connects the highest type of knowledge with the idea of God, and again he affirms the *a priori* procedure of going from the knowledge of God to the adequate knowledge of the essences of things.

[17]The use of propositions, proofs, and corollaries indicate Spinoza's "geometrical" fashion and his hope to obtain at least as much certitude in his philosophy as he finds in mathematics.

he, who has an adequate idea or knows a thing truly, must at the same time have an adequate idea or true knowledge of his knowledge; that is, obviously, he must be assured. Q.E.D.

Note.—I explained in the note to II. xxi. what is meant by the idea of an idea; but we may remark that the foregoing proposition is in itself sufficiently plain. No one, who has a true idea, is ignorant that a true idea involves the highest certainty. For to have a true idea is only another expression for knowing a thing perfectly, or as well as possible. No one, indeed, can doubt of this, unless he thinks that an idea is something lifeless, like a picture on a panel, and not a mode of thinking—namely, the very act of understanding. And who, I ask, can know that he understands anything, unless he do first understand it? In other words, who can know that he is sure of a thing, unless he be first sure of that thing? Further, what can there be more clear, and more certain, than a true idea as a standard of truth? Even as light displays both itself and darkness, so is truth a standard both of itself and of falsity.[18]

I think I have thus sufficiently answered these questions—namely, if a true idea is distinguished from a false idea, only in so far as it is said to agree with its object, a true idea has no more reality or perfection than a false idea (since the two are only distinguished by an extrinsic mark); consequently, neither will a man who has true ideas have any advantage over him who has only false ideas. Further, how comes it that men have false ideas? Lastly, how can any one be sure, that he has ideas which agree with their objects? These questions, I repeat, I have, in my opinion, sufficiently answered. The difference between a true idea and a false idea is plain: the former is related to the latter as being is to not-being. The causes of falsity I have set forth very clearly in II. xix. and II. xxxv. with the note. From what is there stated, the difference between a man who has true ideas, and a man who has only false ideas, is made apparent. As for the last question—as to how a man can be sure that he has ideas that agree with their objects, I have just pointed out, with abundant clearness, that his knowledge arises from the simple fact, that he has an idea which corresponds with its object—in other words, that truth is its own standard. We may add that our mind, in so far as it perceives things truly, is part of the infinite intellect of God; therefore, the clear and distinct ideas of the mind are as necessarily true as the ideas of God.

Prop. XLIV. It is not in the nature of reason to regard things as contingent, but as necessary.[19]

Proof.—It is in the nature of reason to perceive things truly, namely, as they are in themselves—that is, not as contingent, but as necessary. Q.E.D.

---

[18]For Spinoza, the having of a true idea is sufficient in itself, and a true idea needs no prior process or justification. In other words, he rejects the painful process of methodic doubt advocated by Descartes and urges his readers to have the courage to entertain a true idea; for reflection on knowledge already presupposes true ideas clearly had, and "for the certitude of truth, no further sign is necessary beyond the possession of a true idea." Cf. *supra*, p. 99.

[19]This is in keeping with Spinoza's Monism.

Corollary I.—Hence it follows, that it is only through our imagination that we consider things, whether in respect to the future or the past, as contingent.

* * *

Corollary II.—It is in the nature of reason to perceive things under a certain form of eternity *(sub quadam aeternitatis specie)*.

Proof.—It is in the nature of reason to regard things, not as contingent, but as necessary. Reason perceives this necessity of things truly—that is, as it is in itself. But this necessity of things is the very necessity of the eternal nature of God; therefore, it is in the nature of reason to regard things under this form of eternity. We may add that the bases of reason are the notions which answer to things common to all, and which do not answer to the essence of any particular thing: which must therefore be conceived without any relation to time, under a certain form of eternity.

* * *

Part V

Prop. XXIV. The more we understand particular things, the more do we understand God.[20]

Proof.—This is evident from I. xxv. Coroll.

Prop. XXV. The highest endeavor of the mind, and the highest virtue is to understand things by the third kind of knowledge.

Proof.—The third kind of knowledge proceeds from an adequate idea of certain attributes of God to an adequate knowledge of the essence of things; and, in proportion as we understand things more in this way, we better understand God (by the last Prop.); therefore the highest virtue of the mind, that is the power, or nature, or highest endeavor of the mind, is to understand things by the third kind of knowledge. Q.E.D.

Prop. XXVI. In proportion as the mind is more capable of understanding things by the third kind of knowledge, it desires more to understand things by that kind.

Proof.—This is evident. For, in so far as we conceive the mind to be capable of conceiving things by this kind of knowledge, we, to that extent, conceive it as determined thus to conceive things; and consequently, the mind desires so to do, in proportion as it is more capable thereof. Q.E.D.

Prop. XXVII. From this third kind of knowledge arises the highest possible mental acquiescence.

Proof.—The highest virtue of the mind is to know God, or to understand things by the third kind of knowledge, and this virtue is greater in proportion as the mind knows things more by the said kind of knowledge: consequently, he who

[20]From here on Spinoza develops his meaning of the third or highest kind of knowledge, and his development indicat[illegible] the depths and heights of his views [illegible]e power of the human mind. His [illegible]hysical view of the mind as part of [illegible] mind and his equating of knowledge with virtue and perfection are well illustrated in these pages. However, it is hard to find in all this the traces of ordinary human knowledge.

knows things by this kind of knowledge passes to the summit of human perfection, and is therefore affected by the highest pleasure, such pleasure being accompanied by the idea of himself and his own virtue: thus, from this kind of knowledge arises the highest possible acquiescence. Q.E.D.

* * *

Prop. XXX. Our mind, in so far as it knows itself and the body under the form of eternity, has to that extent necessarily a knowledge of God, and knows that it is in God, and is conceived through God.

Proof.—Eternity is the very essence of God, in so far as this involves necessary existence. Therefore to conceive things under the form of eternity, is to conceive things in so far as they are conceived through the essence of God as real entities, or in so far as they involve existence through the essence of God; wherefore our mind, in so far as it conceives itself and the body under the form of eternity, has to that extent necessarily a knowledge of God, and knows, etc. Q.E.D.

* * *

Note.—In proportion, therefore, as a man is more potent in this kind of knowledge, he will be more completely conscious of himself and of God; in other words, he will be more perfect and blessed, as will appear more clearly in the sequel. But we must here observe that, although we are already certain that the mind is eternal, in so far as it conceives things under the form of eternity, yet, in order that what we wish to show may be more readily explained and better understood, we will consider the mind itself, as though it had just begun to exist and to understand things under the form of eternity, as indeed we have done hitherto; this we may do without any danger of error, so long as we are careful not to draw any conclusion, unless our premises are plain.

Prop. XXXII. Whatsoever we understand by the third kind of knowledge, we take delight in, and our delight is accompanied by the idea of God as cause.

Proof.—From this kind of knowledge arises the highest possible mental acquiescence, that is, pleasure, and this acquiescence is accompanied by the idea of the mind itself, and consequently the idea also of God as cause. Q.E.D.

Corollary.—From the third kind of knowledge necessarily arises the intellectual love of God.[21] From this kind of knowledge arises pleasure accompanied by the idea of God as

[21]This presentation of the doctrine of the *intellectual love of God* is the culminating point in Spinoza's philosophy, and it results from the intuitive knowledge of the eternal essence of mind and body as modes of God. This love is said to be eternal, and it is one with God's love for Himself.

This love is also said to be man's salvation, in that true moral advance is made identical with the philosophical clarification of ideas. This is a religious Rationalism which makes growth in knowledge the same as growth in moral living.

This love also constitutes our freedom. But here freedom loses all meaning, since it amounts to the possession of the clear knowledge that we are in all things fully determined by God and inwardly determined as modes of the divine being.

cause, that is, the love of God; not in so far as we imagine him as present, but in so far as we understand him to be eternal; this is what I call the intellectual love of God.

Prop. XXXIII. The intellectual love of God, which arises from the third kind of knowledge, is eternal.

Proof.—The third kind of knowledge is eternal; therefore, the love which arises therefrom is also necessarily eternal. Q.E.D.

Note.—Although this love toward God has (by the foregoing Prop.) no beginning, it yet possesses all the perfections of love, just as though it had arisen as we feigned in the Corollary of the last Proposition. Nor is there here any difference, except that the mind possesses as eternal those same perfections which we feigned to accrue to it, and they are accompanied by the idea of God as eternal cause. If pleasure consists in the transition to a greater perfection, assuredly blessedness must consist in the mind being endowed with perfection itself.

* * *

Prop. XXXVI. The intellectual love of the mind toward God is that very love of God whereby God loves himself, not in so far as he is infinite, but in so far as he can be explained through the essence of the human mind regarded under the form of eternity; in other words, the intellectual love of the mind toward God is part of the infinite love wherewith God loves himself.

Proof.—This love of the mind must be referred to the activities of the mind; it is itself, indeed, an activity whereby the mind regards itself accompanied by the idea of God a cause; that is an activity whereb God, in so far as he can be explaine through the human mind, regard himself accompanied by the idea o himself; therefore (by the las Prop.), this love of the mind is par of the infinite love wherewith Go loves himself. Q.E.D.

Corollary.—Hence it follows tha God, in so far as he loves himself loves man, and consequently, tha the love of God toward men, and th intellectual love of the mind towar God are identical.

Note.—From what has been sai we clearly understand, wherein ou salvation, or blessedness, or free dom, consists: namely, in the con stant and eternal love toward God or in God's love toward men. Thi love or blessedness is, in the Bible called Glory, and not undeservedly For whether this love be referre to God or to the mind, it may rightl be called acquiescence of spirit which is not really distinguishe from glory. In so far as it is referre to God, it is pleasure, if we ma still use that term, accompanied b the idea of itself, and, in so far as i is referred to the mind, it is th same.

Again, since the essence of ou mind consists solely in knowledge whereof the beginning and the foun dation is God, it becomes clear t us, in what manner and way ou mind, as to its essence and exist ence, follows from the divine natur and constantly depends on God. have thought it worth while here t call attention to this, in order t show by this example how the knowl edge of particular things, which have called intuitive or of the thir kind, is potent, and more powerfu than the universal knowledge, which I have styled knowledge of the second kind. For, although in Part I. I showed in general terms, that all things (and consequently, also, the human mind) depend as to their essence and existence on God, yet that demonstration, though legitimate and placed beyond the chances of doubt, does not affect our mind so much, as when the same conclusion is derived from the actual essence of some particular thing, which we say depends on God.

6

The Power of Mind

Gottfried Wilhelm Leibnitz (1646-1716)

Characteristic of Leibnitz' life and writings is the desire to promote peace and harmony in religion, in politics, and even in metaphysics. As he sees it, the universe is made up of countless substances, or beings capable of action, which are simple, inextended sources of energy whose activity is "to perceive." God has chosen to give existence only to those things which promote the greatest possible perfection, and which thus assure the best possible world. All substances are interrelated, each one reflects all else, and yet each proceeds in its own characteristic activity of perceiving[1], without causal influence from any other being except God.

Hence, in those substances which have self-conscious activity--knowledge—there can be no question of *receiving* impulses from outside. Knowledge becomes the unfolding from within the being of ideas or perceptions which are already pre-contained in it from the moment of its creation. Knowledge, as described by Leibnitz, very much resembles Platonic reminiscence and is open to the objections usually urged against an innatist, a priori, rationalistic philosophy.

The selections now offered serve to illustrate Leibnitz' views on the ideal of knowledge and to show how he has earned the title of innatist.

---

[1]In his *Monadology*, n. 14, Leibnitz speaks of *perception* as "the passing state, which involves and represents a multitude in unity or in the simple substance." That is to say that each simple substance, or Monad, is a living representation or expression of the universe; not that all things are conscious of this activity. Where there is awareness of the act of perceiving and awareness of the substantial self which is acting, there is a special type of knowledge or perception called by Leibnitz *reflective knowledge* or *apperception*. This notion of a living, perceiving universe indicates the stress found in Leibnitz on the dynamic aspects of being. (Cf. also *Monadology*, nn. 19, 21.)

DISCOURSE ON METAPHYSICS[2]

VIII. In order to distinguish between the activities of God and the activities of created things we must explain the conception of an individual substance.

It is quite difficult to distinguish God's actions from those of his creatures. Some think that God does everything; others imagine that he only conserves the force that he has given to created things. How far can we say either of these opinions is right?

In the first place since activity and passivity pertain properly to individual substances (*actiones sunt suppositorum*) it will be necessary to explain what such a substance is. It is indeed true that when several predicates are attributes of a single subject and this subject is not an attribute of another, we speak of it as an individual substance, but this is not enough, and such an explanation is merely nominal. We must therefore inquire what it is to be an attribute in reality of a certain subject. Now it is evident that every true predication has some basis in the nature of things, and even when a proposition is not identical, that is, when the predicate is not expressly contained in the subject, it is still necessary that it be virtually contained in it, and this is what the philosophers call *in-esse*, saying thereby that the predicate is in the subject. Thus the content of the subject must always include that of the predicate in such a way that if one understands perfectly the concept of the subject, he will know that the predicate appertains to it also. This being so, we are able to say that this is the nature of an individual substance or of a complete being, namely, to afford a conception so complete that the concept shall be sufficient for the understanding of it and for the deduction of all the predicates of which the substance is or may become the subject.[3] Thus the quality of king, which belonged to Alexander the Great, an abstraction from the subject, is not sufficiently determined to constitute an individual, and does not contain the other qualities of the same subject, nor everything which the idea of this

[2]Selected from *Discourse on Metaphysics* (1686), as found in Gottfried Leibnitz, *Discourse on Metaphysics* and *Monadology*, trans. by George Montgomery (La Salle, Ill.: Open Court Publishing Co., 1957), pp. 12-23, 44-48.

[3]This is one of the points stressed by Leibnitz, and it is connected with his view that all true judgments are basically analytic, so that in knowing the subject one can (at least ideally) know all the predicates which can be affirmed about it. The reason for this is given a few sentences later where by way of example it is said that the soul of Alexander contains marks of all that had happened or would happen to him, as well as traces of all that occurs in the universe. Leibnitz admits that only God can actually have such knowledge; and it must be admitted that He does know all things. However, the difficulty which is implicit here and which comes out with more force later on in his writings is this: If God knows what will happen, and if the "marks" are already precontained in the subject, so that even "free" activity becomes merely the necessitated and foreordained unfolding of what is already there, then what becomes of human liberty?

prince includes. God, however, seeing the individual concept, or haecceity, of Alexander, sees there at the same time the basis and the reason of all the predicates which can be truly uttered regarding him; for instance that he will conquer Darius and Porus, even to the point of knowing *a priori* (and not by experience) whether he died a natural death or by poison, - facts which we can learn only through history. When we carefully consider the connection of things we see also the possibility of saying that there was always in the soul of Alexander marks of all that had happened to him and evidences of all that would happen to him and traces even of everything which occurs in the universe, although God alone could recognize them all.

IX. That every individual substance expresses the whole universe in its own manner and that in its full concept is included all its experiences together with all the attendent circumstances and the whole sequence of exterior events.

There follow from these considerations several noticeable paradoxes; among others that it is not true that two substances may be exactly alike and differ only numerically,[4] *solo numero*, and that what St. Thomas says on this point regarding angels and intelligences *(quod ibi omne individuum sit species infima)* is true of all substances, provided that the specific difference is understood as Geometers understand it in the case of figures; again that a substance will be able to commence only through creation and perish only through annihilation; that a substance cannot be divided into two nor can one be made out of two, and that thus the number of substances neither augments nor diminishes through natural means, although they are frequently transformed. Furthermore every substance is like an entire world and like a mirror of God, or indeed of the whole world it portrays, each one in its own fashion; almost as the same city is variously represented according to the various situations of him who is regarding it. Thus the universe is multiplied in some sort as many times as there are substances, and the glory of God is multiplied in the same way by as many wholly different representations of his works. It can indeed be said that every substance bears in some sort the character of God's infinite wisdom and omnipotence, and imitates him as much as it is able to; for it expresses, although confusedly, all

[4]Behind this thinking is Leibnitz' doctrine on the relations between "essences" prior to creation. Before creation each "essence" is looked upon as striving for existence. However, only those will reach actual existence which, interacting with one another, will guarantee the greatest amount of perfection and assure the "best possible" world. As Leibnitz presents his views, it seems that God *must* select only those essences which promote maximum perfection. Hence, if any two substances are exactly alike on the same level of being, there would be no reason for *two*, since their perfection would be equal. Moreover, because each substance is related to all others, each reflects and is a mirror of the entire universe. Now, if God is required to create the best possible world and no other, if His decision is determined by relations between "essences," then to speak of God's freedom in creating loses all meaning. On "essence prior to creation," cf. *Leibnitz Selections*, Philip Wiener, ed. (New York Charles Scribner's Sons, 1951), pp. 91-93.

that happens in the universe, past, present and future, deriving thus a certain resemblance to an infinite perception or power of knowing. And since all other substances express this particular substance and accommodate themselves to it, we can say that it exerts its power upon all the others in imitation of the omnipotence of the creator.

X. That the belief in substantial forms has a certain basis in fact, but that these forms effect no changes in the phenomena and must not be employed for the explanation of particular events.

It seems that the ancients, able men, who were accustomed to profound meditations and taught theology and philosophy for several centuries and some of whom recommend themselves to us on account of their piety, had some knowledge of that which we have just said and this is why they introduced and maintained the substantial forms so much decried to-day. But they were not so far from the truth nor so open to ridicule as the common run of our new philosophers imagine. I grant that the consideration of these forms is of no service in the details of physics and ought not to be employed in the explanation of particular phenomena. In regard to this last point, the schoolmen were at ault, as were also the physicians of imes past who followed their example, thinking they had given the reason for the properties of a body in mentioning the forms and qualities without going to the trouble of examining the manner of operation; as if ne should be content to say that a lock had a certain amount of clockess derived from its form, and hould not inquire in what that clockness consisted. This is indeed enough for the man who buys it, provided he surrenders the care of it to someone else. The fact, however, that there was this misunderstanding and misuse of the substantial forms should not bring us to throw away something whose recognition is so necessary in metaphysics. Since without these we will not be able, I hold, to know the ultimate principles nor to lift our minds to the knowledge of the incorporeal natures and of the marvels of God. Yet as the geometer does not need to encumber his mind with the famous puzzle of the composition of the continuum, and as no moralist, and still less a jurist or a statesman has need to trouble himself with the great difficulties which arise in conciliating free will with the providential activity of God, (since the geometer is able to make all his demonstrations and the statesman can complete all his deliberations without entering into these discussions which are so necessary and important in Philosophy and Theology), so in the same way the physicist can explain his experiments, now using simpler experiments already made, now employing geometrical and mechanical demonstrations without any need of the general considerations which belong to another sphere, and if he employs the co-operation of God, or perhaps of some soul or animating force, or something else of a similar nature, he goes out of his path quite as much as that man who, when facing an important practical question would wish to enter into profound argumentations regarding the nature of destiny and of our liberty; a fault which men quite frequently commit without realizing it when they cumber their minds with considerations regarding fate, and thus they are even sometimes turned from a good resolution or from some necessary provision.

XI. That the opinions of the theologians and of the so-called scholastic philosophers are not to be wholly despised.

I know that I am advancing a great paradox in pretending to resuscitate in some sort the ancient philosophy, and to recall *postliminio* the substantial forms almost banished from our modern thought. But perhaps I will not be condemned lightly when it is known that I have long meditated over the modern philosophy and that I have devoted much time to experiments in physics and to the demonstrations of geometry and that I, too, for a long time was persuaded of the baselessness of those "beings" which, however, I was finally obliged to take up again in spite of myself and as though by force. The many investigations which I carried on compelled me to recognize that our moderns do not do sufficient justice to Saint Thomas and to the other great men of that period and that there is in the theories of the scholastic philosophers and theologians far more solidity than is imagined, provided that these theories are employed *a propos* and in their place. I am persuaded that if some careful and meditative mind were to take the trouble to clarify and direct their thoughts in the manner of analytic geometers, he would find a great treasure of very important truths, wholly demonstrable.

XII. That the conception of the extension of a body is in a way imaginary and does not constitute the substance of the body.

But to resume the thread of our discussion, I believe that he who will meditate upon the nature of substance, as I have explained it above, will find that the whole nature of bodies is not exhausted in their extension, that is to say, in their size, figure and motion, but that we must recognize something which corresponds to soul, something which is commonly called substantial form, although these forms effect no change in the phenomena, any more than do the souls of beasts, that is if they have souls. It is even possible to demonstrate that the ideas of size, figure, and motion are not so distinctive as is imagined, and that they stand for something imaginary relative to our preceptions as do, although to a greater extent, the ideas of color, heat, and the other similar qualities in regard to which we may doubt whether they are actually to be found in the nature of the things outside of us. This is why these latter qualities are unable to constitute "substance" and if there is no other principle of identity in bodies than that which has just been referred to a body would not subsist more than for a moment.

The souls and the substance-forms of other bodies are entirely different from intelligent souls which alone know their actions, and not only do not perish through natural means but indeed always retain the knowledge of what they are; a fact which makes them alone open to chastisement or recompense, and makes them citizens of the republic of the universe whose monarch is God. Hence it follows that all the other creatures should serve them, a point which we shall discuss more amply later.

XIII. As the individual concept of each person includes once for all everything which can ever happen to him, in it can be seen, a priori *the evidences or the reasons for the reality of each event, and why one happened sooner than the other. But these events, however certain, are nevertheless contingent, being based on the free choice of God and of his creatures. It is true that their choices always have their reasons, but they incline to the choices under no compulsion of necessity.*

But before going further it is necessary to meet a difficulty which may arise regarding the principles which we have set forth in the preceding. We have said that the concept of an individual substance includes once for all everything which can ever happen to it and that in considering this concept one will be able to see everything which can truly be said concerning the individual, just as we are able to see in the nature of a circle all the properties which can be derived from it. But does it not seem that in this way the difference between contingent and necessary truths will be destroyed, that there will be no place for human liberty, and that an absolute fatality will rule as well over all our actions as over all the rest of the events of the world?[5] To this I reply that a distinction must be made between that which is certain and that which is necessary. Every one grants that future contingencies are assured since God foresees them, but we do not say just because of that that they are necessary. But it will be objected, that if any conclusion can be deduced infallibly from some definition or concept, it is necessary; and now since we have maintained that everything which is to happen to anyone is already virtually included in his nature or concept, as all the properties are contained in the definition of a circle, therefore, the difficulty still remains. In order to meet the objection completely, I say that the connection or sequence is of two kinds; the one, absolutely necessary, whose contrary implies contradiction, occurs in the eternal verities like the truths of geometry; the other is necessary only *ex hypothesi*, and so to speak by accident, and in itself it is contingent since the contrary is not implied. This latter sequence is not founded upon ideas wholly pure and upon the pure understanding of God, but upon his free decrees and upon the processes of the universe. Let us give an example. Since Julius Caesar will become perpetual Dictator and master of the Republic and will overthrow the liberty of Rome, this action is contained in his concept, for we have supposed that it is the nature of such a perfect concept of a subject to involve everything, in fact so that the predicate may be included in the subject *ut possit inesse subjecto*. We may say that it is not in virtue of this concept or idea that he is obliged to perform this action,

---

[5]Leibnitz here attacks the objection that his doctrine destroys liberty. He insists that the substance does precontain all its predicates, so all that a free agent will ever do can be known a priori in knowing the subject. However, Leibnitz insists that man's free acts occur with hypothetical necessity, not with absolute necessity; and in this sense the opposite is not impossible, but it just *will not happen.* The reconciliation of God's foreknowledge with man's freedom is a thorny philosophical question, and it is not at all clear that Leibnitz' solution does allow for human liberty.

since it pertains to him only because God knows everything. But it will be insisted in reply that his nature or form responds to this concept, and since God imposes upon him this personality, he is compelled henceforth to live up to it. I could reply by instancing the similar case of the future contingencies which as yet have no reality save in the understanding and will of God, and which, because God has given them in advance this form, must needs correspond to it. But I prefer to overcome a difficulty rather than to excuse it by instancing other difficulties, and what I am about to say will serve to clear up the one as well as the other. It is here that must be applied the distinction in the kind of relation, and I say that that which happens conformably to these decrees is assured, but that it is not therefore necessary, and if anyone did the contrary, he would do nothing impossible in itself, although it is impossible *ex hypothesi* that that other happen. For if anyone were capable of carrying out a complete demonstration by virtue of which he could prove this connection of the subject, which is Caesar, with the predicate, which is his successful enterprise, he would bring us to see in fact that the future dictatorship of Caesar had its basis in his concept or nature, so that one would see there a reason why he resolved to cross the Rubicon rather than to stop, and why he gained instead of losing the day at Pharsalus, and that it was reasonable and by consequence assured that this would occur, but one would not prove that it was necessary in itself, nor that the contrary implied a contradiction, almost in the same way in which it is reasonable and assured that God will always do what is best although that which is less perfect is not thereby implied. For it would be found that this demonstration of this predicate as belonging to Caesar is not as absolute as are those of numbers or of geometry, but that this predicate supposes a sequence of things which God has shown by his free will. This sequence is based on the first free decree of God which was to do always that which is the most perfect and upon the decree which God made following the first one, regarding human nature, which is that men should always do, although freely, that which appears to be the best. Now every truth which is founded upon this kind of decree is contingent, although certain, for the decrees of God do not change the possibilities of things and, as I have already said, although God assuredly chooses the best, this does not prevent that which is less perfect from being possible in itself. Although it will never happen, it is not its impossibility but its imperfection which causes him to reject it. Now nothing is necessitated whose opposite is possible. One will then be in a position to satisfy these kinds of difficulties, however great they may appear (and in fact they have not been less vexing to all other thinkers who have ever treated this matter), provided that he considers well that all contingent propositions have reasons why they are thus, rather than otherwise, or indeed (what is the same thing) that they have proof *a priori* of their truth, which render them certain and show that the connection of the subject and predicate in these propositions has its basis in the nature of the one and of the other, but he must further remember that such contingent propositions have not the demonstrations of necessity, since their reasons are founded only on the principle of contingency or of the existence of things, that is to say, upon that which is, or which appears to be the best among several things equally possible. Necessary truths, on the other hand, are founded upon the principle of contradiction, and upon the possibility or impossibility of the essences themselves, without regard here to the free will of God or of creatures.

* * *

XXVI. Ideas are all stored up within us. Plato's doctrine of reminiscence.

In order to see clearly what an idea is, we must guard ourselves against a misunderstanding. Many regard the idea as the form or the differentiation of our thinking, and according to this opinion we have the idea in our mind, in so far as we are thinking of it, and each separate time that we think of it anew we have another idea although similar to the preceding one. Some, however, take the idea as the immediate object of thought, or as a permanent form which remains even when we are no longer contemplating it. As a matter of fact our soul has the power of representing to itself any form or nature whenever the occasion comes for thinking about it, and I think that this activity of our soul is, so far as it expresses some nature, form or essence, properly the idea of the thing. This is in us, and is always in us, whether we are thinking of it or no. (Our soul expresses God and the universe and all essences as well as all existences.) This position is in accord with my principles that naturally nothing enters into our minds from outside.

It is a bad habit we have of thinking as though our minds receive certain messengers, as it were, or as if they had doors or windows. We have in our minds all those forms for all periods of time because the mind at every moment expresses all its future thoughts and already thinks confusedly of all that of which it will ever think distinctly. Nothing can be taught us of which we have not already in our minds the idea.[6] This idea is as it were the material out of which the thought will form itself. This is what Plato has excellently brought out in his doctrine of reminiscence, a doctrine which contains a great deal of truth, provided that it is properly understood and purged of the error of pre-existence, and provided that one does not conceive of the soul as having already known and thought at some other time what it learns and thinks now. Plato has also confirmed his position by a beautiful experiment. He introduces a small boy, whom he leads by short

[6]This view stresses both the independence of thought from sensation and the doctrine of innate ideas. Leibnitz held that no finite substance could act on another, that ideas have no point of origin in the senses, but that they are merely the unfolding of what is already precontained in the mind from the beginning. This rationalist explanation of knowledge denies rather than explains the human experience of knowing. Leibnitz' description of substance allows no possibility for abstraction as a way of getting at essential structures. Hence, any note of necessity or universality in knowledge must be due to a priori factors in knowledge; they must, in fact, be innate.

steps, to extremely difficult truths of geometry bearing on incommensurables, all this without teaching the boy anything, merely drawing out replies by a well arranged series of questions. This shows that the soul virtually knows those things, and needs only to be reminded (animadverted) to recognize the truths. Consequently it possesses at least the idea upon which these truths depend. We may say even that it already possesses those truths, if we consider them as the relations of the ideas.

XXVII. In what respect our souls can be compared to blank tablets and how conceptions are derived from the senses.

Aristotle preferred to compare our souls to blank tablets prepared for writing, and he maintained that nothing is in the understanding which does not come through the senses. This position is in accord with the popular conceptions as Aristotle's positions usually are. Plato thinks more profoundly. Such tenets or practicologies are nevertheless allowable in ordinary use somewhat in the same way as those who accept the Copernican theory still continue to speak of the rising and setting of the sun. I find indeed that these usages can be given a real meaning containing no error, quite in the same way as I have already pointed out that we may truly say particular substances act upon one another. In this same sense we may say that knowledge is received from without through the medium of the senses because certain exterior things contain or express more particularly the causes which determine us to certain thoughts. Because in the ordinary uses of life we attribute to the soul only that which belongs to it most manifestly and particularly, and there is no advantage in going further. When, however, we are dealing with the exactness of metaphysical truths, it is important to recognize the powers and independence of the soul which extend infinitely further than is commonly supposed. In order, therefore, to avoid misunderstandings it would be well to choose separate terms for the two. These expressions which are in the soul whether one is conceiving of them or not may be called ideas, while those which one conceives of or constructs may be called conceptions, *conceptus*. But whatever terms are used, it is always false to say that all our conceptions come from the so-called external senses, because those conceptions which I have of myself and of my thoughts, and consequently of being, of substance, of action, of identity, and of many others came from an inner experience.[7]

[7]Although Leibnitz admits that substances or monads advance from perception to perception, and that in some beings — men — this can be fully conscious and so constitute an advance in human knowledge, yet he insists here, and even more clearly in the next paragraph, that this growth in knowledge is in no way due to any influence from beings "outside" the knower, except God alone. Substances, for Leibnitz, "have no windows through which anything can enter or depart" (*Monadology*, n. 7); no one created substance can act directly on another. Hence, any change proceeds "from an *internal principle*" (*Monadology*, n. 11). By this, Leibnitz denies the Aristotelico-Thomistic position that all we know is somehow derived through the senses and really presents human knowledge as the unfolding of what is innate in each one from the beginning. Thus, while Leibnitz may be looked upon as a realist in the sense that he admits

XXVIII. The only immediate object of our perceptions which exists outside of us is God, and in him alone is our light.

In the strictly metaphysical sense no external cause acts upon us excepting God alone, and he is in immediate relation with us only by virtue of our continual dependence upon him. Whence it follows that there is absolutely no other external object which comes into contact with our souls and directly excites perceptions in us. We have in our souls ideas of everything, only because of the continual action of God upon us, that is to say, because every effect expresses its cause and therefore the essences of our souls are certain expressions, imitations or images of the divine essence, divine thought and divine will, including all the ideas which are there contained. We may say, therefore, that God is for us the only immediate external object, and that we see things through him. For example, when we see the sun or the stars, it is God who gives to us and preserves in us the ideas and whenever our senses are affected according to his own laws in a certain manner, it is he, who by his continual concurrence, determines our thinking.[8] God is the sun and the light of souls, *lumen illuminans omnem hominem venientem in hunc mundum*, although this is not the current conception. I think I have already remarked that during the scholastic period many believed God to be the light of the soul, *intellectus agens animæ rationalis*, following in this the Holy Scriptures and the fathers who were always more Platonic than Aristotelian in their mode of thinking. The Averroists misused this conception, but others, among whom were several mystic theologians, and William of Saint Amour, also I think, understood this conception in a manner which assured the dignity of God and was able to raise the soul to a knowledge of its welfare.

XXIX. Yet we think directly by means of our own ideas and not through God's.

Nevertheless I cannot approve of the position of certain able philosophers who seem to hold that our ideas themselves are in God and not at all in us.[9] I think that in taking this position they have neither sufficiently considered the nature of substance, which we have just explained, nor the entire extension and independence of the soul which includes all that happens to it, and expresses God, and with him all possible and actual beings in the same way that an effect expresses its

an "external" world, his theory of knowledge allows for no influence from that world on our knowledge except through God, and so human knowledge can proceed just as if there were no such world.

[8]Leibnitz himself admits earlier that we have no awareness of this in ordinary living (no. XXVII), but he is forced to such a position by his metaphysical considerations on the nature of substance, according to which no monad "can be altered or changed in its inner being by any other creature" (*Monadology*, n. 7). Locke, in his *Essay*, will take the whole innatist position to task. It is not only that we do not experience such Innatism, but it cannot be reconciled with what we do experience.

[9]This seems to be aimed at Spinoza, whose extremes Leibnitz wished to avoid. Yet in his desire to avoid a Monism of substance and to stress the dynamic aspects of reality and of knowledge, Leibnitz himself goes to the extreme of denying any creaturely passivity or receptivity relative to the action of other creatures.

cause. It is indeed inconceivable that the soul should think using the ideas of something else. The soul when it thinks of anything must be affected effectively in a certain manner, and it must needs have in itself in advance not only the passive capacity of being thus affected, a capacity already wholly determined but it must have besides an active power by virtue of which it has always had in its nature the marks of the future production of this thought, and the disposition to produce it at its proper time. All of this shows that the soul already includes the idea which is comprised in any particular thought.

7

Ideas as Objects of Experience

John Locke (1632-1704)

Locke introduces British Empiricism with its emphasis on "experience." He is opposed to all sorts of Innatism, to apriorism, and to grandiose philosophical systems. His aim is to examine and determine the extent of human knowledge, and this he does by examining ideas, which he considers to be the immediate objects of knowledge.

He is famous for propagating the distinction between primary and secondary qualities; the former, according to Locke, resemble what is in reality; the latter do not. This position prepares the way for Berkeley's denial of the objectivity of all qualities and for Hume's sceptical views touching on substance and causality.

Locke feels that knowledge demands the admission of general ideas, and he seeks to find in the likenesses between things the foundation for the formation of such ideas; however, his rejection of any human ability to know anything about the essential structures of things leaves him without any truly metaphysical foundation for these universals.

The following selections present Locke's discussions about sensible qualities and his views on general ideas.

BOOK II: OF IDEAS[1]

Chapter I

OF IDEAS IN GENERAL, AND THEIR ORIGINAL

1. *Idea is the object of thinking.*—Every man being conscious to himself that he thinks, and that which his mind is applied about whilst thinking being the ideas that are there,[2] it is past doubt that men have in their minds several ideas, such as are those expressed by the words whiteness, hardness, sweetness, thinking, motion, man, elephant, army, drunkenness, and others: it is in the first place then to be inquired, How he comes by them? I know it is a received doctrine, that men have native ideas and original characters stamped upon their minds in their very first being. This opinion I have at large examined already[3]; and, I suppose, what I have said in the foregoing book will be much more easily admitted, when I have shown whence the understanding may get all the ideas it has, and by what ways and degrees they may come into the mind; for which I shall appeal to everyone's own observation and experience.

2. *All ideas come from sensation or reflection.*—Let us then suppose the mind to be, as we say, white paper, void of all characters, without any ideas; how comes it to be furnished? Whence comes it by that vast store, which the busy and boundless fancy of man has painted on it with an almost endless variety? Whence has it all the materials of reason and knowledge? To this I answer, in one word, from experience. In that all our knowledge is founded, and from that it ultimately derives itself.[4] Our observation, employed either about external sensible objects, or about the internal operations of our minds, perceived and reflected on by ourselves, is that which supplies our understandings

[1]The following selections are from Locke's *An Essay Concerning Human Understanding* (1690). A handy edition of extensive selections of this work can be found in: *Locke's Essay*, Mary W. Calkins, ed. (La Salle, Ill.: Open Court Publishing Co., 1927).

[2]This view, that ideas themselves are the objects known, became a commonplace and a landmark of British Empiricism. In the last analysis it denies all immediate contact with sensible reality and thus closes the door to verification of ideas; it will logically lead to the Immaterialism of Berkeley and the Scepticism of Hume. Basically, it means a confusion between *what* is known and *that by which* we know what is known.

[3]In Book I of the present *Essay* where he has delivered a devastating blow to the whole theory of Innatism.

[4]So although Locke considers ideas to be the immediate objects known, he does not hold that ideas are the only existents. For there is the external world from which ideas are derived through *sensation*, and there are real internal operations of the mind of which ideas are formed by *reflection*. These two, sensation and reflection, are the only two sources or operations of *experience*, and all the materials of knowledge come to the mind through them. Incidentally, as Locke sees it, sensation has absolute priority, for the mind must receive its initial data through sensation, and only afterwards can the understanding operate in its own distinctive way, observe its operations, and thus acquire ideas of reflection.

with all the materials of thinking. These two are the fountains of knowledge, from whence all the ideas we have, or can naturally have, do spring.

3. *The object of sensation one source of ideas.*—First, our senses, conversant about particular sensible objects, do convey into the mind several distinct perceptions of things, according to those various ways wherein those objects do affect them; and thus we come by those ideas we have of yellow, white, heat, cold, soft, hard, bitter, sweet, and all those which we call sensible qualities; which when I say the senses convey into the mind, I mean, they from external objects convey into the mind what produces there those perceptions. This great source of most of the ideas we have, depending wholly upon our senses, and derived by them to the understanding, I call *sensation.*

4. *The operations of our minds the other source of them.*—Secondly, the other fountain, from which experience furnisheth the understanding with ideas, is the perception of the operations of our own mind within us, as it is employed about the ideas it has got; which operations when the soul comes to reflect on and consider, do furnish the understanding with another set of ideas which could not be had from things without; and such are perception, thinking, doubting, believing, reasoning, knowing, willing, and all the different actings of our own minds; which we, being conscious of, and observing in ourselves, do from these receive into our understandings as distinct ideas, as we do from bodies affecting our senses. This source of ideas every man has wholly in himself; and though it be not sense as having nothing to do with external objects, yet it is very like it, and might properly enough be called *internal sense.* But as I call the other sensation, so I call this *reflection,* the ideas its affords being such only as the mind gets by reflecting on its own operations within itself. By reflection, then, in the following part of this discourse, I would be understood to mean that notice which the mind takes of its own operations, and the manner of them, by reason whereof there come to be ideas of these operations in the understanding. These two, I say, viz., external material things as the object of sensation, and the operations of our own minds within as the objects of reflection, are, to me, the only originals from whence all our ideas take their beginnings. The term *operations* here, I use in a large sense, as comprehending not barely the actions of the mind about its ideas, but some sort of passions arising sometimes from them, such as is the satisfaction or uneasiness arising from any thought.

5. *All our ideas are of the one or the other of these.*—The understanding seems to me not to have the least glimmering of any ideas which it doth not receive from one of these two. *External objects* furnish the mind with the ideas of sensible qualities, which are all those different perceptions they produce in us; and *the mind* furnishes the understanding with ideas of its own operations.

These, when we have taken a full survey of them, and their several modes, [combinations, and relations,] we shall find to contain all our whole stock of ideas; and that we have nothing in our minds which did not come in one of these two ways. Let anyone examine his own thoughts, and thoroughly search into his understanding, and then let him tell me, whether all the original ideas he has there, are any other than of the objects of his senses, or of the operations of his mind considered as objects of his reflection; and how great a mass of knowledge soever he imagines to be lodged there, he will, upon taking a strict view, see that he has not any idea in his mind but what one of these two have imprinted, though perhaps with infinite variety compounded and enlarged by the understanding, as we shall see hereafter.

6. *Observable in children.*—He that attentively considers the state of a child at his first coming into the world, will have little reason to think him stored with plenty of ideas that are to be the matter of his future knowledge. It is by degrees he comes to be furnished with them; and though the ideas of obvious and familiar qualities imprint themselves before the memory begins to keep a register of time or order, yet it is often so late before some unusual qualities come in the way, that there are few men that cannot recollect the beginning of their acquaintance with them: and, if it were worth while, no doubt a child might be so ordered as to have but a very few even of the ordinary ideas till he were grown up to a man. But all that are born into the world being surrounded with bodies that perpetually and diversely affect them, variety of ideas, whether care be taken about it or not, are imprinted on the minds of children. Light and colors are busy at hand everywhere when the eye is but open; sounds and some tangible qualities fail not to solicit their proper senses; and force an entrance to the mind; but yet I think it will be granted easily, that if a child were kept in a place where he never saw any other but black and white till he were a man, he would have no more ideas of scarlet or green than he that from his childhood never tasted an oyster or a pineapple has of those particular relishes.

7. *Men are differently furnished with these according to the different objects they converse with.*—Men then come to be furnished with fewer or more simple ideas from without, according as the objects they converse with afford greater or less variety; and from the operations of their minds within, according as they more or less reflect on them. For, though he that contemplates the operations of his mind cannot but have plain and clear ideas of them; yet, unless he turn his thoughts that way, and considers them attentively, he will no more have clear and distinct ideas of all the operations of his mind, and all that may be observed therein, than he will have all the particular ideas of any landscape, or of the parts and motions of a clock, who will not turn his eyes to it, and with attention heed all the parts of it. The picture or clock may be so placed, that they may come in his way every day; but yet he will have but a confused idea of all the parts they are made of, till he applies himself with attention to consider them each in particular.

8. *Ideas of reflection later, because they need attention.*—And hence we see the reason why it is pretty late before most children get ideas of the operations of their own minds; and some have not any very clear or perfect ideas of the greatest part of them all their lives; because, though they pass there con-

tinually, yet floating visions, they make not deep impressions enough to leave in the mind, clear, distinct, lasting ideas, till the understanding turns inwards upon itself, reflects on its own operations, and makes them the objects of its own contemplation. Children, when they come first into it, are surrounded with a world of new things, which, by a constant solicitation of their senses, draw the mind constantly to them, forward to take notice of new, and apt to be delighted with the variety of changing objects. Thus the first years are usually employed and diverted in looking abroad. Men's business in them is to acquaint themselves with what is to be found without; and so, growing up in a constant attention to outward sensations, seldom make any considerable reflection on what passes within them till they come to be of riper years; and some scarce ever at all.

9. *The soul begins to have ideas when it begins to perceive.*—To ask, at what time a man has first any ideas, is to ask when he begins to perceive; *having ideas,* and *perception,* being the same thing. I know it is an opinion, that the soul always thinks; and that it has the actual perception of ideas in itself constantly, as long as it exists; and that actual thinking is as inseparable from the soul, as actual extension is from the body: which if true, to inquire after the beginning of a man's ideas is the same as to inquire after the beginning of his soul. For by this account, soul and its ideas, as body and its extension, will begin to exist both at the same time.

10. *The soul thinks not always; for this wants proofs.*—But whether the soul be supposed to exist antecedent to, or coeval with, or some time after, the first rudiments or organization, or the beginnings of life in the body, I leave to be disputed by those who have better thought of that matter. I confess myself to have one of those dull souls that doth not perceive itself always to contemplate ideas; nor can conceive it any more necessary for the soul always to think, than for the body always to move; the perception of ideas being, as I conceive, to the soul, what motion is to the body: not its essence, but one of its operations; and, therefore, though thinking be supposed never so much the proper action of the soul, yet it is not necessary to suppose that it should be always thinking, always in action. That, perhaps, is the privilege of the infinite Author and Preserver of all things, "who never slumbers nor sleeps;" but it is not competent to any finite being, at least not to the soul of man. We know certainly, by experience, that we sometimes think; and thence draw this infallible consequence—that there is something in us that has a power to think. But whether that substance perpetually thinks, or no, we can be no farther assured than experience informs us. For to say that actual thinking is essential to the soul, and inseparable from it, is to beg what is in question, and not to prove it by reason; which is necessary to be done, if it be not a self-evident proposition. But whether this—that "the soul always thinks," be a self-evident proposition, that everybody assents to on first hearing, I appeal to mankind. [It is doubted whether I thought all last night, or no; the question being about a matter of fact, it is begging it to bring as a proof for it an hypothesis which is the very thing in dispute;

by which way one may prove anything; and it is but supposing that all watches, whilst the balance beats, think, and it is sufficiently proved, and past doubt, that my watch thought all last night. But he that would not deceive himself ought to build his hypothesis on matter of fact, and make it out by sensible experience, and not presume on matter of fact because of his hypothesis; that is, because he supposes it to be so; which way of proving amounts to this—that I must necessarily think all last night, because another supposes I always think, though I myself cannot perceive that I always do so.

But men in love with their opinions may not only suppose what is in question, but allege wrong matter of fact. How else could anyone make it an inference of mine, that a thing is not, because we are not sensible of it in our sleep? I do not say, there is no soul in a man because he is not sensible of it in his sleep; but I do say, he cannot think at any time, waking or sleeping, without being sensible of it. Our being sensible of it is not necessary to anything but to our thoughts; and to them it is, and to them it will always be, necessary, till we can think without being conscious of it.]

11. *It is not always conscious of it.*—I grant that the soul in a waking man is never without thought, because it is the condition of being awake; but whether sleeping without dreaming be not an affection of the whole man, mind as well as body, may be worth a waking man's consideration; it being hard to conceive that anything should think and not be conscious of it. If the soul doth think in a sleeping man without being conscious of it, I ask, whether, during such thinking, it has any pleasure or pain, or be capable of happiness or misery? I am sure the man is not, no more than the bed or earth he lies on. For to be happy or miserable without being conscious of it, seems to me utterly inconsistent and impossible. Or if it be possible that the soul can, whilst the body is sleeping, have its thinking, enjoyments, and concerns, its pleasure or pain, apart, which the man is not conscious of, nor partakes in, it is certain that Socrates asleep and Socrates awake is not the same person; but his soul when he sleeps, and Socrates the man, consisting of body and soul, when he is waking, are two persons; since waking Socrates has no knowledge of, or concernment for that happiness or misery of his soul, which it enjoys alone by itself whilst he sleeps, without perceiving anything of it, no more than he has for the happiness or misery of a man in the Indies, whom he knows not. For if we take wholly away all consciousness of our actions and sensations, especially of pleasure and pain, and the concernment that accompanies it, it will be hard to know wherein to place personal identity.

Chapter II

OF SIMPLE IDEAS

1. *Uncompounded appearances.*—The better to understand the nature, manner, and extent of our knowledge, one thing is carefully to be observed concerning the ideas we have; and

that is, that some of them are *simple*, and some *complex*.

Though the qualities that affect our senses are, in the things themselves,[5] so united and blended that there is no separation, no distance between them; yet it is plain the ideas they produce in the mind enter by the senses simple and unmixed. For though the sight and touch often take in from the same object, at the same time, different ideas—as a man sees at once motion and color, the hand feels softness and warmth in the same piece of wax—yet the simple ideas thus united in the same subject are as perfectly distinct as those that come in by different senses; the coldness and hardness which a man feels in a piece of ice being as distinct ideas in the mind as the smell and whiteness of a lily, or as the taste of sugar and smell of a rose: and there is nothing can be plainer to a man than the clear and distinct perception he has of those simple ideas; which, being each in itself uncompounded, contains in it nothing but *one uniform appearance or conception in the mind*, and is not distinguishable into different ideas.

2. *The mind can neither make nor destroy them.*—These simple ideas, the materials of all our knowledge, are suggested and furnished to the mind only by those two ways above mentioned, viz., sensation and reflection. When the understanding is once stored with these simple ideas, it has the power to repeat, compare, and unite them, even to an almost infinite variety, and so can make at pleasure new complex ideas. But it is not in the power of the most exalted wit or enlarged understanding, by any quickness or variety of thought, to *invent* or *frame* one new simple idea in the mind, not taken in by the ways before mentioned; nor can any force of the understanding *destroy* those that are there: the dominion of man in this little world of his own understanding, being muchwhat the same as it is in the great world of visible things; wherein his power, however managed by art and skill, reaches no farther than to compound and divide the materials that are made to his hand but can do nothing towards the making the least particle of new matter, or destroying one atom of what is already in being. The same inability will everyone find in himself, who shall go about to fashion in his understanding any simple idea not received in by his senses from external objects, or by reflection from the operations of his own mind about them. I would have anyone try to fancy any taste which had never affected his palate, or frame the idea of a scent he had never smelt; and when he can do this, I will also conclude that a blind man hath *ideas* of colors, and a deaf man true, distinct notions of sounds.

3. *Only the qualities that affect the senses are imaginable.*—This is the reason why, though we cannot believe it impossible to God to make a creature with other organs, and more ways to convey into the understanding the notice of corporeal things than those five as they are usually counted, which He has given to man; yet I think it is not possible for anyone to imagine any other qualities in bodies, howsoever constituted, whereby they can be taken notice of, besides sounds, tastes,

---

[5]One of the confusions in Locke's writings is that he sometimes speaks of qualities as ideas in the mind and sometimes as objective characteristics of the thing known.

smells, visible and tangible qualities. And had mankind been made with but four senses, the qualities then which are the objects of the fifth sense had been as far from our notice, imagination, and conception, as now any belonging to a sixth, seventh, or eighth sense can possibly be; which, whether yet some other creatures, in some other parts of this vast and stupendous universe, may not have, will be a great presumption to deny. He that will not set himself proudly at the top of all things, but will consider the immensity of this fabric, and the great variety that is to be found in this little and inconsiderable part of it which he has to do with, may be apt to think, that in other mansions of it there may be other and different intelligible beings, of whose faculties he has as little knowledge or apprehension, as a worm shut up in one drawer of a cabinet hath of the senses or understanding of a man; such variety and excellency being suitable to the wisdom and power of the Maker. I have here followed the common opinion of man's having but five senses, though perhaps there may be justly counted more; but either supposition serves equally to my present purpose.

* * *

Chapter VIII

SOME FARTHER CONSIDERATIONS CONCERNING OUR SIMPLE IDEAS OF SENSATION

1. *Positive ideas from privative causes.*—Concerning the simple ideas of sensation, it is to be considered that whatsoever is so constituted in nature as to be able by affecting our senses to cause any perception in the mind, doth thereby produce in the understanding a simple idea; which, whatever be the external cause of it, when it comes to be taken notice of by our discerning faculty, it is by the mind looked on and considered there to be a real positive idea in the understanding, as much as any other whatsoever; though perhaps the cause of it be but a privation in the subject.

2. Thus the ideas of heat and cold, light and darkness, white and black, motion and rest, are equally clear and positive ideas in the mind; though perhaps some of the causes which produce them are barely privations in those subjects from whence our senses derive those ideas. These the understanding, in its view of them, considers all as distinct positive ideas without taking notice of the causes that produce them; which is an inquiry not belonging to the idea as it is in the understanding, but to the nature of the things existing without us. These are two very different things, and carefully to be distinguished; it being one thing to perceive and know the idea of white or black, and quite another to examine what kind of particles they must be, and how ranged in the superficies, to make any object appear white or black.

3. A painter or dyer who never inquired into their causes hath the ideas of white and black and other colors as clearly, perfectly, and distinctly in his understanding, and perhaps more distinctly than the philosopher who hath busied himself in considering their natures, and thinks he knows how far either or

them is in its cause positive or privative; and the idea of black is no less positive in his mind than that of white, however the cause of that color in the external object may be only a privation.

4. If it were the design of my present undertaking to inquire into the natural causes and manner of perception, I should offer this as a reason why a privative cause might, in some cases at least, produce a positive idea; viz., that all sensation being produced in us only by different degrees and modes of motion in our animal spirits, variously agitated by external objects, the abatement of any former motion must as necessarily produce a new sensation as the variation or increase of it; and so introduce a new idea, which depends only on a different motion of the animal spirits in that organ.

5. But whether this be so or not I will not here determine, but appeal to everyone's own experience, whether the shadow of a man, though it consists of nothing but the absence of light (and the more the absence of light is, the more discernible is the shadow), does not, when a man looks on it, cause as clear and positive an idea in his mind as a man himself, though covered over with clear sunshine! And the picture of a shadow is a positive thing. Indeed, we have negative names, [which stand not directly for positive ideas, but for their absence, such as *insipid, silence, nihil,* etc., which words denote positive ideas, v.g., *taste, sound, being,* with a signification of their absence].

6. And thus one may truly be said to see darkness. For, supposing a hole perfectly dark, from whence no light is reflected, it is certain one may see the figure of it, or it may be painted; or whether the ink I write with make any other idea, is a question. The privative causes I have here assigned of positive ideas are according to the common opinion; but, in truth, it will be hard to determine whether there be really any ideas from a privative cause, till it be determined whether rest be any more a privation than motion.

7. *Ideas in the mind, qualities in bodies.*—To discover the nature of our ideas the better, and to discourse them intelligibly, it will be convenient to distinguish them, as they are *ideas or perceptions in our minds,* and as they are *modifications of matter in the bodies that cause such perception in us:* that so we may not think (as perhaps usually is done) that they are exactly the images and resemblances of something inherent in the subject; most of those of sensation being in the mind no more the likeness of something existing without us than the names that stand for them are the likeness of our ideas, which yet upon hearing they are apt to excite in us.

8. Whatsoever the mind perceives in itself, or is the immediate object of perception, thought, or understanding, that I call *idea;* and the power to produce any idea in our mind, I call *quality* of the subject wherein that power is. Thus a snowball having the power to produce in us the ideas of white, cold, and round, the powers to produce those ideas in us as they are in the snowball, I call qualities; and as they are sensations or perceptions in our understandings, I call them ideas; which ideas, if I speak of them sometimes as in the things themselves, I would be understood to mean those

qualities in the objects which produce them in us.

9. *Primary qualities.*[6]—[Qualities thus considered in bodies are: *First* such as are utterly inseparable from the body, in what estate soever it be;] and such as, in all the alterations and changes it suffers, all the force can be used upon it, it constantly keeps; and such as sense constantly finds in every particle of matter which has bulk enough to be perceived, and the mind finds inseparable from every particle of matter, though less than to make itself singly be perceived by our senses: v.g., take a grain of wheat, divide it into two parts, each part has still solidity, extension, figure, and mobility; divide it again, and it retains still the same qualities: and so divide it on till the parts become insensible, they must retain still each of them all those qualities. For, division (which is all that a mill or pestle or any other body does upon another, in reducing it to insensible parts) can never take away either solidity, extension, figure, or mobility from any body, but only makes two or more distinct separate masses of matter of that which was but one before; all which distinct masses, reckoned as so many distinct bodies, after division, make a certain number. [These I call *original* or *primary qualities* of body, which I think we may observe to produce simple ideas in us, viz., solidity, extension, figure, motion or rest, and number.

10. *Secondary qualities.—Secondly*, such qualities, which in truth are nothing in the objects themselves, but powers to produce various sensations in us by their primary qualities, i.e., by the bulk, figure, texture, and motion of their insensible parts, as colors, sounds, tastes, etc., these I call *secondary* qualities. To these might be added a third sort, which are allowed to be barely powers, though they are as much real qualities in the subject as those which I, to comply with the

[6]The rest of this selection (nos. 9-26) goes into a consideration of three sorts of qualities, with special emphasis on the position that *secondary qualities*, such as color or sound, do not exist as such in things sensed, and hence that ideas of these qualities do not resemble the qualities themselves. In general, qualities are said to be powers in things. Ideas of primary qualities — for example, extension, figure, and motion — resemble the corresponding qualities; this is not true of ideas of secondary qualities. Locke's reasons for this latter position are much the same as Descartes', although there is some variation.

In this whole discussion it can be observed that Locke often seems to mix up qualities with ideas of qualities so that his meaning is not always clear. Moreover, in his handling of this matter, he is persistent in treating ideas as instrumental signs rather than as formal signs and, hence, as the primary or perhaps the sole object of knowledge. It is in keeping with this method of viewing ideas that subsequent Empiricism will question Locke's stand on the resemblance found in primary qualities, and will conclude that the same reasons which tell against secondary qualities can also be brought to bear on the primary.

Also, since ideas of qualities have one mode of existence and are themselves the direct objects of knowledge whereas qualities themselves have their own mode of existence in things, just what does Locke mean by the one being "like" the other? This is not clear, and on his own premises it will never be possible to compare the two since the "thing in itself" is really not open to our direct inspection.

As can be seen, Locke very closely associates the secondary qualities with the primary, so that any suspicion cast on the former will or can be brought to bear on the latter.

common way of speaking, call qualities, but, for distinction, *secondary* qualities. For, the power in fire to produce a new color or consistency in wax or clay, by its primary qualities, is as much a quality in fire as the power it has to produce in me a new idea or sensation of warmth or burning, which I felt not before, by the same primary qualities, viz., the bulk, texture, and motion of its insensible parts.]

11. [*How primary qualities produce ideas in us.*—The next thing to be considered is, how bodies produce ideas in us; and that is manifestly by impulse, the only way we can conceive bodies to operate in.]

12. If, then, external objects be not united to our minds when they produce ideas therein, and yet we perceive these original qualities in such of them as singly fall under our senses, it is evident that some motion must be thence continued by our nerves, or animal spirits, by some parts of our bodies, to the brain or the seat of sensation, there to produce in our minds the particular ideas we have of them. And since the extension, figure, number, and motion of bodies of an observable bigness, may be perceived at a distance by the sight, it is evident some singly imperceptible bodies must come from them to the eyes, and thereby convey to the brain some motion which produces these ideas which we have of them in us.

13. *How secondary.*—After the same manner that the ideas of these original qualities are produced in us, we may conceive that the ideas of secondary qualities are also produced, viz., by the operation of insensible particles on our senses. For it being manifest that there are bodies, and good store of bodies, each whereof are so small that we cannot by any of our senses discover either their bulk, figure, or motion (as is evident in the particles of the air and water, and others extremely smaller than those, perhaps as much smaller than the particles of air or water as the particles of air or water are smaller than peas or hailstones): let us suppose at present that the different motions and figures, bulk and number, of such particles, affecting the several organs of our senses, produce in us these different sensations which we have from the colors and smells of bodies, v.g., that a violet, by the impulse of such insensible particles of matter of peculiar figures and bulks, and in different degrees and modifications of their motions, causes the ideas of the blue color and sweet scent of that flower to be produced in our minds; it being no more impossible to conceive that God should annex such ideas to such motions, with which they have no similitude, than that He should annex the idea of pain to the motion of a piece of steel dividing our flesh, with which the idea hath no resemblance.

14. What I have said concerning colors and smells may be understood also of tastes and sounds, and other the like sensible qualities; which, whatever reality we by mistake attribute to them, are in truth nothing in the objects themselves, but powers to produce various sensations in us, and depend on those primary qualities, viz., bulk, figure, texture, and motion of parts [as I have said].

15. *Ideas of primary qualities are resemblances; of secondary, not.*—From whence I think it is easy to draw this observation, that the ideas of primary qualities of bodies are resemblances of them, and their

patterns do really exist in the bodies themselves; but the ideas produced in us by these secondary qualities have no resemblance of them at all. There is nothing like our ideas existing in the bodies themselves. They are, in the bodies we denominate from them, only a power to produce those sensations in us; and what is sweet, blue, or warm in idea, is but the certain bulk, figure, and motion of the insensible parts in the bodies themselves, which we call so.

16. Flame is denominated hot and light; snow, white and cold; and manna, white and sweet, from the ideas they produce in us, which qualities are commonly thought to be the same in those bodies that those ideas are in us, the one the perfect resemblance of the other, as they are in a mirror; and it would by most men be judged very extravagant, if one should say otherwise. And yet he that will consider that the same fire that at one distance produces in us the sensation of warmth, does at a nearer approach produce in us the far different sensation of pain, ought to bethink himself what reason he has to say, that this idea of warmth which was produced in him by the fire, is actually in the fire, and his idea of pain which the same fire produced in him the same way is not in the fire. Why are whiteness and coldness in snow and pain not, when it produces the one and the other idea in us, and can do neither but by the bulk, figure, number, and motion of its solid parts?

17. The particular bulk, number, figure, and motion of the parts of fire or snow are really in them, whether anyone's senses perceive them or no; and therefore they may be called *real* qualities, because they really exist in those bodies. But light, heat, whiteness, or coldness, are no more really in them than sickness or pain is in manna. Take away the sensation of them; let not the eyes see light or colors, nor the ears hear sounds; let the palate not taste, nor the nose smell; and all colors, tastes, odors, and sounds, as they are such particular ideas, vanish and cease, and are reduced to their causes, i.e., bulk, figure, and motion of parts.

18. A piece of manna of a sensible bulk is able to produce in us the idea of a round or square figure; and, by being removed from one place to another, the idea of motion. This idea of motion represents it as it really is in the manna moving; a circle or square are the same, whether in idea or existence, in the mind or in the manna; and this, both motion and figure, are really in the manna, whether we take notice of them or no: this everybody is ready to agree to. Besides, manna, by the bulk, figure, texture, and motion of its parts, has a power to produce the sensations of sickness, and sometimes of acute pains or gripings, in us. That these ideas of sickness and pain are not in the manna, but effects of its operations on us, and are nowhere when we feel them not; this also everyone readily agrees to. And yet men are hardly to be brought to think that sweetness and whiteness are not really in manna, which are but the effects of the operations of manna by the motion, size, and figure of its particles on the eyes and palate; as the pain and sickness caused by manna, are confessedly nothing but the effects of its operations on the stomach and guts by the size, motion, and figure of its insensible parts (for by nothing else can a body operate, as has

been proved): as if it could not operate on the eyes and palate, and thereby produce in the mind particular distinct ideas which in itself it has not, as well as we allow it can operate on the guts and stomach, and thereby produce distinct ideas which in itself it has not. These ideas being all effects of the operations of manna on several parts of our bodies, by the size, figure, number, and motion of its parts, why those produced by the eyes and palate should rather be thought to be really in the manna than those produced by the stomach and guts; or why the pain and sickness, ideas that are the effects of manna, should be thought to be nowhere when they are not felt; and yet the sweetness and whiteness, effects of the same manna on other parts of the body, by ways equally as unknown, should be thought to exist in the manna, when they are not seen nor tasted would need some reason to explain.

19. Let us consider the red and white colors in porphyry; hinder light but from striking on it, and its colors vanish; it no longer produces any such ideas in us. Upon the return of light, it produces these appearances on us again. Can anyone think any real alterations are made in the porphyry by the presence or absence of light, and that those ideas of whiteness and redness are really in porphyry in the light, when it is plain it has no color in the dark? It has indeed such a configuration of particles, both night and day, as are apt, by the rays of light rebounding from some parts of that hard stone, to produce in us the idea of redness, and from others the idea of whiteness. But whiteness or redness are not in it at any time, but such a texture that hath the power to produce such a sensation in us.

20. Pound an almond, and the clear white color will be altered into a dirty one, and the sweet taste into an oily one. What real alteration can the beating of the pestle make in any body, but an alteration of the texture of it?

21. Ideas being thus distinguished and understood, we may be able to give an account how the same water, at the same time, may produce the idea of cold by one hand, and of heat by the other; whereas it is impossible that the same water, if those ideas were really in it, should at the same time be both hot and cold. For if we imagine warmth as it is in our hands, to be nothing but a certain sort and degree of motion in the minute particles of our nerves or animal spirits, we may understand how it is possible that the same water may at the same time produce the sensation of heat in one hand, and cold in the other; which yet figure never does, that never producing the idea of a square by one hand which has produced the idea of a globe by another. But if the sensation of heat and cold be nothing but the increase or diminution of the motion of the minute parts of our bodies, caused by the corpuscles of any other body, it is easy to be understood that if that motion be greater in one hand than in the other, if a body be applied to the two hands, which has in its minute particles a greater motion than in those of one of the hands, and a less than in those of the other, it will increase the motion of the one hand, and lessen it in the other, and so cause the different sensations of heat and cold that depend thereon.

22. I have, in what just goes before, been engaged in physical in-

quiries a little farther than perhaps I intended. But it being necessary to make the nature of sensation a little understood, and to make the difference between the qualities in bodies, and the ideas produced by them in the mind, to be distinctly conceived, without which it were impossible to discourse intelligibly of them, I hope I shall be pardoned this little excursion into natural philosophy, it being necessary in our present inquiry to distinguish the primary and real qualities of bodies, which are always in them (viz., solidity, extension, figure, number, and motion or rest, and are sometimes perceived by us, viz., when the bodies they are in are big enough singly to be discerned), from those secondary and imputed qualities, which are but the powers of several combinations of those primary ones, when they operate without being distinctly discerned; whereby we also may come to know what ideas are, and what are not, resemblances of something really existing in the bodies we denominate from them.

23. *Three sorts of qualities in bodies.*—The qualities then that are in bodies, rightly considered, are of three sorts:

First, the bulk, figure, number, situation, and motion or rest of their solid parts; those are in them, whether we perceive them or not; and when they are of that size that we can discover them, we have by these ideas of the thing as it is in itself, as is plain in artificial things. These I call *primary qualities.*

Secondly, the power that is in any body, by reason of its insensible primary qualities, to operate after a peculiar manner on any of our senses, and thereby produce in us the different ideas of several colors, sounds, smells, tastes, etc. These are usually called *sensible qualities.*

Thirdly, the power that is in any body, by reason of the particular constitution of its primary qualities, to make such a change in the bulk, figure, texture, and motion of another body, as to make it operate on our senses differently from what it did before. Thus the sun has a power to make wax white, and fire, to make lead fluid. [These are usually called *powers.*]

The first of these, as has been said, I think may be properly called real, original, or primary qualities, because they are in the things themselves, whether they are perceived or no; and upon their different modifications it is that the secondary qualities depend.

The other two are only powers to act differently upon other things, which powers result from the different modifications of those primary qualities.

24. *The first are resemblances; the second thought resemblances, but are not; the third neither are, nor are thought so.*—But though these two latter sorts of qualities are powers barely, and nothing but powers, relating to several other bodies, and resulting from the different modifications of the original qualities, yet they are generally otherwise thought of. For the second sort, viz., the powers to produce several ideas in us by our senses, are looked upon as real qualities in the things thus affecting us; but the third sort are called and esteemed barely powers. V.g., the idea of heat or light which we receive by our eyes or touch from the sun, are commonly thought real qualities existing in the sun, and something more than mere powers in it. But

when we consider the sun in reference to wax, which it melts or blanches, we look upon the whiteness and softness produced in the wax, not as qualities in the sun, but effects produced by powers in it: whereas, if rightly considered, these qualities of light and warmth, which are perceptions in me when I am warmed or enlightened by the sun, are no otherwise in the sun than the changes made in the wax, when it is blanched or melted, are in the sun. They are all of them equally powers in the sun, depending on its primary qualities, whereby it is able in the one case so to alter the bulk, figure, texture, or motion of some of the insensible parts of my eyes or hands as thereby to produce in me the idea of light or heat, and in the other it is able so to alter the bulk, figure, texture, or motion of the insensible parts of the wax as to make them fit to produce in me the distinct ideas of white and fluid.

25. The reason why the one are ordinarily taken for real qualities, and the other only for bare powers, seems to be because the ideas we have of distinct colors, sounds, etc., containing nothing at all in them of bulk, figure, or motion, we are not apt to think them the effects of these primary qualities which appear not, to our senses, to operate in their production, and with which they have not any apparent congruity, or conceivable connection. Hence it is that we are so forward to imagine that those ideas are the resemblances of something really existing in the objects themselves, since sensation discovers nothing of bulk, figure, or motion of parts, in their production, nor can reason show how bodies by their bulk, figure, and motion, should produce in the mind the ideas of blue or yellow, etc. But, in the other case, in the operations of bodies changing the qualities one of another, we plainly discover that the quality produced hath commonly no resemblance with anything in the thing producing it; wherefore, we look on it as a bare effect of power. For though, receiving the idea of heat or light from the sun, we are apt to think it is a perception and resemblance of such a quality in the sun, yet when we see wax, or a fair face, receive change of color from the sun, we cannot imagine that to be the reception or resemblance of anything in the sun, because we find not those different colors in the sun itself. For, our senses being able to observe a likeness or unlikeness of sensible qualities in two different external objects, we forwardly enough conclude the production of any sensible quality in any subject to be an effect of bare power, and not the communication of any quality which was really in the efficient, when we find no such sensible quality in the thing that produced it. But our senses not being able to discover any unlikeness between the idea produced in us and the quality of the object producing it, we are apt to imagine that our ideas are resemblances of something in the objects, and not the effects of certain powers placed in the modification of their primary qualities, with which primary qualities the ideas produced in us have no resemblance.

26. *Secondary qualities twofold: first, immediately perceivable; secondly, mediately perceivable.*— To conclude: Beside those before-mentioned primary qualities in bodies, viz., bulk, figure, extension, number, and motion of their solid parts, all the rest whereby we take

notice of bodies and distinguish them one from another, are nothing else but several powers in them depending on those primary qualities, whereby they are fitted, either by immediately operating on our bodies, to produce several different ideas in us; or else by operating on other bodies, so to change their primary qualities as to render them capable of producing ideas in us different from what before they did. The former of these, I think, may be called secondary qualities *immediately perceivable;* the latter, secondary qualities *mediately perceivable.*

* * *

BOOK III: OF WORDS

Chapter III

OF GENERAL TERMS

1. *The greatest part of words general.*—All things that exist being particulars, it may perhaps be thought reasonable that words, which ought to be conformed to things, should be so too. I mean in their signification: but yet we find the quite contrary. The far *greatest part of words,* that make all languages, *are general terms:* which has not been the effect of neglect, or chance, but of reason, and necessity.

* * *

6. *How general words are made.*—The next thing to be considered is, *how general words come to be made.* For since all things that exist are only particulars, how come we by general terms, or where find we those general natures they are supposed to stand for? Words become general, by being made the signs of general *ideas:* and *ideas* become general, by separating from them the circumstances of time, and place, and any other *ideas,* that may determine them to this or that particular existence. By this way of abstraction they are made capable of representing more individuals than one; each of which, having in it a conformity to that abstract *idea,* is (as we call it) of that sort.

7. But to deduce this a little more distinctly, it will not perhaps be amiss to trace our notions, and names, from their beginning, and observe by what degrees we proceed, and by what steps we enlarge our *ideas* from our first infancy. There is nothing more evident, than that the *ideas* of the persons children converse with, (to instance in them alone) are like the persons themselves, only particular. The *ideas* of the nurse, and the mother, are well framed in their minds; and, like pictures of them there, represent only those individuals. The names they first gave to them, are confined to these individuals; and the names of *nurse* and *mamma,* the

child uses, determine themselves to those persons. Afterwards, when time and a large acquaintance has made them observe, that there are a great many things in the world, that in some common agreements of shape, and several other qualities, resemble their father and mother, and those persons they have been used to, they frame an *idea,* which they find those many particular do partake in; and to that they give, with others, the name *man* for example. And *thus they come to have a general name,* and a general *idea.* Wherein they make nothing new, but only leave out of the complex *idea* they had of *Peter* and *James, Mary* and *Jane,* that which is peculiar to each, and retain only what is common to them all.

* * *

9. *General natures are nothing but abstract ideas.*[7]—That this is the *way, whereby men first formed general* ideas, *and general names to them,* I think, is so evident, that there needs no other proof of it, but the considering of a man's self, or others, and the ordinary proceedings of their minds in knowledge: and he that thinks general natures or notions, are any thing else but such abstract and partial *ideas* of more complex ones, taken at first from particular existences, will, I fear, be at a loss where to find them. For let anyone reflect, and then tell me, wherein does his *idea of man* differ from that of *Peter* and *Paul;* or his *idea of horse* from that of *Bucephalus,* but in the leaving out something that is peculiar to each individual; and retaining so much of those particular complex *ideas,* of several particular existences, as they are found to agree in? Of the complex *ideas,* signified by the names *man,* and *horse,* leaving out but those particulars wherein they differ, and retaining only those wherein they agree, and of those making a new distinct complex *idea,* and giving the name *animal* to it, one has a more general term, that comprehends, with man, several other crea-

[7]Locke has just presented what he considers to be the psychological process whereby general names and general ideas are formed. He now attempts to justify this process by presenting his doctrine on abstraction as the intellect's way of forming general ideas, and he further justifies this abstraction on the score that things are alike in nature. In keeping with his Empiricism, Locke insists that we cannot have even a minimal knowledge of the real essences of things; we get ideas only of their "qualities." So any general idea must in fact be in itself only a particular idea, to which the mind contributes a general meaning.

In these pages Locke rejects Nominalism by his admission of general ideas. He rightly insists on the fact that only individual things can exist, and so the mind somehow introduces formal universality. He encounters real difficulty, however, when he seeks to explain the foundation for this universality. The sort of abstraction proposed by Locke actually *presupposes* the apprehension of similarities as such, else there would be no ground for isolating and combining only certain ideas. But this demands some intellectual grasp of the essential structure of things.

Locke will not grant any such apprehension, even though he comes close to it when he asserts that nature makes things to be alike (Cf. sect. 13, p. 140). His view that bundles of qualities constitute the nominal essence of a thing, and that these qualities hide rather than reveal something about the real essence, prevents his giving a firm metaphysical foundation to his views on general ideas.

tures. Leave out of the *idea* of *animal*, sense and spontaneous motion, and the remaining complex *idea*, made up of the remaining simple ones of body, life, and nourishment, becomes a more general one, under the more comprehensive term, *vivens*. And not to dwell longer upon this particular, so evident in itself, by the same way the mind proceeds to *body, substance*, and at last to *being, thing*, and such universal terms, which stand for any of our *ideas* whatsoever. To conclude, this whole *mystery of genera* and *species*, which make such a noise in the schools, and are, with justice, so little regarded out of them, is nothing else but abstract *ideas*, more or less comprehensive, with names annexed to them. In all which, this is constant and unvariable. That every more general term stands for such an *idea*, as is but a part of any of those contained under it.

* * *

11. *General and universal are creatures of the understanding.*—To return to general words, it is plain, by what has been said, that *general and universal*, belong not to the real existence of things; but *are the inventions* and *creatures of the understanding*, made by it for its own use, *and concern only signs*, whether words, or *ideas*. Words are general, as has been said, when used for signs of general *ideas;* and so are applicable indifferently to many particular things; and *ideas*, are general, when they are set up as the representatives of many particular things: but universality belongs not to things themselves, which are all of them particular in their existence, even those words, and *ideas*, which in their signification, are general. When therefore we quit particulars, the generals that rest, are only creatures of our own making, their general nature being nothing but the capacity they are put into by the understanding of signifying or representing many particulars. For the signification they have, is nothing but a relation, that by the mind of man is added to them.

* * *

13. *They are the workmanship of the understanding, but have their foundation in the similitude of things.*—I would not here be thought to forget, much less to deny, that nature in the production of things, makes several of the alike: there is nothing more obvious, especially in the races of animals, and all things propagated by seed. But yet, I think, we may say, the *sorting* of them under names is the *workmanship of the understanding, taking occasion from the similitude* it observes amongst them, to make abstract general *ideas*, and set them up in the mind, with names annexed to them, as patterns or forms, (for in that sense the word *form* has a very proper signification,) to which, as particular things existing are found to agree, so they come to be of that species, have that denomination, or are put into that *classis*. For when we say, that is a *man*, that a *horse;* this *justice*, that *cruelty;* this a *watch*, that a *jack;* what do we else but rank things under different specific names, as agreeing to those abstract *ideas*, of which we have made those names the signs? And what are the essences of those species,

set out and marked by names, but those abstract ideas in the mind; which are, as it were, the bonds between particular things that exist, and the names they are to be ranked under? And when general names have any connection with particular beings, these abstract *ideas* are the *medium* that unites them: so that the essences of species, as distinguished and denominated by us, neither are, nor can be any thing but those precise abstract *ideas* we have in our minds. And therefore the supposed real essences of substances, if different from our abstract *ideas*, cannot be the essences of the species we rank things into. For two species may be one, as rationally, as two different essences be the essence of one species: And I demand, what are the alterations which may, or may not be in a *horse* or *lead*, without making either of them to be another species? In determining the species of things by our abstract *ideas*, this is easy to resolve: but if anyone will regulate himself herein, by supposed real essences, he will, I suppose, be at a loss: and he will never be able to know when any thing precisely ceases to be of the species of a *horse*, or *lead*.

* * *

15. *Real and nominal essence.*—But since the *essences* of things are thought by some, (and not without reason,) to be wholly unknown: it may not be amiss to consider the *several significations of the word* essence.

First, *essence* may be taken for the being of any thing, whereby it is, what it is. And thus the real internal, but generally in substances, unknown constitution of things, whereon their discoverable qualities depend, may be called their *essence*. This is the proper original signification of the word, as is evident from the formation of it; *essentia*, in its primary notation, signifying properly *being*. And in this sense it is still used, when we speak of the *essence* of particular things, without giving them any name.

Secondly, the learning and disputes of the schools, having been much busied about *genus* and *species*, the word *essence* has almost lost its primary signification; and instead of the real constitution of things, has been almost wholly applied to the artificial constitution of *genus* and *species*. It is true, there is ordinarily supposed a real constitution of the sorts of things; and it is past doubt, there must be some real constitution, on which any collection of simple *ideas* co-existing, must depend. But it being evident, that things are ranked under names into sorts of species, only as they agree to certain abstract *ideas*, to which we have annexed those names, the *essence* of each *genus*, or sort, comes to be nothing but that abstract *idea*, which the general, or *sortal* (if I may have leave so to call it from *sort*, as I do *general* from *genus*,) name stands for. And this we shall find to be that which the word *essence* imports, in its most familiar use. These two sorts of *essences*, I suppose, may not unfitly be termed, the one the *real*, the other the *nominal essence*.

16. *Constant connection between the name and nominal essence.*—*Between the nominal essence, and the name*, there is so *near a connection*, that the name of any sort of things cannot be attributed to any

particular being, but what has this *essence*, whereby it answers that abstract *idea*, whereof that name is the sign.

17. *Supposition that species are distinguished by their real essences, useless.*—Concerning the real essences of corporeal substances, (to mention those only,) there are, if I mistake not, two opinions. The one is of those, who using the word *essence*, for they know not what, suppose a certain number of those essences, according to which, all natural things are made, and wherein they do exactly every one of them partake, and so become of this or that *species*. The other, and more rational opinion, is of those, who look on all natural things to have a real, but unknown constitution of their insensible parts, from which flow those sensible qualities, which serve us to distinguish them one from another, according as we have occasion to rank them into sorts, under common denominations.[8] The former of these opinions, which supposes these *essences*, as a certain number of forms or molds, wherein all natural things, that exist, are cast, and do equally partake, has, I imagine, very much perplexed the knowledge of natural things. The frequent production of monsters, in all the species of animals, and of changelings, and other strange issues of humane birth, carry with them difficulties, not possible to consist with this *hypothesis:* since it is as impossible, that two things partaking exactly of the same real *essence*, should have different properties, as that two figures partaking in the same real *essence* of a circle should have different properties. But were there no other reason against it, yet the *supposition of essences, that cannot be known;* and the making them nevertheless to be that which distinguishes the species of things, *is so wholly useless*, and unserviceable to any part of our knowledge, that that alone were sufficient to make us lay it by, and content ourselves with such *essences* of the sorts or species of things, as come within the reach of our knowledge; which, when seriously considered, will be found as I have said, to be nothing else but those abstract complex *ideas*, to which we have annexed distinct general names.

* * *

20. *Recapitulation.*—To conclude, this is that which in short I would

---

[8]Locke's view on the difference between real and nominal essences, which has frequently recurred in the previous pages, is presented briefly in this sentence: (1) It may be true to say that all natural things "have a real, but unknown constitution . . . ." Hence, there may well be *real* essences, which he earlier refers to as "the real, internal . . . constitution of things, whereon their discoverable qualities depend." However, even if there are, these real essences are *unknown*. (2) In fact, objects are known and linked together because of their "sensible qualities . . . according as we have occasion to rank them into sorts." So, as he said earlier, "the *essence* of each genus . . . comes to be nothing but that abstract idea . . . which the general . . . name stands for." This is the nominal essence. Hence, (3) there are general *terms;* these are signs of abstract *ideas;* however, these ideas do not represent real (unknown) essences but are made by the mind linking similar sensible qualities together. Briefly, words are general, there are general ideas, but these do not represent a nature or essence really existing as that whereby a being is what it is.

say, (viz.) that all the great business of *genera* and *species*, and their *essences*, amount to no more but this, that men making abstract *ideas*, and settling them in their minds, with names annexed to them, do thereby enable themselves to consider things, and discourse of them, as it were in bundles, for the easier and readier improvement and communication of their knowledge, which would advance but slowly, were their words and thoughts confined only to particulars.

8

Ideas as the Sole Objects of Experience

George Berkeley (1685-1753)

That ideas are the only objects immediately known is a basic empiricist position taken over directly from Locke and pushed a good step forward by Berkeley. Starting thus from the mind, Berkeley does not ask how one can bridge the gap between mind and things; rather, he refused to suppose that sensible things and ideas are really different, and his aim was to present a coherent account of the world in the light of the position that the mental object and the real sensible thing are one and the same.

Our only world, then, is a world of *ideas* which are perceived and of spirits or minds which perceive the ideas. This is Berkeley's basic stand that all *esse* is either *percipi* (ideas) or *percipere* (spirits), and so there is only a spiritual realm of finite minds governed and directed by the Infinite Spirit or Mind of God. Therefore, he feels there is no further materialistic grounds to justify either Atheism or Scepticism.

Berkeley's views on the activity of mind, his insight into the logical implications of Locke's basic ideas, and his insistence on the basic unintelligibility of matter understood as totally inert and mere passivity, indicate the depth of his thought. What must be brought into question and submitted to critical analysis is the basic empirical assumption that ideas are the sole immediate objects of knowledge. This will indicate an oversimplification of the data at the very starting point of Empiricism.

THE ROLE OF IDEAS[1]

1. It is evident to any one who takes a survey of the *objects* of human knowledge, that they are either ideas actually imprinted on the senses; or else such as are perceived by attending to the passions and operations of the mind; or lastly, ideas formed by help of memory and imagination—either compounding, dividing, or barely representing those originally perceived in the aforesaid ways.[2] By sight I have the ideas of light and colours, with their several degrees and variations. By touch I perceive hard and soft, heat and cold, motion and resistance, and of all these more and less either as to quantity or degree. Smelling furnishes me with odours; the palate with tastes; and hearing conveys sounds to the mind in all their variety of tone and composition. And as several of these are observed to accompany each other, they come to be marked by one name, and so to be reputed as one thing. Thus, for example, a certain colour, taste, smell, figure and consistence having been observed to go together, are accounted one distinct thing, signified by the name *apple*; other collections of ideas constitute a stone, a tree, a book, and the like sensible things—which as they are pleasing or disagreeable excite the passions of love, hatred, joy, grief, and so forth.

2. But, besides all that endless variety of ideas or objects of knowledge, there is likewise something which knows or perceives them, and exercises divers operations, as willing, imagining, remembering, about them. This perceiving, active being is what I call *mind, spirit, soul* or *myself.*[3] By which words I do not denote any one of my ideas, but a thing entirely distinct from them, wherein, they exist, or, which is the same thing, whereby they are perceived—for the existence of an idea consists in being perceived.

3. That neither our thoughts, nor passions, nor ideas formed by the imagination, exist without the mind, is what everybody will allow.[4] And it seems no less evident that the various sensations or ideas imprinted on the sense, however blended or combined together (that is, whatever

---

[1]Selections are from George Berkeley, *A Treatise Concerning the Principles of Human Knowledge* [1710] (La Salle, Ill.: Open Court Publishing Co., 1946).

[2]Berkeley continues the empiricist doctrine that ideas are the objects immediately known, and he will go on to develop his doctrine showing that sensible things are immaterial in nature.

[3]This completes Berkeley's stand on what exists. There are two sorts of "things": (1) ideas or objects of knowledge, whose *esse* is *percipi*, and (2) minds or spirits, whose *esse* is *percipere*.

[4]The burden of Berkeley's present development is to convince his readers of the truth of his immaterialist view, that the *to-be-known* is the very *being* of sensible objects. This he seeks to prove at repetitious length by many illustrations of the truism that a thing cannot be known without being known. We might say, however, that from this it nowise follows that a thing cannot be known without *being an idea*. That something has a relation to consciousness indicates its intelligibility; it does not prove that its only existence is its existence *in* consciousness. In this matter, Berkeley assumes his basic principle that *esse est percipi* and then proceeds as if it is already established.

objects they compose), cannot exist otherwise than in a mind perceiving them.—I think an intuitive knowledge may be obtained of this by any one that shall attend to what is meant by the term *exists*, when applied to sensible things. The table I write on I say exists, that is, I see and feel it; and if I were out of my study I should say it existed—meaning thereby that if I was in my study I might perceive it, or that some other spirit actually does perceive it. There was an odour, that is, it was smelt; there was a sound, that is, it was heard; a colour or figure, and it was perceived by sight or touch. This is all that I can understand by these and the like expressions. For as to what is said of the absolute existence of unthinking things without any relation to their being perceived, that seems perfectly unintelligible. Their *esse* is *percipi*, nor is it possible they should have any existence out of the minds or thinking things which perceive them.

4. It is indeed an opinion strangely prevailing amongst men, that houses, mountains, rivers, and in a word all sensible objects, have an existence, natural or real, distinct from their being perceived by the understanding. But, with how great an assurance and acquiescence soever this principle may be entertained in the world, yet whoever shall find in his heart to call it in question may, if I mistake not, perceive it to involve a manifest contradiction. For, what are the fore-mentioned objects but the things we perceive by sense? and what do we perceive besides our own ideas or sensations? and is it not plainly repugnant that any one of these, or any combination of them, should exist unperceived?

5. If we thoroughly examine this tenet it will, perhaps, be found at bottom to depend on the doctrine of *abstract ideas*. For can there be a nicer strain of abstraction than to distinguish the existence of sensible objects from their being perceived, so as to conceive them existing unperceived? Light and colours, heat and cold, extension and figures—in a word the things we see and feel—what are they but so many sensations, notions, ideas, or impressions on the sense? and is it possible to separate, even in thought, any of these from perception? For my part, I might as easily divide a thing from itself. I may, indeed, divide in my thoughts, or conceive apart from each other, those things which, perhaps I never perceived by sense so divided. Thus, I imagine the trunk of a human body without the limbs, or conceive the smell of a rose without thinking on the rose itself. So far, I will not deny, I can abstract—if that may properly be called *abstraction* which extends only to the conceiving separately such objects as it is possible may really exist or be actually perceived asunder. But my conceiving or imagining power does not extend beyond the possibility of real existence or perception. Hence, as it is impossible for me to see or feel anything without an actual sensation of that thing, so is it impossible for me to conceive in my thoughts any sensible thing or object distinct from the sensation or perception of it. In truth, the object and the sensation are the same thing, and cannot therefore be abstracted from each other.

6. Some truths there are so near and obvious to the mind that a man need only open his eyes to see them. Such I take this important one to be, viz., that all the choir of heaven and furniture of the earth, in a word all those bodies which compose the

nighty frame of the world, have not ny subsistence without a mind, that heir *being* is to be perceived or nown; that consequently so long as hey are not actually perceived by ne, or do not exist in my mind or hat of any other created spirit, hey must either have no existence t all, or else subsist in the mind f some Eternal Spirit—it being erfectly unintelligible, and involving all the absurdity of abstraction, o attribute to any single part of hem an existence independent of a pirit. (To be convinced of which, he reader need only reflect, and ry to separate in his own thoughts he *being* of a sensible thing from ts *being perceived*.)

7. From what has been said it ollows there is not any other Substance than *Spirit*, or that which erceives. But, for the fuller proof of this point, let it be considered the sensible qualities are colour, figure, motion, smell, taste, etc., *i.e.* the deas perceived by sense. Now, for an idea to exist in an unperceiving hing is a manifest contradiction, for o have an idea is all one as to perceive; that therefore wherein colour, igure, and the like qualities exist nust perceive them; hence it is clear there can be no unthinking substance or *substratum* of those ideas.

8. But, say you, though the ideas themselves do not exist without the mind, yet there may be things like them, whereof they are copies or resemblances, which things exist without the mind in an unthinking substance. I answer, an idea can be like nothing but an idea;[5] a colour or figure can be like nothing but another colour or figure. If we look but never so little into our thoughts, we shall find it impossible for us to conceive a likeness except only between our ideas. Again, I ask whether those supposed originals or external things, of which our ideas are the pictures or representations, be themselves perceivable or no? If they are, then they are ideas and we have gained our point; but if you say they are not, I appeal to any one whether it be sense to assert a colour is like something which is invisible; hard or soft, like something which is intangible; and so of the rest.

9. Some there are who make a distinction betwixt *primary* and *secondary* qualities.[6] By the former they mean extension, figure, motion, rest, solidity or impenetrability, and number; by the latter they denote all other sensible qualities, as colours, sounds, tastes, and so forth. The ideas we have of these they acknowledge not to be the resemblances of anything existing without the mind, or unperceived, but they will have our ideas of the primary qualities to be patterns or images of things which exist without the mind, in an unthinking substance

---

[5]This basic postulate of Berkeley neans that minds and ideas or things known do not differ in ontological rank. Hence, sensible things must be immaterial, and the problem of how an immaterial faculty can come to know material things does not arise for him.

[6]Berkeley, here and in the sequel, attacks Locke's views on the reality of primary qualities. Taking the empirical standpoint—that ideas are the objects of knowledge—he has no trouble in defeating Locke. He merely indicates how secondary and primary qualities are so fused that there is as much reason for denying reality to the primary as to the secondary. The answer to Berkeley must be one which goes to the very root of the empirical position on ideas as the sole immediate object of knowledge.

which they call Matter. By Matter, therefore, we are to understand an inert, senseless substance, in which extension, figure, and motion do actually subsist. But it is evident from what we have already shown, that extension, figure, and motion are only ideas existing in the mind, and that an idea can be like nothing but another idea, and that consequently neither they nor their archetypes can exist in an unperceiving substance. Hence, it is plain that the very notion of what is called *Matter* or *corporeal substance*, involves a contradiction in it.

10. They who assert that figure, motion, and the rest of the primary or original qualities do exist without the mind in unthinking substances, do at the same time acknowledge that colours, sounds, heat, cold, and such-like secondary qualities, do not - which they tell us are sensations existing in the mind alone, that depend on and are occasioned by the different size, texture, and motion of the minute particles of matter. This they take for an undoubted truth, which they can demonstrate beyond all exception. Now, if it be certain that those original qualities are inseparably united with the other sensible qualities, and not, even in thought, capable of being abstracted from them, it plainly follows that they exist only in the mind. But I desire any one to reflect and try whether he can, by any abstraction of thought, conceive the extension and motion of a body without all other sensible qualities. For my own part, I see evidently that it is not in my power to frame an idea of a body extended and moving, but I must withal give it some colour or other sensible quality which is acknowledged to exist only in the mind. In short, extension, figure, and motion, abstracted from all other qualities, are inconceivable. Where therefore the other sensible qualities are, there must these be also, to wit, in the mind and nowhere else.

11. Again, *great* and *small*, *swift* and *slow*, are allowed to exist nowhere without the mind, being entirely relative, and changing as the frame or position of the organs of sense varies. The extension therefore which exists without the mind is neither great nor small, the motion neither swift nor slow, that is, they are nothing at all. But, say you, they are extension in general, and motion in general: thus we see how much the tenet of extended movable substances existing without the mind depends on the strange doctrine of *abstract ideas*. And here I cannot but remark how nearly the vague and indeterminate description of Matter or corporeal substance, which the modern philosophers are run into by their own principles, resembles that antiquated and so much ridiculed notion of *materia prima*, to be met with in Aristotle and his followers. Without extension solidity cannot be conceived; since therefore it has been shown that extension exists not in an unthinking substance, the same must also be true of solidity.

* * *

16. But let us examine a little the received opinion.—It is said extension is a mode or accident of Matter, and that Matter is the *substratum* that supports it. Now I desire that you would explain to me what is meant by Matter's *supporting* extension. Say you, I have no idea of Matter and therefore cannot explain it. I answer, though you have no

ositive, yet, if you have any meanng at all, you must at least have a elative idea of Matter; though you now not what it is, yet you must be upposed to know what relation it ears to accidents, and what is neant by its supporting them. It is vident "support" cannot here be aken in its usual or literal sense—s when we say that pillars support building; in what sense therefore nust it be taken?

17. If we inquire into what the nost accurate philosophers declare hemselves to mean by *material subtance*, we shall find them acknowldge they have no other meaning anexed to those sounds but the idea of eing in general, together with the elative notion of its supporting acidents. The general idea of Being ppeareth to me the most abstract nd incomprehensible of all other; nd as for its supporting accidents, his, as we have just now observed, annot be understood in the common ense of those words; it must thereore be taken in some other sense, ut what that is they do not explain. o that when I consider the two parts r branches which make the signifiation of the words *material subtance*, I am convinced there is no istinct meaning annexed to them. ut why should we trouble ourselves ny farther, in discussing this maerial *substratum* or support of figre and motion, and other sensible ualities? Does it not suppose they ave an existence without the mind? nd is not this a direct repugnancy, nd altogether inconceivable?[7]

18. But, though it were possible that solid, figured, movable substances may exist without the mind, corresponding to the ideas we have of bodies, yet how is it possible for us to know this? Either we must know it by sense or by reason. As for our senses, by them we have the knowledge only of our sensations, ideas, or those things that are immediately perceived by sense, call them what you will: but they do not inform us that things exist without the mind, or unperceived, like to those which are perceived. This the materialists themselves acknowledge. It remains therefore that if we have any knowledge at all of external things, it must be by reason, inferring their existence from what is immediately perceived by sense. But what reason can induce us to believe the existence of bodies without the mind, from what we perceive, since the very patrons of Matter themselves do not pretend there is any necessary connexion betwixt them and our ideas? I say it is granted on all hands (and what happens in dreams, phrensies, and the like, puts it beyond dispute) that it is possible we might be affected with all the ideas we have now, though there were no bodies existing without resembling them. Hence, it is evident the supposition of external bodies is not necessary for the producing our ideas; since it is granted they are produced sometimes, and might possibly be produced always in the same order, we see them in at present, without their concurrence.

---

[7]Because of his historical context there s much confusion in the way Berkeley peaks of matter and of material subtance. For one thing, he does not seem understand the meaning of *principles f being* in an act-potency relationship. Also, when he speaks of matter, he does not seem to distinguish *prime matter*, which is mere potency and is unintelligible in itself, from the composite material entity, in which matter is known by its relation to form or act.

19. But, though we might possibly have all our sensations without them, yet perhaps it may be thought easier to conceive and explain the manner of their production, by supposing external bodies in their likeness rather than otherwise; and so it might be at least probable there are such things as bodies that excite their ideas in our minds. But neither can this be said; for, though we give the materialists their external bodies, they by their own confession are never the nearer knowing how our ideas are produced; since they own themselves unable to comprehend in what manner body can act upon spirit, or how it is possible it should imprint any idea in the mind. Hence it is evident the production of ideas or sensations in our minds can be no reason why we should suppose Matter or corporeal substances, since that is acknowledged to remain equally inexplicable with or without this supposition. If therefore it were possible for bodies to exist without the mind, yet to hold they do so, must needs be a very precarious opinion; since it is to suppose, without any reason at all, that God has created innumerable beings that are entirely useless, and serve to no manner of purpose.

20. In short, if there were external bodies, it is impossible we should ever come to know it; and if there were not, we might have the very same reasons to think there were that we have now.[8] Suppose—what no one can deny possible—an intelligence without the help of external bodies, to be affected with the same train of sensations or ideas that you are, imprinted in the same order and with like vividness in his mind. I ask whether that intelligence hath not all the reason to believe the existence of corporeal substances, represented by his ideas, and exciting them in his mind, that you can possibly have for believing the same thing? Of this there can be no question - which one consideration were enough to make any reasonable person suspect the strength of whatever arguments he may think himself to have, for the existence of bodies without the mind

21. Were it necessary to add any farther proof against the existence of Matter after what has been said I could instance several of those errors and difficulties (not to mentio impieties) which have sprung fron that tenet. It has occasioned numberless controversies and dispute in philosophy, and not a few of fa greater moment in religion. But shall not enter into the detail of then in this place, as well because I thin arguments *a posteriori* are unnecessary for confirming what has been if I mistake not, sufficiently demonstrated *a priori*, as because I shal

[8]The rejection of external bodies, of the entire material world, is not as illogical as it may sound if the context in which it is developed is kept in mind. Berkeley accepts the empiricist position that ideas are the sole object of knowledge. He relentlessly insists on what this logically involves. For one thing, it means that philosophy is concerned solely wit *perceptions*. If so, anything beyond the or behind them is out of contact; in fac there might just as well be no behind o beyond them at all. Berkeley asserts th there *is* nothing material outside ou ideas. He could have gone farther, a Hume did. What needs to be done, however, is to face up to the very startin point and method of Empiricism and b a critical analysis see what aspect the noetic data is being slighted.

ereafter find occasion to speak
omewhat of them.

* * *

25. All our ideas, sensations, no-
ions, or the things which we per-
eive, by whatsoever names they
nay be distinguished, are visibly
nactive—there is nothing of power
r agency included in them. So that
ne idea or object of thought cannot
roduce or make any alteration in
nother. To be satisfied of the truth
f this, there is nothing else requi-
ite but a bare observation of our
deas. For, since they and every
art of them exist only in the mind,
t follows that there is nothing in
hem but what is perceived: but who-
ver shall attend to his ideas,
vhether of sense or reflexion, will
ot perceive in them any power or
ctivity; there is, therefore, no
uch thing contained in them. A
ittle attention will discover to us
hat the very being of an idea im-
lies passiveness and inertness in
t, insomuch that it is impossible for
n idea to do anything, or, strictly
peaking, to be the cause of any-
hing; neither can it be the resem-
lance or pattern of any active being,
s is evident from sect. 8. Whence
t plainly follows that extension, figre, and motion cannot be the cause
f our sensations. To say, thereore, that these are the effects of
owers resulting from the configu-
ation, number, motion, and size of
orpuscles, must certainly be false.

26. We perceive a continual suc-
ession of ideas, some are anew ex-
ited, others are changed or totally
isappear. There is therefore some
ause of these ideas, whereon they
epend, and which produces and changes them. That this cause cannot be any quality or idea or combination of ideas, is clear from the preceding section. It must therefore be a substance; but it has been shown that there is no corporeal or material substance: it remains therefore that the cause of ideas is an incorporeal active substance or Spirit.[9]

27. A spirit is one simple, undivided, active being—as it perceives ideas it is called the *understanding*, and as it produces or otherwise operates about them it is called the *will*. Hence there can be no *idea* formed of a soul or spirit; for all ideas whatever, being passive and inert (Vide sect. 25), they cannot represent unto us, by way of image or likeness, that which acts. A little attention will make it plain to any one, that to have an idea which shall be like that active principle of motion and change of ideas is absolutely impossible. Such is the nature of *spirit*, or that which acts, that it cannot be of itself perceived, but only by the effects which it produceth. If any man shall doubt of the truth of what is here delivered, let him but reflect and try if he can frame the idea of any power or active being, and whether he has ideas of two principal powers, marked by the names *will* and *understanding*, distinct from each other as well as from a third

[9]Having rejected all material substance, Berkeley now introduces his views on minds or spiritual substances. These are required as the active beings which have or entertain ideas which, being perceived, are passive. Obviously we cannot have an *idea* of spirit in itself; yet, since we are conscious of self and do somehow know other minds, Berkeley admits *notion* as a new means of knowledge. His Immaterialism will leave him with a realm of finite minds and an infinite Mind.

idea of Substance or Being in general, with a relative notion of its supporting or being the subject of the aforesaid powers—which is signified by the name *soul* or *spirit*. This is what some hold; but, so far as I can see, the words *will, soul, spirit*, do not stand for different ideas, or, in truth, for any idea at all, but for something which is very different from ideas, and which, being an agent, cannot be like unto, or represented by, any idea whatsoever. Though it must be owned at the same time that we have some *notion* of soul, spirit, and the operations of the mind: such as willing, loving, hating—inasmuch as we know or understand the meaning of these words.

28. I find I can excite ideas in my mind at pleasure, and vary and shift the scene as oft as I think fit. It is no more than willing, and straightway this or that idea arises in my fancy; and by the same power it is obliterated and makes way for another. This making and unmaking of ideas doth very properly denominate the mind active. Thus much is certain and grounded on experience; but when we think of unthinking agents or of exciting ideas exclusive of volition, we only amuse ourselves with words.

29. But, whatever power I may have over my own thoughts, I find the ideas actually perceived by Sense have not a like dependence on my will. When in broad daylight I open my eyes, it is not in my power to choose whether I shall see or no, or to determine what particular objects shall present themselves to my view; and so likewise as to the hearing and other senses; the ideas imprinted on them are not creatures of my will. There is therefore some *other* Will or Spirit that produces them.

30. The ideas of Sense are more strong, lively, and distinct than those of the imagination; they have likewise a steadiness, order, and coherence, and are not excited at random, as those which are the effects of human wills often are, but in a regular train or series, the admirable connexion whereof sufficiently testifies the wisdom and benevolence of its Author. Now the set rules or established methods wherein the Mind we depend on excites in us the ideas of sense, are called the *laws of nature*; and these we learn by experience, which teaches us that such and such ideas are attended with such and such other ideas, in the ordinary course of things.[10]

31. This gives us a sort of foresight which enables us to regulate our actions for the benefit of life. And without this we should be eternally at a loss; we could not know how to act anything that might procure us the least pleasure, or remove the least pain of sense. That food nourishes, sleep refreshes, and fire warms us; that to sow in the seed-time is the way to reap in the harvest; and in general that to obtain such or such ends, such or such means are conducive—all this we know, not by discovering any necessary connexion between our ideas, but only by the observation of the settled laws of nature, without which we should be all in uncertainty and confusion, and a grown man no more know how to manage himself in the affairs of life than an infant just born.

[10] To explain the distinctness, order and coherence of sense ideas, Berkeley introduces the laws of nature—which are said to be the work of God, the Governing Spirit.

32. And yet this consistent uniform working, which so evidently displays the goodness and wisdom of that Governing Spirit whose Will constitutes the laws of nature, is so far from leading our thoughts to Him, that it rather sends them wandering after second causes. For, when we perceive certain ideas of Sense constantly followed by other ideas and we know this is not of our own doing, we forthwith attribute power and agency to the ideas themselves, and make one the cause of another, than which nothing can be more absurd and unintelligible. Thus, for example, having observed that when we perceive by sight a certain round luminous figure we at the same time perceive by touch the idea or sensation called heat, we do from thence conclude the sun to be the cause of heat. And in like manner perceiving the motion and collision of bodies to be attended with sound, we are inclined to think the latter the effect of the former.

33. The ideas imprinted on the Senses by the Author of nature are called *real things*; and those excited in the imagination being less regular, vivid, and constant, are more properly termed *ideas*, or *images of things*, which they copy and represent. But then our sensations, be they never so vivid and distinct, are nevertheless ideas, that is, they exist in the mind, or are perceived by it, as truly as the ideas of its own framing. The ideas of Sense are allowed to have more reality in them, that is, to be more strong, orderly, and coherent than the creatures of the mind; but this is no argument that they exist without the mind. They are also less dependent on the spirit, or thinking substance which perceives them, in that they are excited by the will of another and more powerful spirit; yet still they are *ideas*, and certainly no idea, whether faint or strong, can exist otherwise than in a mind perceiving it.[11]

34. Before we proceed any farther it is necessary we spend some time in answering objections which may probably be made against the principles we have hitherto laid down. In doing of which, if I seem too prolix to those of quick apprehensions; I hope it may be pardoned, since all men do not equally apprehend things of this nature, and I am willing to be understood by every one.

First, then, it will be objected that by the foregoing principles all that is real and substantial in nature is banished out of the world, and instead thereof a chimerical scheme of *ideas* takes place. All things that exist, exist only in the mind, that is, they are purely notional. What therefore becomes of the sun, moon, and stars? What must we think of houses, rivers, mountains, trees, stones; nay, even of our own bodies? Are all these but so many chimeras and illusions on the fancy? To all which, and whatever else of the same sort may be objected, I answer, that by the principles premised we are not deprived of any one thing in nature. Whatever we see, feel, hear, or anywise conceive or understand remains as secure as ever, and is as real as ever. There is a *rerum natura*, and the distinction between realities and chimeras retains its full force. This is evident from sect. 29, 30, and 33, where we have shown what is meant by *real*

---

[11]This merely reiterates what he has said from the very beginning. Cf. paragraph 3 and footnote 4.

things in opposition to *chimeras* or ideas of our own framing; but then they both equally exist in the mind, and in that sense they are alike *ideas*.

35. I do not argue against the existence of any one thing that we can apprehend either by sense or reflexion. That the things I see with my eyes and touch with my hands do exist, really exist, I make not the least question. The only thing whose existence we deny is that which *philosophers* call Matter or corporeal substance.[12] And in doing of this there is no damage done to the rest of mankind, who, I dare say, will never miss it. The Atheist indeed will want the colour of an empty name to support his impiety; and the Philosophers may possibly find they have lost a great handle for trifling and disputation. But that is all the harm that I can see done.

36. If any man thinks this detracts from the existence or reality of things, he is very far from understanding what hath been premised in the plainest terms I could think of. Take here an abstract of what has been said:—There are spiritual substances, minds, or human souls, which will or excite ideas in themselves at pleasure; but these are faint, weak, and unsteady in respect of others they perceive by sense - which, being impressed upon them according to certain rules or laws of nature, speak themselves the effects of a mind more powerful and wise than human spirits. These latter are said to have more *reality* in them than the former:— by which is meant that they are more affecting, orderly, and distinct, and that they are not fictions of the mind perceiving them. And in this sense the sun that I see by day is the real sun, and that which I imagine by night is the idea of the former. In the sense here given of *reality* it is evident that every vegetable, star, mineral, and in general each part of the mundane system, is as much a *real being* by our principles as by any other. Whether others mean anything by the term *reality* different from what I do, I entreat them to look into their own thoughts and see.

37. It will be urged that thus much at least is true, to wit, that we take away all corporeal substances. To this my answer is, that if the word *substance* be taken in the vulgar sense—for a combination of sensible qualities, such as extension, solidity, weight, and the like—this we cannot be accused of taking away: but if it be taken in a philosophic sense—for the support of accidents or qualities without the mind—then indeed I acknowledge that we take it away, if one may be said to take away that which never had any existence, not even in the imagination.[13]

38. But after all, say you, it sounds very harsh to say we eat and drink ideas, and are clothed with

---

[12]As was indicated in footnote 8, there remains some ambiguity in Berkeley's notion of matter. His rejection of the existence of "pure passivity" is quite understandable, but it would seem that one inspiration for his denial of the existence of material beings is indicated in the very next sentence where he refers to "the Atheist." He was much concerned for religious truths and beliefs in the face of developing Scepticism and Atheism, but if we obtain evident knowledge of the only real world by knowing our ideas, and if the world of sensible bodies is one of mind-dependent ideas based on infinite Spirit, then the grounds for these errors are gone.

[13]Cf. footnote 8.

ideas. I acknowledge it does so—the word *idea* not being used in common discourse to signify the several combinations of sensible qualities which are called *things*; and it is certain that any expression which varies from the familiar use of language will seem harsh and ridiculous. But this doth not concern the truth of the proposition, which in other words is no more than to say, we are fed and clothed with those things which we perceive immediately by our senses. The hardness or softness, the colour, taste, warmth, figure, or suchlike qualities, which combined together constitute the several sorts of victuals and apparel, have been shewn to exist only in the mind that perceives them; and this is all that is meant by calling them *ideas*; which word if it was as ordinarily used as *thing*, would sound no harsher nor more ridiculous than it. I am not for disputing about the propriety, but the truth of the expression. If therefore you agree with me that we eat and drink and are clad with the immediate objects of sense, which cannot exist unperceived or without the mind, I shall readily grant it is more proper or conformable to custom that they should be called things rather than ideas.

39. If it be demanded why I make use of the word *idea*, and do not rather in compliance with custom call them *things*; I answer, I do it for two reasons:—first, because the term *thing* in contradistinction to *idea*, is generally supposed to denote somewhat existing without the mind; secondly, because *thing* hath a more comprehensive signification than *idea*, including spirit or thinking things as well as ideas. Since therefore the objects of sense exist only in the mind, and are withal thoughtless and inactive, I chose to mark them by the word *idea*, which implies those properties.

40. But, say what we can, some one perhaps may be apt to reply, he will still believe his senses, and never suffer any arguments, how plausible soever, to prevail over the certainty of them. Be it so; assert the evidence of sense as high as you please, we are willing to do the same. That what I see, hear, and feel doth exist, that is to say, is perceived by me, I no more doubt than I do of my own being. But I do not see how the testimony of sense can be alleged as a proof for the existence of anything which is not perceived by sense. We are not for having any man turn sceptic and disbelieve his senses; on the contrary, we give them all the stress and assurance imaginable; nor are there any principles more opposite to Scepticism than those we have laid down, as shall be hereafter clearly shewn.[14]

41. *Secondly*, it will be objected that there is a great difference betwixt real fire for instance, and the idea of fire, betwixt dreaming or imagining oneself burnt, and actually being so: if you suspect it to be only the idea of fire which you see, do but put your hand into it and you will be convinced with a witness. This and

[14]The hope of refuting Scepticism was another goal which inspired Berkeley. In his day contemporary Scepticism used, as one of its grounds, the claim that if we can know only our ideas then we can never come to know a world distinct from and independent of those ideas. Berkeley's reply is that there is no such material world, and we can know the only real world, which is made up of our ideas. Thus Scepticism is defeated.

the like may be urged in opposition to our tenets. To all which the answer is evident from what hath been already said; and I shall only add in this place, that if real fire be very different from the idea of fire, so also is the real pain that it occasions very different from the idea of the same pain, and yet nobody will pretend that real pain either is, or can possibly be, in an unperceiving thing, or without the mind, any more than its idea.

* * *

45. *Fourthly*, it will be objected that from the foregoing principles it follows things are every moment annihilated and created anew. The objects of sense exist only when they are perceived; the trees therefore are in the garden, or the chairs in the parlour, no longer than while there is somebody by to perceive them. Upon shutting my eyes all the furniture in the room is reduced to nothing, and barely upon opening them it is again created. In answer to all which, I refer the reader to what has been said in sect. 3, 4, &c., and desire he will consider whether he means anything by the actual existence of an idea distinct from its being perceived. For my part, after the nicest inquiry I could make, I am not able to discover that anything else is meant by those words; and I once more entreat the reader to sound his own thoughts, and not suffer himself to be imposed on by words. If he can conceive it possible either for his ideas or their archetypes to exist without being perceived, then I give up the cause; but if he cannot, he will acknowledge it is unreasonable for him to stand up in defence of he knows not what, and pretend to charge on me as an absurdity the not assenting to those propositions which at bottom have no meaning in them.

46. It will not be amiss to observe how far the received principles of philosophy are themselves chargeable with those pretended absurdities. It is thought strangely absurd that upon closing my eyelids all the visible objects around me should be reduced to nothing; and yet is not this what philosophers commonly acknowledge, when they agree on all hands that light and colours, which alone are the proper and immediate objects of sight, are mere sensations that exist no longer than they are perceived?[15] Again, it may to some perhaps seem very incredible that things should be every moment creating, yet this very notion is commonly taught in the schools. For the Schoolmen, though they acknowledge the existence of Matter, and that the whole mundane fabric is framed out of it, are nevertheless of opinion that it cannot subsist without the divine conservation, which by them is expounded to be a continual creation.[16]

47. Farther, a little thought will discover to us that though we allow

---

[15]This is a point well made against Locke's views on the subjectivity of secondary qualities.

[16]It is true that the expression "continual creation" is used by the men to whom Berkeley refers, but his use of it in this context does not convey a correct understanding of it. For those who used it, it did not mean a constant annihilation and a constant re-creation; rather, it referred to the fact that the same divine power which accounted for the beginning of existence for contingent beings is needed at every moment of their existence to account for their continuing to exist.

the existence of Matter or corporeal substance, yet it will unavoidably follow, from the principles which are now generally admitted, that the particular bodies, of what kind soever, do none of them exist whilst they are not perceived. For, it is evident from sect. 11 and the following sections, that the Matter philosophers contend for is an incomprehensible somewhat, which hath none of those particular qualities whereby the bodies falling under our senses are distinguished one from another. But, to make this more plain, it must be remarked that the infinite divisibility of Matter is now universally allowed, at least by the most approved and considerable philosophers, who on the received principles demonstrate it beyond all exception. Hence, it follows there is an infinite number of parts in each particle of Matter which are not perceived by sense.[17] The reason therefore that any particular body seems to be of a finite magnitude, or exhibits only a finite number of parts to sense, is, not because it contains no more, since in itself it contains an infinite number of parts, but because the sense is not acute enough to discern them. In proportion therefore as the sense is rendered more acute, it perceives a greater number of parts in the object, that is, the object appears greater, and its figure varies, those parts in its extremities which were before unperceivable appearing now to bound it in very different lines and angles from those perceived by an obtuser sense. And at length, after various changes of size and shape, when the sense becomes infinitely acute the body shall seem infinite. During all which there is no alteration in the body, but only in the sense. Each body therefore, considered in itself, is infinitely extended, and consequently void of all shape or figure. From which it follows that, though we should grant the existence of Matter to be never so certain, yet it is withal as certain, the materialists themselves are by their own principles forced to acknowledge, that neither the particular bodies perceived by sense, nor anything like them, exists without the mind. Matter, I say, and each particle thereof, is according to them infinite and shapeless, and it is the mind that frames all that variety of bodies which compose the visible world, any one whereof does not exist longer than it is perceived.

48. If we consider it, the objection proposed in sect. 45 will not be found reasonably charged on the principles we have premised, so as in truth to make any objection at all against our notions. For, though we hold indeed the objects of sense to be nothing else but ideas which cannot exist unperceived; yet we may not hence conclude they have no existence except only while they are perceived by us, since there may be some other spirit that perceives them though we do not. Wherever bodies are said to have no existence without the mind, I would not be understood to mean this or that particular mind, but all minds whatsoever. It does not therefore follow from the foregoing principles that bodies are annihilated and created every moment, or exist not at all during the intervals between our perception of them.

---

[17] One should keep in mind the distinction between the *actual* and the *potential* respecting the divisibility of matter and the presence of parts in the whole.

9

A Sceptical Conclusion

David Hume (1711-1776)

In keeping with his empirical predecessors, Hume looks upon internal perceptions as the immediate objects of knowledge. His phenomenal analyses of these perceptions leads him to the denial of the knowledge of substances and in particular of any extramental order of causes. Human insistence on the cause-effect relationship is due to custom and to the intramental association of ideas, because, as Hume sees it, actual experience is only of loose, disconnected perceptions.

Thus Hume leads Empiricism to a logically phenomenal conclusion, and, per se, deprives all general truths and all scientific inference of their bases in extramental reality. Only on the subjective side is there found some basis for relations between perceptions.

The selections offered indicate Hume's atomization of perceptions in his discovery of the basic elements of cognition, his development of mental association to provide some basis of unification, and especially the application of his Phenomenalism to the cause-effect relation. The results of this philosophy for both science and metaphysics were clearly seen by Kant, and in order to save knowledge from total shipwreck, Kant faced the need of reappraising the basic insights of Empiricism in terms of a fuller human experience.

AN ENQUIRY CONCERNING HUMAN UNDERSTANDING[1]

Section II

OF THE ORIGIN OF IDEAS

Every one will readily allow, that there is a considerable difference between the perceptions of the mind, when a man feels the pain of excessive heat, or the pleasure of moderate warmth, and when he afterwards recalls to his memory this sensation, or anticipates it by his imagination. These faculties may mimic or copy the perceptions of the senses; but they never can entirely reach the force and vivacity of the original sentiment. The utmost we say of them, even when they operate with greatest vigour, is, that they represent their object in so lively a manner, that we could *almost* say we feel or see it: But, except the mind be disordered by disease or madness, they never can arrive at such a pitch of vivacity, as to render these perceptions altogether undistinguishable. All the colours of poetry, however splendid, can never paint natural objects in such a manner as to make the description be taken for a real landscape. The most lively thought is still inferior to the dullest sensation.

We may observe a like distinction to run through all the other perceptions of the mind. A man in a fit of anger, is actuated in a very different manner from one who only thinks of that emotion. If you tell me, that any person is in love, I easily understand your meaning, and form a just conception of his situation; but never can mistake that conception for the real disorders and agitations of the passion. When we reflect on our past sentiments and affections, our thought is a faithful mirror, and copies its objects truly; but the colours which it employs are faint and dull, in comparison of those in which our original perceptions were clothed. It requires no nice discernment or metaphysical head to mark the distinction between them.

Here therefore we may divide all the perceptions[2] of the mind into two classes or species, which are distinguished by their different degrees of force and vivacity. The less forcible and lively are commonly denominated *Thoughts* or *Ideas*. The other species want a name in our language, and in most others; I suppose, because it was not requisite for any, but philosophical purposes, to rank them under a general term or appellation. Let us, therefore, use a little freedom, and call them *Impressions;* employing that word in a sense somewhat different from the

---

[1]Selections are from David Hume, *An Enquiry Concerning Human Understanding* [1748], Charles W. Hendel, ed. (New York: The Liberal Arts Press, Inc.,1955).

[2]Hume, like Locke and Berkeley, begins by breaking down knowledge into its elements, and then proceeds to evaluate these and to reconstruct knowledge from these units. Again, as is general in Empiricism, what we know are our perceptions only; these may be either vivid and strong, which Hume names *impressions*, or languid and weak, which he names *ideas*.

usual. By the term *impression*, then, I mean all our more lively perceptions, when we hear, or see, or feel, or love, or hate, or desire, or will. And impressions are distinguished from ideas, which are the less lively perceptions, of which we are conscious, when we reflect on any of those sensations or movements above mentioned.

Nothing, at first view, may seem more unbounded than the thought of man, which not only escapes all human power and authority, but is not even restrained within the limits of nature and reality. To form monsters, and join incongruous shapes and appearances, costs the imagination no more trouble than to conceive the most natural and familiar objects. And while the body is confined to one planet, along which it creeps with pain and difficulty; the thought can in an instant transport us into the most distant regions of the universe; or even beyond the universe, into the unbounded chaos, where nature is supposed to lie in total confusion. What never was seen, or heard of, may yet be conceived; nor is any thing beyond the power of thought, except what implies an absolute contradiction.

But though our thought seems to possess this unbounded liberty, we shall find, upon a nearer examination, that it is really confined within very narrow limits, and that all this creative power of the mind amounts to no more than the faculty of compounding, transposing, augmenting, or diminishing the materials afforded us by the senses and experience. When we think of a golden mountain, we only join two consistent ideas, *gold* and *mountain*, with which we were formerly acquainted. A virtuous horse we can conceive; because, from our own feeling, we can conceive virtue; and this we may unite to the figure and shape of a horse, which is an animal familiar to us. In short, all the materials of thinking are derived either from our outward or inward sentiment: the mixture and composition of these belongs alone to the mind and will. Or, to express myself in philosophical language, all our ideas or more feeble perceptions are copies of our impressions or more lively ones.

To prove this, the two following arguments will, I hope, be sufficient. First, when we analyze our thoughts or ideas, however compounded or sublime, we always find that they resolve themselves into such simple ideas as were copied from a precedent feeling or sentiment. Even those ideas, which, at first view, seem the most wide of this origin, are found, upon a nearer scrutiny, to be derived from it. The idea of God, as meaning an infinitely intelligent, wise, and good Being, arises from reflecting on the operations of our own mind, and augmenting, without limit, those qualities of goodness and wisdom. We may prosecute this enquiry to what length we please; where we shall always find, that every idea which we examine is copied from a similar impression. Those who would assert that this position is not universally true nor without exception, have only one, and that an easy method of refuting it; by producing that idea, which, in their opinion, is not derived from this source. It will then be incumbent on us, if we would maintain our doctrine, to produce the impression, or lively perception, which corresponds to it.

Secondly. If it happen, from a deect of the organ, that a man is not usceptible of any species of sen- ation, we always find that he is as ittle susceptible of the correspond- nt ideas. A blind man can form no otion of colours; a deaf man of ounds. Restore either of them that ense in which he is deficient; by pening this new inlet for his sen- ations, you also open an inlet for he ideas; and he finds no difficulty n conceiving these objects. The ase is the same, if the object, roper for exciting any sensation, as never been applied to the organ. Laplander or Negro has no no- ion of the relish of wine. And hough there are few or no in- tances of a like deficiency in the nind, where a person has never felt r is wholly incapable of a senti- nent or passion that belongs to his pecies; yet we find the same ob- ervation to take place in a less legree. A man of mild manners can orm no idea of inveterate revenge r cruelty; nor can a selfish heart asily conceive the heights of riendship and generosity. It is eadily allowed, that other beings nay possess many senses of which ve can have no conception; because he ideas of them have never been ntroduced to us in the only man- ıer by which an idea can have ac- ess to the mind, to wit, by the ctual feeling and sensation.

There is, however, one contra- lictory phenomenon, which may rove that it is not absolutely im- ossible for ideas to arise, inde- endent of their correspondent mpressions. I believe it will read- ly be allowed, that the several listinct ideas of colour, which en- er by the eye, or those of sound, vhich are conveyed by the ear, are eally different from each other; though, at the same time, resem- bling. Now if this be true of differ- ent colours, it must be no less so of the different shades of the same colour; and each shade produces a distinct idea, independent of the rest. For if this should be denied, it is possible, by the continual gradation of shades, to run a colour insensibly into what is most re- mote from it; and if you will not allow any of the means to be differ- ent, you cannot, without absurdity, deny the extremes to be the same. Suppose, therefore, a person to have enjoyed his sight for thirty years, and to have become per- fectly acquainted with colours of all kinds except one particular shade of blue, for instance, which it never has been his fortune to meet with. Let all the different shades of that colour, except that single one, be placed before him, descending grad- ually from the deepest to the light- est; it is plain that he will perceive a blank, where that shade is want- ing, and will be sensible that there is a greater distance in that place between the contiguous colours than in any other. Now I ask, whether it be possible for him, from his own imagination, to supply this defi- ciency, and raise up to himself the idea of that particular shade, though it had never been conveyed to him by his senses? I believe there are few but will be of opinion that he can; and this may serve as a proof that the simple ideas are not al- ways, in every instance, derived from the correspondent impres- sions; though this instance is so singular, that it is scarcely worth our observing, and does not merit that for it alone we should alter our general maxim.

Here, therefore, is a proposition,

which not only seems, in itself, simple and intelligible; but, if a proper use were made of it, might render every dispute equally intelligible, and banish all that jargon, which has so long taken possession of metaphysical reasonings, and drawn disgrace upon them. All ideas, especially abstract ones, are naturally faint and obscure: the mind has but a slender hold of them: they are apt to be confounded with other resembling ideas; and when we have often employed any term, though without a distinct meaning, we are apt to imagine it has a determinate idea annexed to it. On the contrary, all impressions, that is, all sensations, either outward or inward, are strong and vivid: the limits between them are more exactly determined: nor is it easy to fall into any error or mistake with regard to them. When we entertain, therefore, any suspicion that a philosophical term is employed without any meaning or idea (as is but too frequent), we need but enquire, *from what impression is that supposed idea derived?*[3] And if it be impossible to assign any, this wi serve to confirm our suspicion. B bringing ideas into so clear a ligh we may reasonably hope to remov all dispute, which may arise, con cerning their nature and reality.

Section III

OF THE ASSOCIATION OF IDEAS

It is evident that there is a prin ciple of connexion between the dif ferent thoughts or ideas of the minc and that, in their appearance to th memory or imagination, they intro duce each other with a certain de gree of method and regularity. I our more serious thinking or dis course this is so observable tha any particular thought, which break in upon the regular tract or chai of ideas, is immediately remarke and rejected. And even in our wild est and most wandering reverie nay in our very dreams, we sha find, if we reflect, that the imagina tion ran not altogether at adven tures, but that there was still connexion upheld among the differ ent ideas, which succeeded eac other. Were the loosest and frees conversation to be transcribe there would immediately be ob

[3] As elsewhere in Hume, the attack in this paragraph on the foundation and validity of metaphysical knowledge is intelligible only in the context of British Empiricism, which Hume drives to its logical conclusion. In keeping with that tradition, Hume limits all human knowledge to *appearances* and to them alone. Hence, he rules out all possibility of acquiring any knowledge of essences or ultimate principles of being. His is a phenomenalistic study of sense appearances, and any further inquiry is rejected as going beyond *experience*. Experience is limited to sense *impressions* and *ideas* which can be traced back to those impressions. Put another way, Hume transfers from the level of empirical science to metaphysics and to all human knowledge the claim that there is no knowledge of the essences of things, even of the sel This view reduces the role of the intel lect to the mere recording and, by wa of the imagination, to the association various ideas. Human *experience* is fa more profound than Empiricism will al low. Our knowledge of existence is n limited to mere sense perceptions, ar the intellect can find in the data presente by the senses an intelligible structur to which it responds.

ɜrved something which connected in all its transitions. Or where ɪis is wanting, the person who roke the thread of discourse might ill inform you, that there had se-cretly revolved in his mind a suc-ɜssion of thought, which had grad-ɪlly led him from the subject of ɔnversation. Among different lan-ɪages, even where we cannot sus-ɜct the least connexion or com-ɪunication, it is found, that the ords, expressive of ideas, the ost compounded, do yet nearly ɔrrespond to each other: a certain roof that the simple ideas, com-rehended in the compound ones, ere bound together by some uni-ɜrsal principle, which had an equal ɪfluence on all mankind.

Though it be too obvious to escape ɔservation, that different ideas are ɔnnected together; I do not find ɪat any philosopher has attempted enumerate or class all the prin-ples of association; a subject, ɔwever, that seems worthy of cu-osity. To me, there appear to be ɪly three principles of connexion nong ideas, namely, *Resemblance*, *ɔntiguity* in time or place, and *ause* or *Effect*.[4]

That these principles serve to connect ideas will not, I believe, be much doubted. A picture naturally leads our thoughts to the original: the mention of one apartment in a building naturally introduces an enquiry or discourse concerning the others: and if we think of a wound, we can scarcely forbear reflecting on the pain which follows it. But that this enumeration is complete, and that there are no other principles of association except these, may be difficult to prove to the satisfaction of the reader, or even to a man's own satisfaction. All we can do, in such cases, is to run over several instances, and examine carefully the principle which binds the different thoughts to each other, never stopping till we render the principle as general as possible. The more instances we examine, and the more care we employ, the more assurance shall we acquire, that the enumeration, which we form from the whole, is complete and entire.

Section IV

SCEPTICAL DOUBTS CONCERNING THE OPERATIONS OF THE UNDERSTANDING.

Part I

All the objects of human reason or enquiry may naturally be divided

---

[4]It must be remembered that Hume, in eping with the empirical tradition, has omized "experience" into its elemen-ry units, perceptions, which in them-lves are loose and unconnected. The nction of these three principles is to ovide, from the subjective or mental de, an account of what holds the uni-rse of perceptions together *for us*. He pposes that all men are endowed with is "cement of the universe" (cf. Hume, *ɪ Abstract of a Treatise of Human Na-re*, to be found in C. Hendel's edition *An Enquiry Concerning Human Under-anding*, p. 198), so we can all have the me experience. This notion of associ-ion will be used by Hume to explain neral ideas, the belief in reality, and the causal relationship. This explanation, however, does not go deep enough to provide a solid foundation for the validity of knowledge. It is open to the same objections which have been urged against making perceptions or ideas the only immediate object of knowledge.

into two kinds, to wit, *Relations of Ideas,* and *Matters of Fact.* Of the first kind are the sciences of Geometry, Algebra, and Arithmetic; and in short, every affirmation which is either intuitively or demonstratively certain. *That the square of the hypothenuse is equal to the squares of the two sides,* is a proposition which expresses a relation between these figures. *That three times five is equal to the half of thirty,* expresses a relation between these numbers. Propositions of this kind are discoverable by the mere operation of thought, without dependence on what is anywhere existent in the universe. Though there never were a circle or triangle in nature, the truths demonstrated by Euclid would for ever retain their certainty and evidence.

Matters of fact, which are the second objects of human reason, are not ascertained in the same manner; nor is our evidence of their truth, however great, of a like nature with the foregoing. The contrary of every matter of fact is still possible; because it can never imply a contradiction, and is conceived by the mind with the same facility and distinctness, as if ever so conformable to reality. *That the sun will not rise to-morrow* is no less intelligible a proposition, and implies no more contradiction than the affirmation, *that it will rise.* We should in vain, therefore, attempt to demonstrate its falsehood. Were it demonstratively false, it would imply a contradiction, and could never be distinctly conceived by the mind.

It may, therefore, be a subject worthy of curiosity, to enquire what is the nature of that evidence which assures us of any real existence and matter of fact, beyond the present testimony of our senses,[5] c the records of our memory. Th part of philosophy, it is observ able, has been little cultivate either by the ancients or modern and therefore our doubts and er rors, in the prosecution of so im portant an enquiry, may be th more excusable; while we marc through such difficult paths witho any guide or direction. They ma even prove useful, by exciting curi osity, and destroying that implic faith and security, which is th bane of all reasoning and free en quiry. The discovery of defects i the common philosophy, if any suc there be, will not, I presume, be discouragement, but rather an in citement, as is usual, to attem something more full and satisfac tory than has yet been proposed t the public.

All reasonings concerning matte of fact seem to be founded on th relation of *Cause and Effect.* B means of that relation alone we ca go beyond the evidence of our mem ory and senses[6]. If you were to as

[5]This limitation of knowledge to sens experience is intimately connected wi the view of experience as one discon nected event after another with no objec tive link between them. In this conte there is room for no specific intellectu apprehension, and there naturally aris problems on general ideas and on caus relationships.

[6]This statement is open to two ve different meanings. By going beyond th evidence of our memory and senses, o can mean to say that human knowledg is not limited to the senses and imag nation, and that in the very sense presen tations, the mind can find its own prope object of knowledge. Thus the give sensed object can also be *known* in re spect to its *dependence for being,* and foundation for the causal relation is in tellectually discovered. However, fro

man, why he believes any matter fact, which is absent; for in- ance, that his friend is in the untry, or in France; he would ve you a reason; and this reason ould be some other fact; as a let- r received from him, or the owledge of his former resolutions d promises. A man finding a atch or any other machine in a sert island, would conclude that ere had once been men in that is- nd. All our reasonings concerning ct are of the same nature. And re it is constantly supposed that ere is a connexion between the esent fact and that which is in- rred from it. Were there nothing bind them together, the inference ould be entirely precarious. The aring of an articulate voice and tional discourse in the dark as- ures us of the presence of some rson: Why? because these are the fects of the human make and fab- c, and closely connected with it. we anatomize all the other rea- nings of this nature, we shall find at they are founded on the rela- on of cause and effect, and that is relation is either near or re- ote, direct or collateral. Heat and ght are collateral effects of fire, d the one effect may justly be in- rred from the other.

If we would satisfy ourselves, erefore, concerning the nature of at evidence, which assures us of atters of fact, we must enquire w we arrive at the knowledge of use and effect.

I shall venture to affirm, as a general proposition, which admits of no exception, that the knowledge of this relation is not, in any instance, attained by reasonings *a priori;* but arises entirely from experience,[7] when we find that any particular objects are constantly conjoined with each other. Let an object be presented to a man of ever so strong natural reason and abilities; if that object be entirely new to him, he will not be able, by the most accurate examination of its sensible qualities, to discover any of its causes or effects. Adam, though his rational faculties be supposed, at the very first, entirely perfect, could not have inferred from the fluidity and transparency of water that it would suffocate him, or from the light and warmth of fire that it would consume him. No object ever discovers, by the qualities which appear to the senses, either the causes which produced it, or the effects which will arise from it; nor can our reason, unassisted by experience, ever draw any inference concerning real existence and matter of fact.

This proposition, *that causes and effects are discoverable, not by*

---

ume's point of view, the mind does not scover this foundation but simply goes *yond* the evidence. For him we get ly loose and disconnected perceptions, d by the association of ideas the caus- relation arises.

[7]This statement, and Hume's entire treatment of the cause-effect relation, indicate that for Hume there is deep opposition between *reason* and *experience*. According to Hume, in line with the tradition he has inherited, reason is supposed to operate in complete independence of sense experience; with an easy glance, reason is supposed to give insights into essences and into the entire causal order of things. While such a view may reflect the position of rationalistic philosophies, it is not the only one possible. Reason can and should be seen as relying on the senses, as gradually learning about the natures of things, and, thus, as contributing to the total and concrete human experience.

reason but by experience,[8] will readily be admitted with regard to such objects, as we remember to have once been altogether unknown to us; since we must be conscious of the utter inability, which we then lay under, of foretelling what would arise from them. Present two smooth pieces of marble to a man who has no tincture of natural philosophy; he will never discover that they will adhere together in such a manner as to require great force to separate them in a direct line, while they make so small a resistance to a lateral pressure. Such events, as bear little analogy to the common course of nature, are also readily confessed to be known only by experience; nor does any man imagine that the explosion of gunpowder, or the attraction of a loadstone, could ever be discovered by arguments *a priori*. In like manner, when an effect is supposed to depend upon an intricate machinery or secret structure of parts, we make no difficulty in attributing all our knowledge of it to experience. Who will assert that he can give the ultimate reason, why milk or bread is proper nourishment for a man, not for a lion or a tiger?

But the same truth may not appear, at first sight, to have the same evidence with regard t events, which have become famil iar to us from our first appearanc in the world, which bear a clos analogy to the whole course of na ture, and which are supposed to de pend on the simple qualities of ob jects, without any secret structur of parts. We are apt to imagine tha we could discover these effects b the mere operation of our reason without experience. We fancy, tha were we brought on a sudden int this world, we could at first hav inferred that one Billiard-ball woul communicate motion to another upo impulse; and that we needed not t have waited for the event, in orde to pronounce with certainty con cerning it. Such is the influence c custom, that, where it is strongest it not only covers our natural ig norance, but even conceals itself and seems not to take place, merel because it is found in the highes degree.

But to convince us that all th laws of nature, and all the opera tions of bodies without exception are known only by experience, th following reflections may, perhaps suffice. Were any object presente to us, and were we required to pro nounce concerning the effect, whic will result from it, without consult ing past observation; after wha manner, I beseech you, must th mind proceed in this operation? I must invent or imagine some event which it ascribes to the object a its effect; and it is plain that thi invention must be entirely arbi trary. The mind can never possibl find the effect in the supposed cause by the most accurate scrutiny an examination. For the effect is totall different from the cause, and con sequently can never be discovere

[8] This statement is ambiguous. If it means that reason apart from experience cannot discover causal relations, it is true, since even here there is dependence on sense data. However, in the context it seems to mean that experience, not reason, discovers them. Of course Hume still has in mind the *a priori* and autonomous sort of reason propounded by the Cartesians, rather than that experienced rational power which functions in co-operation with the sensory powers and discovers intellectual content in the sense presentations.

it. Motion in the second Billiard-ll is a quite distinct event from otion in the first: nor is there ything in the one to suggest the nallest hint of the other. A stone piece of metal raised into the r, and left without any support, mediately falls, but to consider e matter *a priori*, is there any-ing we discover in this situation hich can beget the idea of a down-ard, rather than an upward, or any her motion, in the stone or metal?[9]

And as the first imagination or invention of a particular effect, in all natural operations, is arbitrary, where we consult not experience; so must we also esteem the supposed tie or connexion between the cause and effect, which binds them together, and renders it impossible that any other effect could result from the operation of that cause. When I see, for instance, a Billiard-ball moving in a straight line towards another; even suppose motion in the second ball should by accident be suggested to me, as the result of their contact or impulse; may I not conceive, that a hundred different events might as well follow from that cause? May not both these balls remain at absolute rest? May not the first ball return in a straight line, or leap off from the second in any line or direction? All these suppositions are consistent and conceivable. Why then should we give the preference to one, which is no more consistent or conceivable than the rest? All our reasonings *a priori* will never be able to show us any foundation for this preference.

---

[9]It is clear that here Hume is preoc-pied with particular causes and with e predictability of particular effects om them. His argument may be illus-ated by saying that, if I am presented th something entirely new, I can look it and meditate on it as much as I nt, but I will not know how it will op-ate, what "effects" it will produce, less I let it act, and then, by actually periencing it operating this way or at, I can say "this is what happened." wever, Hume feels that if I could ow the cause-effect relationship, then should be able *a priori* to predict its eration. Hence, the conclusion is that lo not know causality. My experience es me a succession of things in va-ous conditions, but I can never experi-ce *how* that change is brought about. nce, I can never experience causality, I can never know how a cause works, d in particular I can never predict at will happen in any given case. On sense level, and this is Hume's, that true enough. Succession is all that n be observed in change.

However, that is not the whole story uman experience. For in the very ex-rience of change, more than the senses e involved. The passage from potency act must be explained; hence the in-lect knows that there must be some nt to account for it, for in the sensed a the intellect recognizes dependence another and so knows that there must a cause. What that cause is may not be y to decide. It may require detailed dy and many experiences of the given uence. But at times I can come to w which of the antecedents accounts for the change, which means that I can come to know which is the cause.

Hume was most concerned with predictability, and although this is not the most basic element in the causal relationship—the most basic being the recognition, in any case of change, of a dependence for being on the part of the changing thing—we can at times still come to such knowledge as will permit prediction. However, this requires the process of induction whereby, through sufficient observation and analysis, one comes to at least some knowledge of the nature of a given being. Having arrived at this knowledge, we can know how the being works naturally and, hence, how it will work; therefore we can and do predict its future activity in given circumstances.

In a word, then, every effect is a distinct event from its cause. It could not, therefore, be discovered in the cause, and the first invention or conception of it, *a priori*, must be entirely arbitrary. And even after it is suggested, the conjunction of it with the cause must appear equally arbitrary; since there are always many other effects, which, to reason, must seem fully as consistent and natural. In vain, therefore, should we pretend to determine any single event, or infer any cause or effect, without the assistance of observation and experience.[10]

Hence we may discover the reason why no philosopher, who is rational and modest, has ever pretended to assign the ultimate cause of any natural operation, or to show distinctly the action of that power, which produces any single effect in the universe. It is confessed, that the utmost effort of human reason is to reduce the principles, productive of natural phenomena, to a greater simplicity, and to resolve the many particular effects into a few general causes, by means of reasonings from analogy, experience, and observation. But as to the causes of these general causes, we should in vain attempt their discovery; nor shall we ever be able t satisfy ourselves, by any particula explication of them. These ultimat springs and principles are totall shut up from human curiosity an enquiry. Elasticity, gravity, cohesion of parts, communication o motion by impulse; these are probably the ultimate causes and prinI ciples which we ever discover i nature; and we may esteem ourselves sufficiently happy, if, by accurate inquiry and reasoning, w can trace up the particular phenomena to, or near to, these general principles. The most perfec philosophy of the natural kind onl staves off our ignorance a littl longer; as perhaps the most perfec philosophy of the moral or metaphysical kind serves only to discove larger portions of it. Thus the observation of human blindness an weakness is the result of all philosophy, and meets us at every turn in spite of our endeavours to elud or avoid it.

Nor is geometry, when taken int the assistance of natural philosophy ever able to remedy this defect, o lead us into the knowledge of ultimate causes, by all thataaccurac of reasoning for which it is s justly celebrated. Every part mixed mathematics proceeds upo the supposition that certain laws ar established by nature in her operations; and abstract reasonings ar employed, either to assist experience in the discovery of these law or to determine their influence particular instances, where it depends upon any precise degree distance and quantity. Thus, it is law of motion, discovered by experience, that the moment or forc of any body in motion is in the com

[10]Leaving aside Hume's general view on the unknowability of causality, it must be admitted that he is quite right in demanding experience and observation where some succession is newly experienced in order to determine in particular what the precise cause or effect is in any given situation. So far as that goes, it is only a restatement of the fact that potency is known from act. Still that does not mean to imply that objectively the operating of that cause is arbitrary, nor does it mean that I cannot, by observation and experiment, come to know precisely how it does operate and so finally be able to predict the effect which it will produce.

pound ratio or proportion of its solid contents and its velocity; and consequently, that a small force may remove the greatest obstacle or raise the greatest weight, if, by any contrivance or machinery, we can increase the velocity of that force, so as to make it an overmatch for its antagonist. Geometry assists us in the application of this law, by giving us the just dimensions of all the parts and figures which can enter into any species of machine; but still the discovery of the law itself is owing merely to experience, and all the abstract reasonings in the world could never lead us one step towards the knowledge of it. When we reason *a priori*, and consider merely any object or cause, as it appears to the mind, independent of all observation, it never could suggest to us the notion of any distinct object, such as its effect; much less, show us the inseparable and inviolable connexion between them. A man must be very sagacious who could discover by reasoning that crystal is the effect of heat, and ice of cold, without being previously acquainted with the operation of these qualities.

Part II

But we have not yet attained any tolerable satisfaction with regard to the question first proposed. Each solution still gives rise to a new question as difficult as the foregoing, and leads us on to farther enquiries. When it is asked, *What is the nature of all our reasonings concerning matter of fact?* the proper answer seems to be, that they are founded on the relation of cause and effect. When again it is asked, *What is the foundation of all our reasonings and conclusions concerning that relation?* it may be replied in one word, Experience. But if we still carry on our sifting humour, and ask, *What is the foundation of all conclusions from experience?* this implies a new question, which may be of more difficult solution and explication. Philosophers, that give themselves airs of superior wisdom and sufficiency, have a hard task when they encounter persons of inquisitive dispositions, who push them from every corner to which they retreat, and who are sure at last to bring them to some dangerous dilemma. The best expedient to prevent this confusion, is to be modest in our pretensions; and even to discover the difficulty ourselves before it is objected to us. By this means, we may make a kind of merit of our very ignorance.

I shall content myself, in this section, with an easy task, and shall pretend only to give a negative answer to the question here proposed. I say then, that, even after we have experience of the operations of cause and effect, our conclusions from that experience are *not* founded on reasoning, or any process of the understanding. This answer we must endeavour both to explain and to defend.

It must certainly be allowed, that nature has kept us at a great distance from all her secrets, and has afforded us only the knowledge of a few superficial qualities of objects; while she conceals from us those powers and principles on which the influence of those objects entirely depends. Our senses inform us of the colour, weight, and consistence of bread; but neither sense nor reason can ever inform us of those qualities which fit it for the nourishment and support of a human body. Sight or feeling conveys an idea of the actual motion of bodies; but as to that wonderful force or power, which would carry on a moving body for ever in a continued change of place, and which bodies never lose but by communicating it to others; of this we cannot form the most distant conception. But notwithstanding this ignorance of natural powers and principles, we always presume, when we see like sensible qualities, that they have like secret powers, and expect that effects, similar to those which we have experienced, will follow from them. If a body of like colour and consistence with that bread, which we have formerly eat, be presented to us, we make no scruple of repeating the experiment, and foresee, with certainty, like nourishment and support. Now this is a process of the mind or thought, of which I would willingly know the foundation. It is allowed on all hands that there is no known connexion between the sensible qualities and the secret powers; and consequently, that the mind is not led to form such a conclusion concerning their constant and regular conjunction, by anything which it knows of their nature.[11] As to past *Experience*, it can be allowed to give *direct* and *certain* information of those precise objects only, and that precise period of time, which fell under its cognizance: but why this experience should be extended to future times, and to other objects, which, for aught we know, may be only in appearance similar; this is the main question on which I would insist. The bread, which I formerly eat, nourished me; that is, a body of such sensible qualities was, at that time, endued with such secret powers: but does it follow, that other bread must also nourish me at another time, and that like sensible qualities must always be attended with like secret powers? The consequence seems nowise necessary. At least, it must be acknowledged that there is here a consequence drawn by the mind; that there is a certain step taken; a process of thought, and an inference, which wants to be explained. These two propositions are far from being the same, *I have found that such an object has always been attended with such an effect*, and *I foresee, that other objects, which are, in appearance, similar, will be attended with similar effects*. I shall allow, if you please, that the one proposition may justly be inferred from the other; I know, in fact, that it always is inferred. But if you insist that the inference is made by a chain of reasoning, I desire you to produce that reasoning. The connexion between these propositions is not intuitive. There is required a medium, which may enable the mind to draw such an inference, if indeed it be drawn by reasoning and argument. What that medium is, I must confess, passes my comprehension; and it is incumbent on those

[11] For Hume the mind can know nothing of natures, and there is no "connexion between the sensible qualities and the secret powers." So, even if natures do exist, sensible qualities are reified and, by definition and postulation, are set up as obstacles and hindrances to the knowledge of substance, instead of being looked on as revealing at least a minimal knowledge of the nature. (Cf. Reginald F. O'Neill, *Theories of Knowledge* (Englewood Cliffs, N. J.: Prentice-Hall, Inc., 1960), pp. 188-195.

to produce it, who assert that it really exists, and is the origin of all our conclusions concerning matter of fact.[12]

This negative argument must certainly, in process of time, become altogether convincing, if many penetrating and able philosophers shall turn their enquiries this way and no one be ever able to discover any connecting proposition or intermediate step, which supports the understanding in this conclusion. But as the question is yet new, every reader may not trust so far to his own penetration, as to conclude, because an argument escapes his enquiry, that therefore it does not really exist. For this reason it may be requisite to venture upon a more difficult task; and enumerating all the branches of human knowledge, endeavour to show that none of them can afford such an argument.

All reasonings may be divided into two kinds, namely, demonstrative reasoning, or that concerning relations of ideas, and moral reasoning, or that concerning matter of fact and existence. That there are no demonstrative arguments in the case seems evident; since it implies no contradiction that the course of nature may change, and that an object, seemingly like those which we have experienced, may be attended with different or contrary effects. May I not clearly and distinctly conceive that a body, falling from the clouds, and which, in all other respects, resembles snow, has yet the taste of salt or feeling of fire? Is there any more intelligible proposition than to affirm, that all the trees will flourish in December and January, and decay in May and June? Now whatever is intelligible, and can be distinctly conceived, implies no contradiction, and can never be proved false by any demonstrative argument or abstract reasoning *a priori*.

If we be, therefore, engaged by arguments to put trust in past experience, and make it the standard of our future judgement, these arguments must be probable only, or such as regard matter of fact and real existence, according to the division above mentioned. But that there is no argument of this kind, must appear, if our explication of that species of reasoning be admitted as solid and satisfactory. We have said that all arguments concerning existence are founded on the relation of cause and effect; that our knowledge of that relation is derived entirely from experience; and that all our experimental conclusions proceed upon the supposition that the future will be conformable to the past. To endeavour,

[12] As has been said, Hume's insistence on the need of experience to see how a thing does act is a point well made, for we do need to observe how a being concretely operates. But Hume is not so ready to admit what this involves. For it means that from these activities we do come to some knowledge of potencies or capacities, and by the process of induction we can come to some knowledge of natures or essences. As Hume warns, we must be very careful in this matter, because hasty generalizations can easily be erroneous. However, realizing that natures are determined in their way of being and of operating (since they do not have the only power which can introduce novelty, freedom), and that man does have the power of abstraction whereby he can come to know beings under various intelligible aspects, both accidental and substantial, we can at times by way of induction come to the knowledge of a law of nature or to the knowledge of how a given being operates, has operated, and will operate.

therefore, the proof of this last supposition by probable arguments, or arguments regarding existence, must be evidently going in a circle, and taking that for granted, which is the very point in question.

In reality, all arguments from experience are founded on the similarity which we discover among natural objects, and by which we are induced to expect effects similar to those which we have found to follow from such objects. And though none but a fool or madman will ever pretend to dispute the authority of experience, or to reject that great guide of human life, it may surely be alloweda philosopher to have so much curiosity at least as to examine the principle of human nature, which gives this mighty authority to experience, and makes us draw advantage from that similarity which nature has placed among different objects. From causes which appear *similar* we expect similar effects. This is the sum of all our experimental conclusions. Now it seems evident that, if this conclusion were formed by reason, it would be as perfect at first, and upon the instance, as after ever so long a course of experience. But the case is far otherwise. Nothing so like as eggs; yet no one, on account of this appearing similarity, expects the same taste and relish in all of them. It is only after a long course of uniform experiments in any kind, that we attain a firm reliance and security with regard to a particular event. Now where is that process of reasoning which, from one instance, draws a conclusion, so different from that which it infers from a hundred instances that are nowise different from that single one? This question I propose as much for the sake of information, as with an intention of raising difficulties. I cannot find, I cannot imagine any such reasoning. But I keep my mind still open to instruction, if any one will vouchsafe to bestow it on me.

Should it be said that, from a number of uniform experiments, we *infer* a connexion between the sensible qualities and the secret powers; this, I must confess, seems the same difficulty, couched in different terms. The question still recurs, on what process of argument this *inference* is founded? Where is the medium, the interposing ideas, which join propositions so very wide of each other? It is confessed that the colour, consistence, and other sensible qualities of bread appear not, of themselves, to have any connexion with the secret powers of nourishment and support. For otherwise we could infer these secret powers from the first appearance of these sensible qualities, without the aid of experience; contrary to the sentiment of all philosophers, and contrary to plain matter of fact. Here, then, is our natural state of ignorance with regard to the powers and influence of all objects. How is this remedied by experience? It only shows us a number of uniform effects, resulting from certain objects, and teaches us that those particular objects, at that particular time, were endowed with such powers and forces. When a new object, endowed with similar sensible qualities, is produced, we expect similar powers and forces, and look for a like effect. From a body of like colour and consistence with bread we expect like nourishment and support. But this surely is a step or progress of the mind, which wants to be explained. When a man says, *I have found, in all past instances, such sensible qualities conjoined with such secret powers:* And when he says, *Similar sensible qualities will always be conjoined with similar secret powers,* he is not guilty of a tautology, nor are these propositions in any respect the same. You say that the one proposition is an inference from the other. But you must confess that the inference is not intuitive; neither is it demonstrative: Of what nature is it, then? To say it is experimental, is begging the question. For all inferences from experience suppose, as their foundation, that the future will resemble the past, and that similar powers will be conjoined with similar sensible qualities. If there be any suspicion that the course of nature may change, and that the past may be no rule for the future, all experience becomes useless, and can give rise to no inference or conclusion. It is impossible, therefore, that any arguments from experience can prove this resemblance of the past to the future; since all these arguments are founded on the supposition of that resemblance. Let the course of things be allowed hitherto ever so regular; that alone, without some new argument or inference, proves not that, for the future, it will continue so. In vain do you pretend to have learned the nature of bodies from your past experience. Their secret nature, and consequently all their effects and influence, may change, without any change in their sensible qualities. This happens sometimes, and with regard to some objects: Why may it not happen always, and with regard to all objects? What logic, what process of argument secures you against this supposition? My practice, you say, refutes my doubts. But you mistake the purport of my question. As an agent, I am quite satisfied in the point; but as a philosopher, who has some share of curiosity, I will not say scepticism, I want to learn the foundation of this inference. No reading, no enquiry has yet been able to remove my difficulty, or give me satisfaction in a matter of such importance.[13] Can I do better than propose the difficulty to the public, even though, perhaps, I have small hopes of obtaining a solution? We shall, at least, by this means, be sensible of our ignorance, if we do not augment our knowledge.

I must confess that a man is guilty of unpardonable arrogance who concludes, because an argument has escaped his own investigation, that therefore it does not really exist. I must also confess that, though all the learned, for several ages, should have employed themselves in fruitless search upon any subject, it may still, perhaps, be rash to conclude positively that the subject must, therefore, pass human comprehension. Even though we examine all the sources of our knowledge, and conclude them unfit

---

[13]Kant came to realize what the empirical views (especially Hume's) meant for scientific knowledge. If all that can be known is one event after another, then there can be no universality or necessity characteristic of human knowledge, and scientific knowledge would be nonexistent. To remedy this, Kant began a reappraisal of the situation. As a result of his studies, he was convinced that he had found the means for reinstating scientific knowledge and at the same time preserving what was valid in the empirical emphasis on the need for experience.

for such a subject, there may still remain a suspicion, that the enumeration is not complete, or the examination not accurate. But with regard to the present subject, there are some considerations which seem to remove all this accusation of arrogance or suspicion of mistake.

It is certain that the most ignorant and stupid peasants—nay infants, nay even brute beasts—improve by experience, and learn the qualities of natural objects, by observing the effects which result from them. When a child has felt the sensation of pain from touching the flame of a candle, he will be careful not to put his hand near any candle; but will expect a similar effect from a cause which is similar in its sensible qualities and appearance. If you assert, therefore, that the understanding of the child is led into this conclusion by any process of argument or ratiocination, I may justly require you to produce that argument; nor have you any pretense to refuse so equitable a demand. You cannot say that the argument is abtruse, and may possibly escape your enquiry; since you confess that it is obvious to the capacity of a mere infant. If you hesitate, therefore, a moment, or if, after reflection, you produce any intricate or profound argument, you, in a manner, give up the question, and confess that it is not reasoning which engages us to suppose the past resembling the future, and to expect similar effects from causes which are, to appearance, similar. This is the proposition which I intended to enforce in the present section. If I be right, I pretend not to have made any mighty discovery. And if I be wrong, I must acknowledge myself to be indeed a very backward scholar; since I cannot now discover an argument which, it seems, was perfectly familiar to me long before I was out of my cradle.

10

Mind and Experience Reintegrated

Emmanuel Kant (1724-1804)

By the middle of the eighteenth century, studies in the nature and meaning of human knowledge had become almost the only concern of philosophers. British Empiricism had quite logically developed into a Scepticism concerning not only causality but also general ideas, universal judgments, and the knowledge of substances or natures. On the other hand, Rationalism had insisted on the a priori power of the mind and thus proposed a dogmatic type of philosophy which sought to disavow its empirical origins. Faced with this situation, Kant sought to save what might be the valid insights of both developments and, at the same time, to avoid their excesses.

Accepting the existence of mathematics as factual and the physical sciences as true sciences, and noting that in metaphysics there was at once a lack of progress being made and a long history of violent disagreements among metaphysicians, Kant proceeded to ask two questions: (1) *How* are mathematics and physics possible as sciences; and (2) *Is* metaphysics possible as a science? To answer those questions, Kant made the natural sciences the criterion or norm for all scientific knowledge. In studying scientific judgments, he found two factors: there is an increase in knowledge, rather than a tautological repetition in the predicate of what was already known in the subject of the judgment (and on this score he called these judgments *synthetic*), and there are also the notes of universality and necessity rather than the particularity and contingency which characterize the objects of sense experience (and on this score he called these judgments *a priori*). Hence, the physical sciences *are possible* precisely because they are enunciated in *synthetic a priori* judgments.

When Kant applies this to metaphysics, as he does in the *Critique of Pure Reason,* he concludes that metaphysics *as a science* is impossible. As he sees the situation, what the metaphysician does is to ignore experience entirely, to take as his objects certain "categories" or "principles of unity" with which the mind is equipped, and to project these mental categories outside the mind as though they were characteristics of reality. The true function of these categories is to make possible the integration of various sense presentations. Metaphysics uses them as though they belonged to extramental reality, and hence its procedure is not scientific.

Actually, Kant's attempt to reconcile empirical or experiential elements of knowledge with intellectual dynamism was greatly needed. The basic difficulty underlying his philosophy is his uncritical acceptance of a rationalistic concept of reason. Human reason is not the totally independent a priori power which Rationalism has pictured. In its concrete functions, even in metaphysical considerations, it is dependent upon and works in close collaboration with sense experience. In what can be sensibly grasped, the human mind is able to discover intelligible aspects, so that it is neither subject to the limits of sensation nor arbitrary or a priori in its pronouncements.

Kant developed his studies in his three famous Critiques. The following selection, however, is taken from his *Prolegomena*, not only because it is somewhat easier to grasp but also because he himself wrote this as an introduction for teachers of his philosophy. It contains his basic views and his reasons for them, and it presents them in manageable form and in a relatively intelligible style.

PROLEGOMENA TO ANY FUTURE METAPHYSICS[1]

Introduction

My object is to persuade all those who think Metaphysics worth studying, that it is absolutely necessary to pause a moment, and, neglecting all that has been done, to propose first the preliminary question, "Whether such a thing as metaphysics be at all possible?"

If it be a science, how comes it that it cannot, like other sciences, obtain universal and permanent recognition? If not, how can it maintain its pretensions, and keep the human mind in suspense with hopes, never ceasing, yet never fulfilled? Whether then we demonstrate our knowledge or our ignorance in this field, we must come once for all to a definite conclusion respecting the nature of this so-called science, which cannot possibly remain on its

[1]The selections are from *Prolegomena to Any Future Metaphysics* (trans. Paul Carus, 1783), as found in the edition edited by Lewis White Beck (New York: Liberal Arts Press, Inc., 1950), pp. 3-9, 13-17, 20-27, 45-54, 61-64. For a brief analysis of Kant's position, cf. O'Neill, *Theories of Knowledge*, pp. 202-209.

present footing. It seems almost ridiculous, while every other science is continually advancing, that in this, which pretends to be Wisdom incarnate, for whose oracle every one inquires, we should constantly move round the same spot, without gaining a single step. And so its followers having melted away, we do not find men confident of their ability to shine in other sciences venturing their reputation here, where everybody, however ignorant in other matters, may deliver a final verdict, as in this domain there is as yet no standard weight and measure to distinguish sound knowledge from shallow talk.

After all it is nothing extraordinary in the elaboration of a science, when men begin to wonder how far it has advanced, that the question should at last occur, whether and how such a science is possible? Human reason so delights in constructions, that it has several times built up a tower, and then razed it to examine the nature of the foundation. It is never too late to become wise; but if the change comes late, there is always more difficulty in starting a reform.

The question whether a science be possible, presupposes a doubt as to its actuality. But such a doubt offends the men whose whole possessions consist of this supposed jewel; hence he who raises the doubt must expect opposition from all sides. Some, in the proud consciousness of their possessions, which are ancient, and therefore considered legitimate, will take their metaphysical compendia in their hands, and look down on him with contempt; others, who never see anything except it be identical with what they have seen before, will not understand him, and everything will remain for a time, as if nothing had happened to excite the concern, or the hope, for an impending change.

Nevertheless, I venture to predict that the independent reader of these Prolegomena will not only doubt his previous science, but ultimately be fully persuaded, that it cannot exist unless the demands here stated on which its possibility depends, be satisfied; and, as this has never been done, that there is, as yet, no such thing as Metaphysics.[2] But as it can never cease to be in demand,—since the interests of common sense are intimately interwoven with it, he must confess that a radical reform, or rather a new birth of the science after an original plan, are unavoidable, however men may struggle against it for a while.

Since the Essays of Locke and Leibnitz, or rather since the origin of metaphysics so far as we know its history, nothing has ever happened which was more decisive to its fate than the attack made upon it by David Hume. He threw no light on this species of knowledge, but he certainly struck a spark from which light might have been obtained, had it caught some inflammable substance and had its smouldering fire been carefully nursed and developed.

Hume started from a single but important concept in Metaphysics, viz., that of Cause and Effect (including its derivatives force and action, etc.). He challenges reason, which pretends to have given birth to this idea from herself, to answer

---

[2]This position on the nonexistence of a scientific metaphysics is one of the most important consequences of Kant's view of reason, and it follows so logically that to disagree with the conclusion one must disagree with his view of reason.

him by what right she thinks anything to be so constituted, that if that thing be posited, something else also must necessarily be posited; for this is the meaning of the concept of cause. He demonstrated irrefutably that it was perfectly impossible for reason to think *a priori* and by means of concepts a combination involving necessity. We cannot at all see why, in consequence of the existence of one thing, another must necessarily exist, or how the concept of such a combination can arise *a priori*. Hence he inferred, that reason was altogether deluded with reference to this concept, which she erroneously considered as one of her children, whereas in reality it was nothing but a bastard of imagination, impregnated by experience, which subsumed certain representations under the Law of Association, and mistook the subjective necessity of habit for an objective necessity arising from insight. Hence he inferred that reason had no power to think such combinations, even generally, because her concepts would then be purely fictitious, and all her pretended *a priori* cognitions nothing but common experiences marked with a false stamp. In plain language there is not, and cannot be, any such thing as metaphysics at all.

However hasty and mistaken Hume's conclusion may appear, it was at least founded upon investigation, and this investigation deserved the concentrated attention of the brighter spirits of his day as well as determined efforts on their part to discover, if possible, a happier solution of the problem in the sense proposed by him, all of which would have speedily resulted in a complete reform of the science.

But Hume suffered the usual misfortune of metaphysicians, of not being understood. It is positively painful to see how utterly his opponents, Reid, Oswald, Beattie, and lastly Priestley, missed the point of the problem; for while they were ever taking for granted that which he doubted, and demonstrating with zeal and often with impudence that which he never thought of doubting, they so misconstrued his valuable suggestion that everything remained in its old condition, as if nothing had happened.

The question was not whether the concept of cause was right, useful, and even indispensable for our knowledge of nature, for this Hume had never doubted; but whether that concept could be thought by reason *a priori*, and consequently whether it possessed an inner truth, independent of all experience, implying a wider application than merely to the objects of experience. This was Hume's problem. It was a question concerning the *origin*, not concerning the *indispensable need* of the concept. Were the former decided, the conditions of the use and the sphere of its valid application would have been determined as a matter of course.

But to satisfy the conditions of the problem, the opponents of the great thinker should have penetrated very deeply into the nature of reason, so far as it is concerned with pure thinking,—a task which did not suit them. They found a more convenient method of being defiant without any insight, viz., the appeal to *common sense*.[3] It is indeed a great gift of

[3]Besides Reid, Oswald, Beattie, and Priestley, others have rejected Hume's position, and for reasons far deeper than *common sense*. The choice need not be

God, to possess right, or (as they now call it) plain common sense. But this common sense must be shown practically, by well-considered and reasonable thoughts and words, not by appealing to it as an oracle, when no rational justification can be advanced. To appeal to common sense, when insight and science fail, and no sooner—this is one of the subtile discoveries of modern times, by means of which the most superficial ranter can safely enter the lists with the most thorough thinker, and hold his own. But as long as a particle of insight remains, no one would think of having recourse to this subterfuge. For what is it but an appeal to the opinion of the multitude, of whose applause the philosopher is ashamed, while the popular charlatan glories and confides in it? I should think that Hume might fairly have laid as much claim to common sense as Beattie, and in addition to a critical reason (such as the latter did not possess), which keeps common sense in check and prevents it from speculating, or, if speculations are under discussion restrains the desire to decide because it cannot satisfy itself concerning its own arguments. By this means alone can common sense remain sound. Chisels and hammers may suffice to work a piece of wood, but for steel-engraving we require an engraver's needle. Thus common sense and speculative understanding are each serviceable in their own way, the former in judgments which apply immediately to experience, the latter when we judge universally from mere concepts, as in metaphysics, where sound common sense, so called in spite of all inapplicability of the word, has no right to judge at all.

I openly confess, the suggestion of David Hume was the very thing, which many years ago first interrupted my dogmatic slumber, and gave my investigations in the field of speculative philosophy quite a new direction. I was far from following him in the conclusions at which he arrived by regarding, not the whole of his problem, but a part, which by itself can give us no information. If we start from a well-founded, but undeveloped, thought, which another has bequeathed to us, we may well hope by continued reflection to advance farther than the acute man, to whom we owe the first spark of light.

I therefore first tried whether Hume's objections could not be put into a general form, and soon found that the concept of the connexion of cause and effect was by no means the only idea by which the understanding thinks the connexion of things *a priori*, but rather that metaphysics consists altogether of such connexions. I sought to ascertain their number, and when I had satisfactorily succeeded in this by starting from a single principle, I proceeded to the deduction of these concepts, which I was now certain were not deduced from experience, as Hume had apprehended, but sprang from the pure understanding. This deduction (which seemed impossible to my acute predecessor, which had never even occurred to any one else, though no one had hesitated to use the concepts without investigating the basis of their objective validity) was the most difficult task ever un-

---

between a metaphysics which is totally *a priori* and independent of experience and no metaphysics at all. There remains the possibility of a metaphysics developed in connection with and dependent upon sense experience, without being limited to the level of sensation.

dertaken in the service of metaphysics; and the worst was that metaphysics, such as it then existed could not assist me in the least, because this deduction alone can render metaphysics possible. But as soon as I had succeeded in solving Hume's problem not merely in a particular case, but with respect to the whole faculty of pure reason,[4] I could proceed safely, though slowly, to determine the whole sphere of pure reason completely and from general principles, in its circumference as well as in its contents. This was required for metaphysics in order to construct its system according to a reliable method.

* * *

Prolegomena
Preamble on the Peculiarities of All Metaphysical Cognition

1. Of the Sources of Metaphysics.

If it becomes desirable to formulate any cognition as science, it will be necessary first to determine accurately those peculiar features which no other science has in common with it, constituting its characteristics; otherwise the boundaries of all sciences become confused, and none of them can be treated thoroughly according to its nature.

The characteristics of a science may consist of a simple difference of object, or of the sources of cognition, or of the kind of cognition, or perhaps of all three conjointly. On this, therefore, depends the idea of a possible science and its territory.

First, as concerns the sources of metaphysical cognition, its very concept implies that they cannot be empirical. Its principles (including not only its maxims but its basic notions) must never be derived from experience. It must not be physical

---

[4]Speaking of human knowledge, Kant distinguishes between sensation, understanding, and reason, all of which he considers in great detail in his *Critique of Pure Reason.* Sensation, of course, has to do with sense presentations, and, for Kant, all of these must be subsumed under the forms of space and time. More pertinent here is his distinction between understanding and reason. The function of the understanding is to take the many sense intuitions and unify them in various ways. To accomplish this, the understanding is endowed with various principles or rules of unification of the matter of sensation, called *categories* (for example: subsistence, causality, necessity, possibility), and by bringing them to bear on what sensation presents to it, the understanding unites them in definite ways and thereby actually determines the objects of human experience. We may consider the mind, however, precisely insofar as it accounts not for the matter, but for the form of intellectual knowledge. This is called pure reason. Thus we can account for the fact that experience takes place *at all* by concluding critically that pure reason has a *regulative* function, which is the source of the activity and power of the understanding. However, according to Kant, there is a serious danger in another possible use which can be made of pure reason. It can pretend to go beyond its work of guiding the understanding and use its ideas to know or "constitute" real objects, and thus claim to arrive at knowledge of noumena or things-in-themselves. Kant feels that when it does so, it gives rise to metaphysical illusions.

Although Kant rejects this latter use of reason, it can be seen that the function of sensation and understanding is really to construct and determine the objects known, since the forms of sense and the categories of the understanding actually determine the known phenomena.

but metaphysical knowledge, viz., knowledge lying beyond experience.[5] It can therefore have for its basis neither external experience, which is the source of physics proper, nor internal, which is the basis of empirical psychology. It is therefore *a priori* knowledge, coming from pure Understanding and pure Reason.

But so far Metaphysics would not be distinguishable from pure Mathematics; it must therefore be called pure philosophical cognition; and for the meaning of this term I refer to the Critique of the Pure Reason (II. "Method of Transcendentalism," Chap. 1., Sec. i), where the distinction between these two employments of the reason is sufficiently explained. So far concerning the sources of metaphysical cognition.

2. *Concerning the Kind of Cognition which can alone be called Metaphysical.*

a. Of the Distinction between Analytical and Synthetical Judgments in general.—The peculiarity of its sources demands that metaphysical cognition must consist of nothing but *a priori* judgments. But whatever be their origin, or their logical form, there is a distinction in judgments, as to their content, according to which they are either merely explicative, adding nothing to the content of the cognition, or expansive, increasing the given cognition: the former may be called analytical, the latter synthetical, judgments.[6]

Analytical judgments express nothing in the predicate but what has been already actually thought in the concept of the subject, though not so distinctly or with the same (full) consciousness. When I say: All bodies are extended, I have not amplified in the least my concept of body, but have only analysed it, as extension was really thought to belong to that concept before the judgment was made, though it was not expressed; this judgment is therefore analytical. On the contrary, this judgment, All bodies have weight, contains in its predicate something not actually thought in the general concept of the body; it amplifies my knowledge by adding something to my concept, and must therefore be called synthetical.

b. The Common Principle of all Analytical Judgments is the Law of Contradiction.—All analytical judgments depend wholly on the law of Contradiction, and are in their nature *a priori* cognitions, whether the concepts that supply them with matter be empirical or not. For the predicate of an affirmative analytical judgment is already contained in the concept of the subject, of which it cannot be denied without contradiction. In the same way its opposite is necessarily denied of the

[5]This is true only when experience is limited to the level of sense and when the "empirical" view of "experience" is accepted as definitive. Only then must metaphysical knowledge be equivalent to a priori knowledge.

[6]This is Kant's famous division of judgments, and it means that for him all analytical judgments are tautological since the predicate is known in the subject. This is in contradiction with the "traditional" view that both analytic and synthetic judgments are "expansive" of knowledge, the difference between them resting not on whether the predicate pertains to the subject (since in *all* true judgments there must be material identity), but rather on the *motive* for affirming the predicate of the subject. That motive may be either experience (in synthetic judgments) or the mere analysis of the terms (in analytic judgments).

subject in an analytical, but negative, judgment, by the same law of contradiction. Such is the nature of the judgments: all bodies are extended, and no bodies are unextended (i.e., simple).

For this very reason all analytical judgments are *a priori* even when the concepts are empirical, as, for example, Gold is a yellow metal; for to know this I require no experience beyond my concept of gold as a yellow metal: it is, in fact, the very concept, and I need only analyse it, without looking beyond it elsewhere.

c. Synthetical Judgments require a different Principle from the Law of Contradiction.—There are synthetical *a posteriori* judgments of empirical origin; but there are also others which are proved to be certain *a priori*, and which spring from pure Understanding and Reason. Yet they both agree in this, that they cannot possibly spring from the principle of analysis, viz., the law of contradiction, alone; they require a quite different principle, though, from whatever they may be deduced, they must be subject to the law of contradiction, which must never be violated, even though everything cannot be deduced from it. I shall first classify synthetical judgments.

1. *Empirical Judgments* are always synthetical. For it would be absurd to base an analytical judgment on experience, as our concept suffices for the purpose without requiring any testimony from experience. That body is extended, is a judgment established *a priori*, and not an empirical judgment. For before appealing to experience, we already have all the conditions of the judgment in the concept, from which we have but to elicit the predicate according to the law of contradiction, and thereby to become conscious of the necessity of the judgment, which experience could not even teach us.

2. *Mathematical Judgments* are all synthetical. This fact seems hitherto to have altogether escaped the observation of those who have analysed human reason; it even seems directly opposed to all their conjectures, though incontestably certain, and most important in its consequences. For as it was found that the conclusions of mathematicians all proceed according to the law of contradiction (as is demanded by all apodeictic certainty), men persuaded themselves that the fundamental principles were known from the same law. This was a great mistake, for a synthetical proposition can indeed be comprehended according to the law of contradiction, but only by presupposing another synthetical proposition from which it follows, but never in itself.

First of all, we must observe that all proper mathematical judgments are *a priori*, and not empirical, because they carry with them necessity, which cannot be obtained from experience. But if this be not conceded to me, very good; I shall confine my assertion to *pure Mathematics*, the very notion of which implies that it contains pure *a priori* and not empirical cognitions.

It might at first be thought that the proposition 7 + 5 = 12 is a mere analytical judgment, following from the concept of the sum of seven and five, according to the law of contradiction. But on closer examination it appears that the concept of the sum of 7 + 5 contains merely their union in a single number, without its being at all thought what the particular number is that unites them. The concept of twelve is by no means thought by merely thinking of the combination of seven and five; and analyse this possible sum as we may, we shall not discover twelve in the concept. We must go beyond these concepts, by calling to our aid some concrete image *(Anschauung)*, i.e., either our five fingers, or five points (as Segner has it in his Arithmetic), and we must add successively the units of the five, given in some concrete image *(Anschauung)*, to the concept of seven. Hence our concept is really amplified by the proposition $7 + 5 = 12$, and we add to the first a second, not thought in it. Arithmetical judgments are therefore synthetical, and the more plainly according as we take larger numbers; for in such cases it is clear that, however closely we analyse our concepts without calling visual images *(Anschauung)* to our aid, we can never find the sum by such mere dissection.

Nor is any principle of geometry analytical. That a straight line is the shortest path between two points, is a synthetical proposition. For my concept of straight contains nothing of quantity, but only a quality. The attribute of shortness is therefore altogether additional, and cannot be obtained by any analysis of the concept. Here, too, visualisation *(Anschauung)* must come to aid us. It alone makes the synthesis possible.

Some other principles, assumed by geometers, are indeed actually analytical, and depend on the law of contradiction; but they only serve, as identical propositions, as a method of concatenation, and not as principles, e.g., $a = a$, the whole is equal to itself, or $a + b > a$, the whole is greater than its part. And yet even these, though they are recognized as valid from mere concepts, are only admitted in mathematics, because they can be represented in some visual form *(Anschauung)*. What usually makes us believe that the predicate of such apodeictic judgments is already contained in our concept, and that the judgment is therefore analytical, is the duplicity of the expression, requesting us to think a certain predicate as of necessity implied in the thought of a given concept, which necessity attaches to the concept. But the question is not what we are requested to join in thought *to* the given concept, but what we actually think together with and in it, though obscurely; and so it appears that the predicate belongs to these concepts necessarily indeed, yet not directly but indirectly by an added visualisation *(Anschauung)*.

* * *

4. The General Question of the Prolegomena.—Is Metaphysics at all Possible?

Were a metaphysics, which could maintain its place as a science, really in existence; could we say, here is metaphysics, learn it, and it will convince you irresistibly and irrevocably of its truth: this question would be useless, and there would only remain that other question (which would rather be a test of our acuteness, than a proof of the existence of the thing itself), "How is the science possible, and how does reason come to attain it?" But human reason has not been so fortunate in this case. There is no single book to which you can point as you do to Euclid, and say: This is Metaphysics; here you may find the noblest objects of this science, the knowledge of a highest Being, and of a future existence, proved from principles of pure reason.[7] We can be shown indeed many judgments, demonstrably certain, and never questioned; but these are all analytical, and rather concern the materials and the scaffolding for Metaphysics, than the extension of knowledge, which is our proper object in studying it (#2). Even supposing you produce synthetical judgments (such as the law of Sufficient Reason, which you have never proved, as you ought to, from pure reason *a priori* though we gladly concede its truth), you lapse when they come to be employed for your principal object, into such doubtful assertions, that in all ages one Metaphysics has contradicted another, either in its assertions, or their proofs, and thus has itself destroyed its own claim to lasting assent. Nay, the very attempts to set up such a science are the main cause of the early appearance of scepticism, a mental attitude in which reason treats itself with such violence that it could never have arisen save from complete despair of ever satisfying our most important aspirations. For long before men began to inquire into nature methodically, they consulted abstract reason, which had to some extent been exercised by means of ordinary experience; for reason is ever present, while laws of nature must usually be discovered with labor. So Metaphysics floated to the surface, like foam, which dissolved the moment it was scooped off. But immediately there appeared a new supply on the surface, to be ever eagerly gathered up by some, while others, instead of seeking in the depths the cause of the phenomenon, thought they showed their wisdom by ridiculing the idle labor of their neighbors.

The essential and distinguishing feature of pure mathematical cognition among all other *a priori* cognitions is, that it cannot at all proceed from concepts, but only by means of the construction of concepts (see Critique II., "Method of Transcendentalism," Chap. 1, Sec. i). As therefore in its judgments it must proceed beyond the concept to that which its corresponding visualisation *(Anschauung)* contains, these judgments neither can, nor ought to, arise analytically, by dissecting the concept, but are all synthetical.

I cannot refrain from pointing out the disadvantage resulting to philosophy from the neglect of this easy and apparently insignificant observation. Hume being prompted (a task worthy of a philosopher) to cast his eye over the whole field of *a priori* cognitions in which human understanding claims such mighty possessions, heedlessly severed from it a whole, and indeed its most valuable, province, viz., pure mathematics; for he thought its nature, or, so to speak, the state-constitution of this empire, depended on totally different principles, namely, on the law of contradiction alone; and although he did not divide judgments in this manner formally and universally as I have done here, what he said was equivalent to this: that mathematics contains only analytical, but metaphysics synthetical, *a priori* judgments. In this, however, he was greatly mistaken, and the mistake had a decidedly injurious effect upon his whole conception. But for this,

[7] This is an important point. Kant wants these positions proved by *pure reason*—that is, in an extremely rationalistic way—before he will accept them as proved.

he would have extended his question concerning the origin of our synthetical judgments far beyond the metaphysical concept of Causality, and included in it the possibility of mathematics *a priori* also, for this latter he must have assumed to be equally synthetical. And then he could not have based his metaphysical judgments on mere experience without subjecting the axioms of mathematics equally to experience, a thing which he was far too acute to do. The good company into which metaphysics would thus have been brought, would have saved it from the danger of a contemptuous ill-treatment, for the thrust intended for it must have reached mathematics, which was not and could not have been Hume's intention. Thus that acute man would have been led into considerations which must needs be similar to those that now occupy us, but which would have gained inestimably by his inimitably elegant style.

Metaphysical judgments, properly so called, are all synthetical.[8] We must distinguish judgments pertaining to metaphysics from metaphysical judgments properly so called. Many of the former are analytical, but they only afford the means for metaphysical judgments, which are the whole end of the science, and which are always synthetical. For if there be concepts pertaining to metaphysics (as, for example, that of substance), the judgments springing from simple analysis of them also pertain to metaphysics, as, for example, substance is that which only exists as subject; and by means of several such analytical judgments, we seek to approach the definition of the concept. But as the analysis of a pure concept of the understanding pertaining to metaphysics, does not proceed in any different manner from the dissection of any other, even empirical, concepts, not pertaining to metaphysics (such as: air is an elastic fluid, the elasticity of which is not destroyed by any known degree of cold), it follows that the concept indeed, but not the analytical judgment, is properly metaphysical. This science has something peculiar in the production of its *a priori* cognitions, which must therefore be distinguished from the features it has in common with other rational knowledge. Thus the judgment, that all the substance in things is permanent, is a synthetical and properly metaphysical judgment.

If the *a priori* principles, which constitute the materials of metaphysics, have first been collected according to fixed principles, then their analysis will be of great value; it might be taught as a particular part (as a *philosophia definitiva*),

[8]While one may be ready enough to admit with Kant the existence of the science known as Physics and Mathematics, one need not be so ready to admit his equivalent statement that therefore some synthetic *a priori* judgments, as he understands and defines them, are "actual and given." For Kant, such judgments increase our knowledge (synthetic) and are independent of experience (a priori) because of their characteristics of necessity and universality. That the latter characteristics must be arrived at in a purely *a priori* fashion, in no way dependent on and justified by the objective structure of beings experienced, is held by Kant because of his acceptance of the empirical view of experience, and to that extent he fails to take into account the full data received from contact with beings and the ability of the mind to recognize and distinguish between the accidental and the essential in what is known.

containing nothing but analytical judgments pertaining to metaphysics, and could be treated separately from the synthetical which constitute metaphysics proper. For indeed these analyses are not elsewhere of much value, except in metaphysics, i.e., as regards the synthetical judgments, which are to be generated by these previously analysed concepts.

The conclusion drawn in this section then is, that metaphysics is properly concerned with synthetical propositions *a priori*, and these alone constitute its end, for which it indeed requires various dissections of its concepts, viz., of its analytical judgments, but wherein the procedure is not different from that in every other kind of knowledge, in which we merely seek to render our concepts distinct by analysis. But the generation of *a priori* cognition by concrete images as well as by concepts, in fine of synthetical propositions *a priori* in philosophical cognition, constitutes the essential subject of Metaphysics.

Weary therefore as well of dogmatism, which teaches us nothing, as of scepticism, which does not even promise us anything, not even the quiet state of a contented ignorance; disquieted by the importance of knowledge so much needed; and lastly, rendered suspicious by long experience of all knowledge which we believe we possess, or which offers itself, under the title of pure reason: there remains but one critical question on the answer to which our future procedure depends, viz., *Is Metaphysics at all possible?* But this question must be answered not by sceptical objections to the asseverations of some actual system of metaphysics (for we do not as yet admit such a thing to exist), but from the conception, as yet only problematical, of a science of this sort.

In the *Critique of Pure Reason* I have treated this question synthetically, by making inquiries into pure reason itself, and endeavoring in this source to determine the elements as well as the laws of its pure use according to principles. The task is difficult, and requires a resolute reader to penetrate by degrees into a system, based on no data except reason itself, and which therefore seeks, without resting upon any fact, to unfold knowledge from its original germs. *Prolegomena*, however, are designed for preparatory exercises; they are intended rather to point out what we have to do in order if possible to actualise a science, than to propound it. They must therefore rest upon something already known as trustworthy, from which we can set out with confidence, and ascend to sources as yet unknown, the discovery of which will not only explain to us what we knew, but exhibit a sphere of many cognitions which all spring from the same sources. The method of *Prolegomena*, especially of those designed as a preparation for future metaphysics, is consequently analytical.

But it happens fortunately, that though we cannot assume metaphysics to be an actual science, we can say with confidence that certain pure *a priori* synthetical cognitions, pure Mathematics and pure Physics are actual and given;[9] for both contain

---

[9]The final results of Kant's studies will be to show that all scientific knowledge is made up of synthetic *a priori* judgments, that metaphysics, to deserve the name of science, must likewise be made up of that sort of judgment. However, in the Kantian scheme that is im-

propositions, which are thoroughly recognised as apodeictically certain, partly by mere reason, partly by general consent arising from experience, and yet as independent of experience. We have therefore some at least uncontested synthetical knowledge *a priori*, and need not ask *whether* it be possible, for it is actual, but *how* is is possible, in order that we may deduce from the principle which makes the given cognitions possible the possibility of all the rest.[10]

5. *The General Problem: How is Cognition from Pure Reason Possible?*

We have above learned the significant distinction between analytical and synthetical judgments. The possibility of analytical propositions was easily comprehended, being entirely founded on the law of Contradiction. The possibility of synthetical *a posteriori* judgments, of those which are gathered from experience, also requires no particular explanation; for experience is nothing but a continual synthesis of perceptions. There remain therefore only synthetical propositions *a priori*, of which the possibility must be sought or investigated, because they must depend upon other principles than the law of contradiction.

But here we need not first establish the possibility of such propositions so as to ask whether they are possible. For there are enough of them which indeed are of undoubted certainty, and as our present method is analytical, we shall start from the fact, that such synthetical but purely rational cognition actually exists; but we must now inquire into the reason of this possibility, and ask, *how* such cognition is possible, in order that we may from the principles of its possibility be enabled to determine the conditions of its use, its sphere and its limits. The proper problem upon which all depends, when expressed with scholastic precision, is therefore:

How are Synthetic Propositions a priori possible?

For the sake of popularity I have above expressed this problem somewhat differently, as an inquiry into purely rational cognition, which I could do for once without detriment to the desired comprehension, because, as we have only to do here with metaphysics and its sources, the reader will, I hope, after the foregoing remarks, keep in mind that when we speak of purely rational cognition, we do not mean analytical, but synthetical cognition.

---

possible, since he looked upon metaphysics as being completely nonempirical, whereas all true scientific knowledge results from bringing the categories of the understanding to bear on the sense presentations. So, while metaphysical judgments are said to be synthetical, in the sense that they pretend to give new knowledge, they result in illusion because they cannot be brought to bear directly on sense intuitions, and yet they pretend to tell us what things are in themselves. Any such knowledge of things-in-themselves is excluded by the Kantian approach to knowledge.

[10]Here is Kant's profession of the homogeneity of method in *all* kinds of scientific knowledge. Accepting physics as a true science and determining that *synthetic a priori* judgments are what account for its possibility, he proceeds to subject metaphysics to the test of the method proper to physics. Since metaphysics cannot meet these requirements, it is rejected as a science. What should be concluded instead is that the method of physics is not the proper method for metaphysics and that a homogeneity of method is a false desideratum, since reality can be confronted on various levels.

Metaphysics stands or falls with the solution of this problem: its very existence depends upon it. Let any one make metaphysical assertions with ever so much plausibility, let him overwhelm us with conclusions, if he has not previously proved able to answer this question satisfactorily, I have a right to say: this is all vain baseless philosophy and false wisdom. You speak through pure reason, and claim, as it were to create cognitions *a priori* by not only dissecting given concepts, but also by asserting connexions which do not rest upon the law of contradiction, and which you believe you conceive quite independently of all experience; how do you arrive at this, and how will you justify your pretensions? An appeal to the consent of the common sense of mankind cannot be allowed; for that is a witness whose authority depends merely upon rumor. Says Horace:

"Quodcunque ostendis mihi sic, incredulus odi."

"To all that which thou provest me thus, I refuse to give credence."

The answer to this question, though indispensable, is difficult; and though the principal reason that it was not made long ago is, that the possibility of the question never occurred to anybody, there is yet another reason, which is this that a satisfactory answer to this one question requires a much more persistent, profound, and painstaking reflexion, than the most diffuse work on Metaphysics, which on its first appearance promised immortality to its author. And every intelligent reader, when he carefully reflects what this problem requires, must at first be struck with its difficulty, and would regard it as insoluble and even impossible, did there not actually exist pure synthetical cognitions *a priori*. This actually happened to David Hume though he did not conceive the question in its entire universality as is done here, and as must be done should the answer be decisive for all Metaphysics. For how is it possible says that acute man, that when a concept is given me, I can go beyond it and connect with it another, which is not contained in it, in such a manner as if the latter necessarily belonged to the former? Nothing but experience can furnish us with such connexions (thus he concluded from the difficulty which he took to be an impossibility), and all that vaunted necessity, or, what is the same thing, all cognition assumed to be *a priori*, is nothing but a long habit of accepting something as true, and hence of mistaking subjective necessity for objective.

Should my reader complain of the difficulty and the trouble which occasion him in the solution of this problem, he is at liberty to solve it himself in an easier way. Perhaps he will then feel under obligation to the person who has undertaken for him a labor of so profound research and will rather be surprised at the facility with which, considering the nature of the subject, the solution has been attained. Yet it has cost years of work to solve the problem in its whole universality (using the term in the mathematical sense, viz., for that which is sufficient for all cases) and finally to exhibit it in the analytical form, as the reader finds it here.

All metaphysicians are therefore solemnly and legally suspended from their occupations till they shall have answered in a satisfactory manner the question, "How are synthetic cognitions *a priori* possible?" For the answer contains the only credentials which they must show when they have anything to offer in the name of pure reason. But if they do not possess these credentials, they can expect nothing else of reasonable people, who have been deceived so often, than to be dismissed without further ado.

If they on the other hand desire to carry on their business, not as a science, but as an art of wholesome oratory suited to the common sense of man, they cannot in justice be prevented. They will then speak the modest language of a rational belief, they will grant that they are not allowed even to conjecture, far less to know, anything which lies beyond the bounds of all possible experience, but only to assume (not for speculative use, which they must abandon, but for practical purposes only) the existence of something that is possible and even indispensable for the guidance of the understanding and of the will in life. In this manner alone can they be called useful and wise men, and the more so as they renounce the title of metaphysicians; for the latter profess to be speculative philosophers, and since, when judgments *a priori* are under discussion, poor probabilities cannot be admitted (for what is declared to be known *a priori* is thereby announced as necessary), such man cannot be permitted to play with conjectures, but their assertions must be either science, or are worth nothing at all.

It may be said, that the entire transcendental philosophy, which necessarily precedes all metaphysics, is nothing but the complete solution of the problem here propounded, in systematical order and completeness, and hitherto we have never had any transcendental philosophy; for what goes by its name is properly a part of metaphysics, whereas the former science is intended first to constitute the possibility of the latter, and must therefore precede all metaphysics. And it is not surprising that when a whole science, deprived of all help from other sciences, and consequently in itself quite new, is required to answer a single question satisfactorily, we should find the answer troublesome and difficult, nay even shrouded in obscurity.

As we now proceed to this solution according to the analytical method, in which we assume that such cognitions from pure reasons actually exist, we can only appeal to two sciences of theoretical cognition (which alone is under consideration here), pure mathematics and pure natural science (physics). For these alone can exhibit to us objects in a definite and actualisable form (*in der Anschauung*), and consequently (if there should occur in them a cognition *a priori*) can show the truth or conformity of the cognition to the object *in concreto*, that is, its actuality, from which we could proceed to the reason of its possibility by the analytic method. This facilitates our work greatly for here universal considerations are not only applied to facts, but even start from them, while in a synthetic procedure they must strictly be derived *in abstracto* from concepts.

But, in order to rise from these actual and at the same time well-grounded pure cognitions *a priori* to such a possible cognition of the same as we are seeking, viz., to metaphysics as a science, we must comprehend that which occasions it, I mean the mere natural, though in spite of its truth not unsuspected, cognition *a priori* which lies at the bottom of that science, the elaboration of which without any critical investigation of its possibility is commonly called metaphysics. In a word, we must comprehend the natural conditions of such a science as a part of our inquiry, and thus the transcendental problem will be gradually answered by a division into four questions:

1. *How is pure mathematics possible?*
2. *How is pure natural science possible?*
3. *How is metaphysics in general possible?*
4. *How is metaphysics as a science possible?*

It may be seen that the solution of these problems, though chiefly designed to exhibit the essential matter of the Critique, has yet something peculiar, which for itself alone deserves attention. This is the search for the sources of given sciences in reason itself, so that its faculty of knowing something *a priori* may by its own deeds be investigated and measured. By this procedure these sciences gain, if not with regard to their contents, yet as to their proper use, and while they throw light on the higher question concerning their common origin, they give, at the same time, an occasion better to explain their own nature.

* * *

How Is Pure Science of Nature Possible?

We shall here be concerned with experience only, and the universal conditions of its possibility which are given *a priori*. Thence we shall determine nature as the whole object of all possible experience. I think it will be understood that I here do not mean the rules of the observation of a nature that is already given, for these already presuppose experience. I do not mean how (through experience) we can study the laws of nature; for these would not then be laws *a priori*, and would yield us no pure science of nature; but [I mean to ask] how the conditions *a priori* of the possibility of experience are at the same time the sources from which all the universal laws of nature must be derived.

18. In the first place we must state that, while all judgments of experience (*Erfahrungsurtheile*) are empirical (i.e., have their ground in immediate sense-perception), *vice versa*, all empirical judgments (*empirische Urtheile*) are not judgments of experience, but, besides the empirical, and in general besides what is given to the sensuous intuition, particular concepts must yet be superadded—concepts which have their origin quite *a priori* in the pure understanding,[11] and under which every perception must be first of all

[11] Since Kant concedes that all sense presentations are totally contingent and particular, he asserts that the characteristics of universality and necessity found in scientific knowledge must be *a priori*—that is, a contribution from the native power of the human understanding. Concretely, this means that the human mind tends to unify sensations, and it unifies them in various ways. These various ways reflect the "concepts" or "categories" of the understanding. These categories, working with sense presentations, constitute the phenomenon or object known and render scientific experience possible. This means that the

subsumed and then by their means changed into experience.

Empirical judgments, so far as they have objective validity, are *judgments of experience*; but those which are only subjectively valid, I name mere *judgments of perception*. The latter require no pure concept of the understanding, but only the logical connexion of perception in a thinking subject. But the former always require, besides the representation of the sensuous intuition, particular *concepts originally begotten in the understanding*, which produce the objective validity of the judgment of experience.

All our judgments are at first merely judgments of perception; they hold good only for us (i.e., for our subject), and we do not till afterwards give them a new reference (to an object), and desire that they shall always hold good for us and in the same way for everybody else; for when a judgment agrees with an object, all judgments concerning the same object must likewise agree among themselves, and thus the objective validity of the judgment of experience signifies nothing else than its necessary universality of application. And conversely when we have reason to consider a judgment necessarily universal (which never depends upon perception, but upon the pure concept of the understanding, under which the perception is subsumed), we must consider it objective also, that is, that it expresses not merely a reference to our perception to a subject, but a quality of the object. For there would be no reason for the judgments of other men necessarily agreeing with mine, if it were not the unity of the object to which they all refer, and with which they accord; hence they must all agree with one another.

19. Therefore objective validity and necessary universality (for everybody) are equivalent terms, and though we do not know the object in itself, yet when we consider a judgment as universal, and also necessary, we understand it to have objective validity. By this judgment we cognise the object (though it remains unknown as it is in itself) by the universal and necessary connexion of the given perceptions. As this is the case with all objects of sense, judgments of experience take their objective validity not from the immediate cognition of the object (which is impossible), but from the condition of universal validity in empirical judgments, which, as already said, never rests upon empirical, or, in short, sensuous conditions, but upon a pure concept of the understanding. The object always remains unknown in itself; but when by the concept of the understanding the connexion of the representations of the object, which are given to our sensibility, is determined as universally valid, the object is determined by this relation, and it is the judgment that is objective.

To illustrate the matter: When we say, "the room is warm, sugar sweet, and wormwood bitter,"—we have only subjectively valid judgments. I do not at all expect that I or any other person shall always find it as I now do; each of these sentences only expresses a relation of two sensations to the same subject, to myself, and that only in my present state of perception; conse-

---

structure of being is not regulative of knowledge, but rather that *a priori* categories provide the structure and intelligibility of objects.

quently they are not valid of the object. Such are judgments of perception. Judgments of experience are of quite a different nature. What experience teaches me under certain circumstances, it must always teach me and everybody; and its validity is not limited to the subject nor to its state at a particular time. Hence I pronounce all such judgments as being objectively valid. For instance, when I say the air is elastic, this judgment is as yet a judgment of perception only—I do nothing but refer two of my sensations to one another. But, if I would have it called a judgment of experience, I require this connexion to stand under a condition, which makes it universally valid. I desire therefore that I and everybody else should always connect necessarily the same perceptions under the same circumstances.

20. We must consequently analyse experience in order to see what is contained in this product of the senses and of the understanding, and how the judgment of experience itself is possible. The foundation is the intuition of which I become conscious, i.e., perception (*perceptio*), which pertains merely to the senses. But in the next place, there are acts of judging (which belongs only to the understanding). But this judging may be two-fold—first, I may merely compare perceptions and connect them in a particular state of my consciousness; or, secondly, I may connect them in consciousness generally. The former judgment is merely a judgment of perception, and of subjective validity only: it is merely a connexion of perceptions in my mental state, without reference to the object. Hence it is not, as is commonly imagined, enough for experience to compare perceptions and to connect them in consciousness through judgment; there arises no universality and necessity, for which alone judgments can become objectively valid and be called experience.[12]

Quite another judgment therefore is required before perception can become experience. The given intuition must be subsumed under a concept, which determines the form of judging in general relatively to the intuition, connects its empirical consciousness in consciousness generally, and thereby procures universal validity for empirical judgments. A concept of this nature is a pure *a priori* concept of the Understanding, which does nothing but determine for an intuition the general way in which it can be used for judgments. Let the concept be that of cause, then it determines the intuition which is subsumed under it, e.g., that of air, relative to judgments in general, viz., the concept of air serves with regard to its expansion in the relation of antecedent to consequent in a hypothetical judgment. The concept of cause accordingly is a pure concept of the understanding, which is totally disparate from all possible perception, and only serves to determine the representation subsumed under it, relatively to judgments in general, and so to make a universally valid judgment possible.

Before, therefore, a judgment of perception can become a judgment of experience, it is requisite that the perception should be subsumed under some such a concept of the

[12]This view presupposes that in the concrete existent there is no knowable structure that can serve as a foundation for universality and necessity.

nderstanding; for instance, air ranks under the concept of causes, which determines our judgment about t in regard to its expansion as hypothetical. Thereby the expansion f the air is represented not as merely belonging to the perception f the air in my present state or in everal states of mine, or in the tate of perception of others, but as elonging to it necessarily. The udgment, "the air is elastic," beomes universally valid, and a judgment of experience, only by certain udgments preceding it, which subume the intuition of air under the oncept of cause and effect: and they hereby determine the perceptions ot merely as regards one another n me, but relatively to the form of udging in general, which is here ypothetical, and in this way they ender the empirical judgment uniersally valid.

If all our synthetical judgments re analysed so far as they are obectively valid, it will be found that ey never consist of mere intuitions onnected only (as is commonly beeved) by comparison into a judgment; but that they would be impossible were not a pure concept of the nderstanding superadded to the conepts abstracted from intuition, uner which concept these latter are ubsumed, and in this manner only ombined into an objectively valid dgment. Even the judgments of ure mathematics in their simplest xioms are not exempt from this ondition. The principle, "a straight ne is the shortest between two oints," presupposes that the line subsumed under the concept of uantity, which certainly is no mere tuition, but has its seat in the unerstanding alone, and serves to etermine the intuition (of the line) with regard to the judgments which may be made about it, relatively to their quantity, that is, to plurality (as *judicia plurativa*). For under them it is understood that in a given intuition there is contained a plurality of homogeneous parts.

21. To prove, then, the possibility of experience so far as it rests upon pure concepts of the understanding *a priori*, we must first represent what belongs to judgments in general and the various functions of the understanding, in a complete table. For the pure concepts of the understanding must run parallel to these functions,[13] as such concepts are nothing more than concepts of intuitions in general, so far as these are determined by one or other of these functions of judging, in themselves, that is, necessarily and universally. Hereby also the *a priori* principles of the possibility of all experience, as of an objectively valid empirical cognition, will be precisely determined. For they are nothing but propositions by which all perception is (under certain universal conditions of intuition) subsumed under those pure concepts of the understanding.

Logical Table of Judgments

1	2
As to Quantity	*As to Quality*
Universal	Affirmative
Particular	Negative
Singular	Infinite

[13]In determining concretely that there are twelve, and only twelve, "Pure Concepts of the Understanding," Kant merely accepts as final the division of judgments found in the logic texts of his age and relates these to the structure of the understanding.

3	4
As to Relation	*As to Modality*
Categorical	Problematical
Hypothetical	Assertorical
Disjunctive	Apodeictical

Transcendental Table of the Pure Concepts of the Understanding

1	2
As to Quantity	*As to Quality*
Unity (the Measure)	Reality
Plurality (the Quantity)	Negation
Totality (the Whole)	Limitation

3	4
As to Relation	*As to Modality*
Substance	Possibility
Cause	Existence
Community	Necessity

Pure Physiological Table of the Universal Principles of the Science of Nature

1	2
Axioms of Intuition	Anticipations of Perception

3	4
Analogies of Experience	Postulates of Empirical Thinking generally

21a. In order to comprise the whole matter in one idea, it is first necessary to remind the reader that we are discussing not the origin of experience, but of that which lies in experience. The former pertains to empirical psychology, and would even then never be adequately explained without the latter, which belongs to the Critique of cognition, and particularly of the understanding.

Experience consists of intuitions, which belong to the sensibility, and of judgments, which are entirely a work of the understanding. But the judgments, which the understanding forms alone from sensuous intuitions, are far from being judgments of experience. For in the one case the judgment connects only the perceptions as they are given in the sensuous intuition, while in the other the judgments must express what experience in general, and not what the mere perception (which possesses only subjective validity) contains. The judgment of experience must therefore add to the sensuous intuition and its logical connexion in a judgment (after it has been rendered universal by comparison) something that determines the synthetical judgment as necessary and therefore as universally valid. This can be nothing else than that concept which represents the intuition as determined in itself with regard to one form of judgment rather than another, viz., a concept of that synthetical unity of intuitions which can only be represented by a given logical function of judgments.

22. The sum of the matter is this: the business of the senses is to intuite—that of the understanding is to think. But thinking is uniting representations in one consciousness. This union originates either merely relative to the subject, and is accidental and subjective, or is absolute, and is necessary or objective. The union of representations in one consciousness is judgment. Thinking therefore is the same as judging, or

eferring representations to judgments in general. Hence judgments re either merely subjective, when epresentations are referred to a onsciousness in one subject only, nd united in it, or objective, when hey are united in a consciousness enerally, that is, necessarily. The ogical functions of all judgments re but various modes of uniting epresentations in consciousness.[14] But if they serve for concepts, they re concepts of their necessary nion in a consciousness, and so rinciples of objectively valid judgments. This union in a consciousness is either analytical, by identity, r synthetical, by the combination nd addition of various representaions one to another. Experience onsists in the synthetical connexion f phenomena (perceptions) in consciousness, so far as this connexion is necessary. Hence the pure concepts of the understanding are those under which all perceptions must be subsumed ere they can serve for judgments of experience, in which the synthetical unity of the perceptions is represented as necessary and universally valid.

23. Judgments, when considered merely as the condition of the union of given representations in a consciousness, are rules. These rules, so far as they represent the union as necessary, are rules *a priori*, and so far as they cannot be deduced from higher rules, are fundamental principles. But in regard to the possibility of all experience, merely in relation to the form of thinking in it, no conditions of judgments of experience are higher than those which bring the phenomena, according to the various form of their intuition, under pure concepts of the understanding, and render the empirical judgment objectively valid. These concepts are therefore the *a priori* principles of possible experience.

The principles of possible experience are then at the same time universal laws of nature, which can be cognised *a priori*. And thus the problem in our second question, "How is the pure Science of Nature possible?" is solved. For the system which is required for the form of a science is to be met with in perfection here, because, beyond the above-mentioned formal conditions of all judgments in general offered in logic, no others are possible, and these constitute a logical system. The concepts grounded thereupon, which contain the *a priori* conditions of all synthetical and necessary judgments, accordingly constitute a transcendental system. Finally the

[14]Relative to Kant's theory of judgent, the following may be said: Only ense intuition is in immediate relation the object. So, on the level of underanding, no concept or category is ever elated immediately to the object; hence, dgment is always mediate knowledge, a representation of a representation the object. The function of judgment to bring unity to the sense manifold, d any unity which is affirmed is due to e synthesizing consciousness, not to e unknown object. In other words, the t of judging is merely a formal comning of representations, not an intenonal reaffirmation of the being of the her as other. Briefly, then, the judgent, instead of expressing what is or hat is not in reality, guided in its exession by the intelligible structures of ings, merely combines various repreentations into various unities under the rection of the mind's own principles unity. [These ideas can be found in ant's *Critique of Pure Reason,* in the irst Division, Bk. I, Chap. 1, Sec. i; hap. 2, Sec. ii. Cf. Norman Kemp Smith, *manuel Kant's Critique of Pure Reaon* (New York: The Humanities Press, 50), pp. 105, 135, 159.]

principles, by means of which all phenomena are subsumed under these concepts, constitute a physical system, that is, a system of nature, which precedes all empirical cognition of nature, makes it even possible, and hence may in strictness be denominated the universal and pure science of nature.

* * *

32. Since the oldest days of philosophy inquirers into pure reason have conceived, besides the things of sense, or appearances (phenomena), which makes up the sensible world, certain creations of the understanding (*Verstandeswesen*),[15] called noumena, which should constitute an intelligible world. And as appearance and illusion were by those men identified (a thing which we may well excuse in an undeveloped epoch), actuality was only conceded to the creations of thought.

And we indeed, rightly considering objects of sense as mere appearances, confess thereby that they are based upon a thing in itself, though we know not this thing in its internal constitution, but only know its appearances, viz., the way in which our senses are affected by this unknown something. The understanding therefore, by assuming appearances, grants the existence of things in themselves also, and so far we may say, that the representation of such things as form the basis of phenomena, consequently of mere creations of the understanding, is not only admissible, but unavoidable.

Our critical deduction by no means excludes things of that sort (noumena), but rather limits the principles of the Aesthetic (the science of the sensibility) to this, that they shall not extend to all things, as everything would then be turned into mere appearance, but that they shall only hold good of objects of possible experience. Hereby then objects of the understanding are granted, but with the inculcation of this rule which admits of no exception: "that we neither know nor can know anything at all definite of these pure objects of the understanding, because our pure concepts of the understanding as well as our pure intuitions extend to nothing but objects of possible experience, consequently to mere things of sense, and as soon as we leave this sphere these concepts retain no meaning whatever."

33. There is indeed something seductive in our pure concepts of the understanding, which tempts us to a transcendent use,—a use which transcends all possible experience. Not only are our concepts of substance, of power, of action, of reality, and others, quite independent of experience, containing nothing of sense appearance, and so apparently applicable to things in themselves (noumena), but, what strengthens this conjecture, they contain a necessity of determination in themselves, which experience never at-

---

[15]This is the only explanation for Kant at this point. Since metaphysics cannot meet the requirements he has laid down, he must assign to all its findings the status of "creations" of the mind. As he goes on to say, objects of knowledge are the *phenomena* or *appearances* of things which in themselves are unknowable in their internal constitution. Metaphysics seeks to go beyond this mere sense presentation of phenomena to the internal structure of beings. Kant considers such efforts to have no meaning at all since they do go beyond *all possible experience*. What needs basic evaluation is not this last step so much as Kant's initial positions and his understanding of the nature and function of the understanding.

.ins. The concept of cause im-.ies a rule, according to which one ate follows another necessarily; it experience can only show us, iat one state of things often, or at iost, commonly, follows another, id therefore affords neither strict iiversality, nor necessity.

Hence the Categories seem to have deeper meaning and import than in be exhausted by their empirical se, and so the understanding inad-ertently adds for itself to the house experience a much more exten-.ve wing, which it fills with nothing it creatures of thought, without 'er observing that it has trans-:essed with its otherwise lawful oncepts the bounds of their use.

34. Two important, and even in-spensable, though very dry, inves-gations had therefore become in-spensable in the *Critique of Pure eason*,—viz., the two chapters Vom Schematismus der reinen erstandsbegriffe," and "Vom runde der Unterscheidung aller erstandesbegriffe überhaupt in länomena und Noumena." In the rmer it is shown, that the senses rnish not the pure concepts of the .derstanding *in concreto*, but only e schedule for their use, and that e object conformable to it occurs ly in experience (as the product of e understanding from materials of e sensibility). In the latter it is iown, that, although our pure con-pts of the understanding and our inciples are independent of expe-ence, and despite of the apparently eater sphere of their use, still thing whatever can be thought by em beyond the field of experience, cause they can do nothing but erely determine the logical form the judgment relatively to given :uitions. But as there is no intui-tion at all beyond the field of the sensibility, these pure concepts, as they cannot possibly be exhibited *in concreto*, are void of all meaning; consequently all these noumena, to-gether with their complex, the intel-ligible world, are nothing but rep-resentation of a problem, of which the object in itself is possible, but the solution, from the nature of our understanding, totally impossible. For our understanding is not a fac-ulty of intuition, but of the connexion of given intuitions in experience. Experience must therefore contain all the objects for our concepts; but beyond it no concepts have any sig-nificance, as there is no intuition that might offer them a foundation.

35. The imagination may perhaps be forgiven for occasional vagaries, and for not keeping carefully within the limits of experience, since it gains life and vigor by such flights, and since it is always easier to mod-erate its boldness, than to stimulate its languor. But the understanding which ought to *think* can never be forgiven for indulging in vagaries; for we depend upon it alone for as-sistance to set bounds, when neces-sary, to the vagaries of the imagi-nation.

But the understanding begins its aberrations very innocently and modestly. It first elucidates the ele-mentary cognitions, which inhere in it prior to all experience, but yet must always have their application in experience. It gradually drops these limits, and what is there to prevent it, as it has quite freely de-rived its principles from itself? And then it proceeds first to newly-imagined powers in nature, then to beings outside nature; in short to a world, for whose construction the materials cannot be wanting, because fertile fiction furnishes them abundantly, and though not confirmed, is never refuted, by experience. This is the reason that young thinkers are so partial to metaphysics of the truly dogmatical kind, and often sacrifice to it their time and their talents, which might be otherwise better employed.

But there is no use in trying to moderate these fruitless endeavors of pure reason by all manner of cautions as to the difficulties of solving questions so occult, by complaints of the limits of our reason, and by degrading our assertions into mere conjectures. For if their impossibility is not distinctly shown, and reason's cognition of its own essence does not become a true science, in which the field of its right use is distinguished, so to say, with mathematical certainty from that of its worthless and idle use, these fruitless efforts will never be abandoned for good.

THE CONTEMPORARY PERIOD

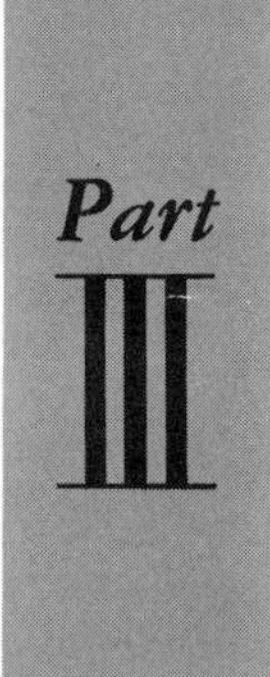

The selections presented in this final section cannot claim to be epresentative of the contemporary status of philosophy. Even a elatively adequate group of selections touching current studies in hu-ıan knowledge would require a complete anthology, and so it is with egret that philosophies such as Existentialism, Idealism, or Person-lism, and philosophers such as Bergson, Whitehead, Sartre, or Gilson annot be included. Even the two selections offered, while important in ıemselves, merely introduce the two philosophers. It can only be oped that the inspiration of lecturers and the personal initiative of tudents will help to remedy these shortcomings.

John Dewey was selected because of his pre-eminence in American hilosophy and because he does stand out as one of the more influ-ntial thinkers of the twentieth century. The material quoted will pro-ide an opportunity to see what his Pragmatism means for truth and ertainty.

Scholastic Realism also has begun to assert itself and has been istened to with more interest than was the case for centuries. Al-ıough there are many points of view to be found among scholastics, ıere is some unanimity concerning the basic principles and the ontinued inheritance from and link with the entire philosophical radition of Western culture. Current analyses of this philosophy re undertaken against a background which, in principle at least, has ɔng proved congenial to the minds of a long line of outstanding think-rs. Therefore, it will be profitable to hear from one of scholastic ealism's most important representatives, M. Jacques Maritain, as e studies the function of concepts in human knowing.

11

Elusive Truth in a Changing World

John Dewey (1859-1952)

John Dewey is surely one of the best known and most influential of American philosophers. His instrumentalism has great appeal because of its apparent vigor and vitality, and his ideas have been spread, particularly in education, through the efforts of countless teachers who studied under him.

Throughout the selections to be offered here, there is a constantly recurring theme to the effect that all "traditional" philosophy has been concerned with a "higher realm of fixed reality," with "the antecedently real," with a "higher and more ultimate form of Being," the knowledge of which is said to be totally divorced from practical action and the world of change. This is, of course, a polemic position adopted for the purpose of providing contrast for Mr. Dewey's emphasis on knowledge as a "making" or a "doing."

It is difficult to evaluate Mr. Dewey's works; it is almost impossible to select any single statement or series of statements which would clearly express his position on any given matter. Hence, any evaluation or criticism must take a rather large view of the tendencies and the developments of his thought.

In his writings, Dewey certainly placed great emphasis upon change and action as pervasive characteristics of human living and of the world in which we live; and it must be admitted that those ideas should be stressed, because they are basic ingredients in experience. The trouble arises, however, when these are treated as the ultimate and exclusive traits of all human experience. Yet in Dewey's thinking there seems to be room for no alternative except the choice between his philosophy of change or action and the static or supramundane philosophy of unchanging essences which he, by an oversimplification, identifies with "traditional" Western philosophy. He thus fails to take into account the possibility of a philosoph which thoroughly respects the contingency and change characterizing th objects of our experience yet recognizes the possibility of a rationall well-founded understanding of basic, eternally true principles of being an of knowledge.

The Pragmatism of John Dewey underlies all his later writings and i exemplified in the pages here quoted. The "making" or "doing," th how-a-thing-works which makes for verifiability and truth in the prag matic sense, leaves unanswered the underlying question of knowledge which is not how a thing works but how we know it at all, how we know it working, how we know its results. If what succeeds is true, then one mus first know what success means, what it is that is working, and what it i that happens.

For Dewey, "the standard of judgment" and of truth is founded upon th "consequents" or upon "intentional construction of a future" rather tha upon a present confrontation with being. This has an appeal, since it ha the appearance of an exciting chase after the ever elusive future. But ma this not also have the inconvenience of treating the present, the past, an even the chase itself as so many fleeting shadows which escape our intel lectual grasp the moment we approach them? Since truth means verifica tion, should not each "success" itself be verified, and, if so, are we nc faced with a never ending process whereby no truth is ever really reached

This is what Bertrand Russell has spoken of as Dewey's "refusal to ad mit 'facts' into his metaphysics, in the sense in which 'facts' are stubbor and cannot be manipulated."

THE QUEST FOR CERTAINTY[1]

I. THE ESCAPE FROM PERIL

If one looks at the foundations of the philosophies of Plato and Aristotle as an anthropologist looks at his material, that is, as cultural subject-matter, it is clear that these philosophies were systematizations in rational form of the content c Greek religious and artistic beliefs The systematization involved purification. Logic provided th patterns to which ultimately rea objects had to conform, while phys ical science was possible in the de gree in which the natural world even in its mutabilities, exhibite exemplification of ultimate immu table rational objects. Thus, alon with the elimination of myths an grosser superstitions, there wer set up the ideals of science and of

[1]From *The Quest for Certainty* by John Dewey. Copyright 1929 by John Dewey. Published by Minton, Balch Co. Used by permission of G. P. Putnam's Sons. Pp. 16-24, 287-304, 309-313.

ife of reason. Ends which could ustify themselves to reason were o take the place of custom as the uide of conduct. These two ideals orm a permanent contribution to vestern civilization.

But with all our gratitude for hese enduring gifts, we cannot for-et the conditions which attended hem. For they brought with them he idea of a higher realm of fixed eality of which alone true science s possible and of an inferior world of changing things with which ex-erience and practical matters are oncerned. They glorified the in-ariant at the expense of change, t being evident that all practical ctivity falls within the realm of hange. It bequeathed the notion, vhich has ruled philosophy ever ince the time of the Greeks, that he office of knowledge is to un-over the antecedently real, rather han, as is the case with our prac-ical judgments, to gain the kind of nderstanding which is necessary o deal with problems as they arise.[2]

In fixing this conception of knowl-edge it established also, as far as philosophies of the classic type are concerned, the special task of phil-osophic inquiry. As a form of knowledge it is concerned with the disclosure of the Real in itself, of Being in and of itself. It is differ-entiated from other modes of know-ing by its preoccupation with a higher and more ultimate form of Being than that with which the sci-ences of nature are concerned. As far as it occupied itself at all with human conduct, it was to superim-pose upon acts ends said to flow from the nature of reason. It thus diverted thought from inquiring into the purposes which experience of actual conditions suggest and from concrete means of their ac-tualization. It translated into a rational form the doctrine of es-cape from the vicissitudes of ex-istence by means of measures which do not demand an active coping with conditions. For deliverance by means of rites and cults, it substi-tuted deliverance through reason. This deliverance was an intellec-tual, a theoretical affair, consti-tuted by a knowledge to be attained apart from practical activity.

The realms of knowledge and ac-tion were each divided into two re-gions. It is not to be inferred that Greek philosophy separated activity from knowing. It connected them. But it distinguished activity from action—that is, from making and doing. Rational and necessary knowledge was treated, as in the celebrations of it by Aristotle, as an ultimate, self-sufficient and self-enclosed form of self-originated and self-conducted activity. It was ideal and eternal, independent of change

---

[2]In these highly polemic pages, Dewey s engaged in an attack upon Greek phi-osophy and also, as becomes very clear n the sequel, upon the whole of Western hought. With the hint here given of his wn position, it might be well to keep in nind from the beginning that, for Dewey, nowledge is part of the evolutionary rocess and must be seen in that light. Moreover, Dewey takes as the ideal in-stance of human knowledge the efforts needed to arrive at a solution in some roblematic situation, where undoubtedly here is need of hypothesis, experimen-ation, and verification, and where the esults may well be merely tentative. This sort of investigation, which surely as its value and is necessary in ap-roaching new problems, he erects into he permanent and total explanation of nan's knowledge.

and hence of the world in which men act and live, the world we experience perceptibly and practically. "Pure activity" was sharply marked off from practical action. The latter, whether in the industrial or the fine arts, in morals or in politics, was concerned with an inferior region of Being in which change rules, and which accordingly has Being only by courtesy, for it manifests deficiency of sure footing in Being by the very fact of change. It is infected with *non*-being.

On the side of knowledge, the division carried with it a difference between knowledge, in its full sense, and belief. The former is demonstrative, necessary—that is, sure. Belief on the contrary is only opinion; in its uncertainty and mere probability, it relates to the world of change as knowledge corresponds to the realm of true reality. This fact brings the discussion around once more to our special theme as far as it affects the conception of the office and nature of philosophy. That man has two modes, two dimensions, of belief, cannot be doubted. He has beliefs about actual existences and the course of events, and he has beliefs about ends to be striven for, policies to be adopted, goods to be attained and evils to be averted. The most urgent of all practical problems concerns the connection the subject-matter of these two kinds of beliefs sustain to each other. How shall our most authentic and dependable cognitive beliefs be used to regulate our practical beliefs? How shall the latter serve to organize and integrate our intellectual beliefs?

There is a genuine possibility that the true problem of philosophy is connected with precisely thi type of question. Man has belief which scientific inquiry vouchsafes beliefs about the actual structur and processes of things; and he als has beliefs about the values whic should regulate his conduct. Th question of how these two ways o believing may most effectively an fruitfully interact with one anothe is the most general and significan of all the problems which life pre sents to us. Some reasoned disci pline, one obviously other than an science, should deal with this issue Thus there is supplied one way c conceiving of the function of phi losophy. But from this mode of de fining philosophy we are estoppe by the chief philosophical tradition For according to it the realms o knowledge and of practical actio have no inherent connection wit each other.[3] Here then is the focu to which the various elements i our discussion converge. We ma then profitably recapitulate. Th realm of the practical is the re

[3]This statement can be questioned The "traditional" philosophy did plac special emphasis upon speculative trut and upon principles of being and of con duct, but it never was totally divorce from action and from the contingent. I began with the sensible, and it sought t explain the world and man's place in i and to provide man with directions fo the proper conduct of his life.

Although earlier in this paragrap Dewey distinguishes between belief about the structure of things and belief about value, it is not clear that he admits any qualitative difference betwee them. The latter may be looked upon a being more "general" and as opening u somewhat wider possibilities, still the must in all cases be vouched for by "scientific inquiry" in the sense of derivin from the positive sciences.

gion of change, and change is always contingent; it has in it an element of chance that cannot be eliminated. If a thing changes, its alteration is convincing evidence of its lack of true or complete Being. What *is,* in the full and pregnant sense of the world, is always, eternally. It is self-contradictory for that which *is* to alter. If it had no defect or imperfection in it how could it change? That which becomes merely *comes* to be, never truly is. It is infected with non-being; with privation of Being in the perfect sense. The world of generation is the world of decay and destruction. Wherever one thing comes into being something else passed out of being.

Thus the depreciation of practice was given a philosophic, an ontological, justification. Practical action, as distinct from self-revolving rational self-activity, belongs in the realm of generation and decay, a realm inferior in value as in Being. In form, the quest for absolute certainty has reached its goal. Because ultimate Being or reality is fixed, permanent, admitting of no change or variation, it may be grasped by rational intuition and set forth in rational, that is, universal and necessary, demonstration. I do not doubt that there was a feeling before the rise of philosophy that the unalterably fixed and the absolutely certain are one, or that change is the source from which comes all our uncertainties and woes. But in philosophy this inchoate feeling was definitely formulated. It was asserted on grounds held to be as demonstrably necessary as are the conclusions of geometry and logic. Thus the predisposition of philosophy toward the universal, invariant and eternal was fixed. It remains the common possession of the entire classic philosophical tradition.

All parts of the scheme hang together. True Being or Reality is complete; in being complete, it is perfect, divine, immutable, the "unmoved mover." Then there are things that change, that come and go, that are generated and perish, because of lack of the stability which participation in ultimate Being alone confers. These changes, however, have form and character and are knowable in the degree in which they tend toward an end which is the fulfillment and completion of the changes in question. Their instability is not absolute but is marked by aspiration toward a goal.

The perfect and complete is rational thought, the ultimate "end" or terminus of all natural movement. That which changes, which becomes and passes away, *is* material; change *defines* the physical. At most and best, it is a potentiality of reaching a stable and fixed end. To these two realms belong two sorts of knowledge. One of them is alone knowledge in the full sense, *science.* This has a rational, necessary and unchanging form. It is *certain.* The other, dealing with change, is belief or opinion; empirical and particular; it is contingent, a matter of probability, not of certainty. The most it can assert is that things are so and so "upon the whole," usually. Corresponding to the division in Being and in knowledge is that in activities. Pure activity is rational; it is theoretical, in the sense in which theory is apart from practical action. Then

there is action in doing and making, occupied with the needs and defects of the lower realm of change in which, in his physical nature, man is implicated.

Although this Greek formulation was made long ago and much of it is now strange in its specific terms, certain features of it are as relevant to present thought as they were significant in their original formulation. For in spite of the great, the enormous changes in the subject-matter and method of the sciences and the tremendous expansion of practical activities by means of arts and technologies, the main tradition of western culture has retained intact this framework of ideas. Perfect certainty is what man wants. It cannot be found by practical doing or making; these take effect in an uncertain future, and involve peril, the risk of misadventure, frustration and failure. Knowledge, on the other hand, is thought to be concerned with a region of being which is fixed in itself. Being eternal and unalterable, human knowing is not to make any difference in it. It can be approached through the medium of the apprehensions and demonstrations of thought, or by some other organ of mind, which does nothing to the real, except just to know it.

There is involved in these doctrines a whole system of philosophical conclusions. The first and foremost is that there is complete correspondence between knowledge in its true meaning and what is real. What is known, what is true for cognition, is what is real in being. The objects of knowledge form the standards of measures of the reality of all other objects of experience. Are the objects of the affections, of desire, effort, choice, that is to say everything to which we attach value, real? Yes, if they can be warranted by knowledge; if we can *know objects* having these value properties, we are justified in thinking them real. But as objects of desire and purpose they have no sure place in Being until they are approached and validated through knowledge. The idea is so familiar that we overlook the unexpressed premise upon which it rests, namely that only the completely fixed and unchanging can be real. The quest for certitude has determined our basic metaphysics.

Secondly, the theory of knowledge has its basic premises fixed by the same doctrine. For knowledge to be certain must relate to that which has antecedent existence or essential being. There are certain things which are alone inherently the proper objects of knowledge and science. Things in the production of which we participate we cannot know in the true sense of the word, for such things succeed instead of preceding our action. What concerns action forms the realm of mere guesswork and probability, as distinct from the warrant of rational assurance which is the ideal of true knowledge. We are so accustomed to the separation of knowledge from doing and making that we fail to recognize how it controls our conceptions of mind, of consciousness and of reflective inquiry. For as relates to genuine knowledge, these must all be defined, on the basis of the premise, so as not to admit of the presence of any overt action that modifies conditions having prior and independent existence.

Special theories of knowledge differ enormously from one another.

Their quarrels with one another fill the air. The din thus created makes us deaf to the way in which they say one thing in common. The controversies are familiar. Some theories ascribe the ultimate test of knowledge to impressions passively received, forced upon us whether we will or no. Others ascribe the guarantee of knowledge to synthetic activity of the intellect. Idealistic theories hold that mind and the object known are ultimately one; realistic doctrines reduce knowledge to awareness of what exists independently, and so on. But they all make one common assumption. They all hold that the operation of inquiry excludes any element of practical activity that enters into the construction of the object known. Strangely enough this is as true of idealism as of realism, of theories of synthetic activity as of those of passive receptivity. For according to them "mind" constructs the known object not in any observable way, or by means of practical overt acts having a temporal quality, but by some occult internal operation.

The common essence of all these theories, in short, is that what is known is antecedent to the mental act of observation and inquiry, and is totally unaffected by these acts; otherwise it would not be fixed and unchangeable[4]. This negative condition, that the processes of search, investigation, reflection, involved in knowledge relate to something having prior being, fixes once for all the main characters attributed to mind, and to the organs of knowing. They *must* be outside what is known, so as not to interact in any way with the object to be known. If the word "interaction" be used, it cannot denote that overt production of change it signifies in its ordinary and practical use.

The theory of knowing is modeled after what was supposed to take place in the act of vision. The object refracts light to the eye and is seen; it makes a difference to the eye and to the person having an optical apparatus, but none to the thing seen. The real object is the object so fixed in its regal aloofness that it is a king to any beholding mind that may gaze upon it. A spectator theory of knowledge is the inevitable outcome.[5] There have been theories which hold that mental activity intervenes, but they have retained the old premise. They have therefore concluded that it is impossible to know reality. Since mind intervenes, we know, according to them, only some modified semblance of the real object, some

---

[4]Here one should distinguish between knowledge of an object and what is known. Things known are not fixed and unchangeable, since all finite beings are mutable beings; yet knowledge—when it affirms what is, no matter how minimal may be the intelligible aspect of being which is grasped—has some stability and immutability, at least in the sense that what it truly affirms is precisely what it is affirmed to be, and it cannot simultaneously be otherwise.

Also, Dewey constantly implies that according to realists the only true knowledge is that of the universal, or of essences, principles, and laws. He hardly does justice to their admission of real knowledge of the contingent particulars in the existential judgment drawn from man's actual experiences of the existing world, or of the realists' practical applications of knowledge and ideas to the particular, concrete cases.

[5]Cf. John Blewett, S. J. (ed.), *John Dewey: His Thought and Influence* (New York: Fordham University Press, 1960), Chap. 3, pp. 71, 78-79.

"appearance." It would be hard to find a more thoroughgoing confirmation than this conclusion provides of the complete hold possessed by the belief that the object of knowledge is a reality fixed and complete in itself, in isolation from an act of inquiry which has in it any element of production of change.

All of these notions about certainty and the fixed, about the nature of the real world, about the nature of the mind and its organs of knowing, are completely bound up with one another, and their consequences ramify into practically all important ideas entertained upon any philosophic question. They all flow—such is my basic thesis—from the separation (set up in the interest of the quest for absolute certainty) between theory and practice, knowledge and actions. Consequently the later problem cannot be attacked in isolation, by itself. It is too thoroughly entangled with fundamental beliefs and ideas in all sorts of fields.

* * *

XI. THE COPERNICAN REVOLUTION

Kant claimed that he had effected a Copernican evolution in philosophy by treating the world and our knowledge of it from the standpoint of the knowing subject. To most critics, the endeavor to make the known world turn on the constitution of the knowing mind, seems like a return to an ultra-Ptolemaic system. But Copernicus, as Kant understood him, effected a straightening out of astronomical phenomena by interpreting their perceived movements from their relation to the perceiving subject, instead of treating them as inherent in the things perceived. The revolution of the sun about the earth as it offers itself to sense-perception was regarded as due to the conditions of human observation and not to the movements of the sun itself. Disregarding the consequences of the changed point of view, Kant settled upon this one feature as characteristic of the method of Copernicus. He thought he could generalize this feature of Copernican method, and thus clear up a multitude of philosophical difficulties by attributing the facts in question to the constitution of the human subject in knowing.

That the consequence was Ptolemaic rather than Copernican is not to be wondered at. In fact, the alleged revolution of Kant consisted in making explicit what was implicit in the classic tradition. In words, the latter had asserted that knowledge is determined by the objective constitution of the universe. But it did so only after it had first assumed that the universe is itself constituted after the pattern of reason. Philosophers first constructed a rational system of nature and then borrowed from it the features by which to characterize their knowledge of it. Kant, in effect, called attention to the borrowing; he insisted that credit for the borrowed material be assigned to human reason instead of to divine.[6] His "rev-

[6]The argument here centers upon the fact that in the Western tradition things have been considered to be intelligible. Before Kant, the basis of that intelligibility was found in the doctrine that all

lution" was a shift from a theo-ogical to a human authorship; be-ond that point, it was an explicit cknowledgement of what philoso-hers in the classic line of descent ad been doing unconsciously before im. For the basic assumption of his tradition was the inherent orrespondence subsisting between *ntellectus* and the structure of Vature—the principle so definitely tated by Spinoza. By the time of Kant difficulties in this rationalis-ic premise had become evident. He hought to maintain the underlying dea and remedy the perplexities it ntailed by placing the locus of in-ellect in man as a knowing subject. The irritation which this perform-nce arouses in some minds is due ather to this transfer than to any loubt about the valid function of eason in the constitution of nature.

Kant refers incidentally to the xperimental method of Galileo as n illustration of the way in which hought actually takes the lead, so hat an object is known because of onformity to a prior conception:—ecause of its conformity to the pecifications of the latter. The re-erence makes clear by contrast the enuine reversal contained in the xperimental way of knowing. It is rue that experimentation proceeds n the basis of a directive idea. But he difference between the office of the idea in determining a known ob-ject and the office assigned to it in Kant's theory is as great as between the Copernican and the Ptolemaic systems. For an idea in experiment is tentative, conditional, not fixed and rigorously determinative. It controls an action to be performed, but the consequences of the opera-tion determine the worth of the di-rective idea; the latter does not fix the nature of the object.[7]

Moreover, in experiment every-thing takes place aboveboard, in the open. Every step is overt and cap-able of being observed. There is a specified antecedent state of things; a specified operation using means, both physical and symbolic, which are externally exhibited and re-ported. The entire process by which the conclusion is reached that such and such a judgment of an object is valid is overt. It can be repeated step by step by any one. Thus every one can judge for himself whether or not the conclusion reached as to

hings reflect in some way the divine deas; according to Kant, the human nind, by the imposition of its categorial n material presentations, accounts for he intelligibility of things. In Dewey's iew, our relation to things is not one of nowledge in the traditional sense of a onformity to what is; knowledge is only reaction to an environment or a series f controlled operations whose "truth" s to be determined by the consequences.

[7]This discussion indicates the new and even revolutionary view of knowledge proposed by Dewey. He insists against Kant that the human mind "does not fix the nature of the object" and thus make it intelligible by the imposition of a mental category, but he himself looks upon knowledge as having the exclusive function of directing and reconstructing the reality in which man finds himself. Dewey sees everything in a purely evo-lutionary context, and even knowledge is only a manifestation of the organism's ability to adapt itself to its environment. He admits that human knowledge can evaluate its various operations or ac-tions by their consequences. Yet, knowl-edge is always in process, it is always tentative or hypothetical, for any appar-ent results become only new hypotheses which must seek new verification in their new consequences; and so, for all time and in all fields, "truth" remains an ever elusive and constantly receding goal.

the object justifies assertion of knowledge, or whether there are gaps and deflections. Moreover, the whole process goes on where other existential processes go on, in time. There is a temporal sequence as definitely as in any art, as in, say, the making of cotton cloth from ginning of raw material, through carding and spinning to the operation of the loom. A public and manifest series of definite operations, all capable of public notice and report, distinguishes scientific knowing from the knowing carried on by inner "mental" processes accessible only to introspection, or inferred by dialectic from assumed premises.

There is accordingly opposition rather than agreement between the Kantian determination of objects by thought and the determination by thought that takes place in experimentation. There is nothing hypothetical or conditional about Kant's forms of perception and conception. They work uniformly and triumphantly; they need no differential testing by consequences. The reason Kant postulates them is to secure universality and necessity instead of the hypothetical and the probable. Nor is there anything overt, observable and temporal or historical in the Kantian machinery. Its work is done behind the scenes. Only the result is observed, and only an elaborate process of dialectic inference enables Kant to assert the existence of his apparatus of forms and categories. These are as inaccessible to observation as were the occult forms and essences whose rejection was a prerequisite of development of modern science.[8]

These remarks are not directed particularly against Kant. For, as has been already said, he edited a new version of old conceptions about mind and its activities in knowing rather than evolved a brand new theory. But since he happens to be the author of the phrase "Copernican revolution," his philosophy forms a convenient point of departure for consideration of a genuine reversal of traditional ideas about the mind, reason, conceptions and mental processes. Phases of this revolution have concerned us in the previous lectures. We have seen how the opposition between knowing and doing, theory and practice, has been abandoned in the actual enterprise of scientific inquiry how knowing goes forward by means of doing. We have seen how the cognitive quest for absolute certainty by purely mental means has been surrendered in behalf of search for a security, having a high degree of probability, by means of preliminary active regulation of conditions. We have considered some of the definite steps by which security has come to attach to regulation of change rather than absolute certainty to the unchangeable. We have noted how in consequence of this transformation the standard of judgment has been transferred from antecedents to consequents, from inert dependence upon the past to intentional construction of a future.

If such changes do not constitute, in the depth and scope of their significance, a reversal compara-

---

[8]The influence of the empirical mentality on Dewey's philosophy is seen in this statement. Like the empiricists, he will not admit the potency-act relationship of principles of being, nor the ability of the human mind to gain at least some minimal knowledge of essences in what is sensibly observed.

ble to a Copernican revolution, I am at a loss to know where such a change can be found or what it would be like. The old center was mind knowing by means of an equipment of powers complete within itself, and merely exercized upon an antecedent external material equally complete in itself. The new center is indefinite interactions taking place within a course of nature which is not fixed and complete, but which is capable of direction to new and different results through the mediation of intentional operations. Neither self nor world, neither soul nor nature (in the sense of something isolated and finished in its isolation) is the center, any more than either earth or sun is the absolute center of a single universal and necessary frame of reference. There is a moving whole of interacting parts; a center emerges wherever there is effort to change them in a particular direction.

The reversal has many phases, and these are interconnected. It cannot be said that one is more important than another. But one change stands out with an extraordinary distinctness. Mind is no longer a spectator beholding the world from without and finding its highest satisfaction in the joy of self-sufficing contemplation. The mind is within the world as a part of the latter's own on-going process. It is marked off as mind by the fact that wherever it is found, changes take place in a *directed* way, so that a movement in a definite one-way sense—from the doubtful and confused to the clear, resolved and settled—takes place. From knowing as an outside beholding to knowing as an active participant in the drama of an on-moving world is the historical transition whose record we have been following.

As far as philosophy is concerned, the first direct and immediate effect of this shift from knowing which makes a difference to the knower but none in the world, to knowing which is a directed change within the world, is the complete abandonment of what we may term the intellectualist fallacy. By this is meant something which may also be termed the ubiquity of knowledge as a measure of reality. Of the older philosophies, framed before experimental knowing had made any significant progress, it may be said that they made a definite separation between the world in which man thinks and knows and the world in which he lives and acts. In his needs and in the acts that spring from them, man *was* a part of the world, a sharer in its fortunes, sometimes willingly, sometimes perforce; he was exposed to its vicissitudes and at the mercy of its irregular and unforeseeable changes. By acting in and upon the world he made his earthly way, sometimes failing, sometimes achieving. He was acted upon by it, sometimes carried forward to unexpected glories and sometimes overwhelmed by its disfavor.

Being unable to cope with the world in which he lived, he sought some way to come to terms with the universe as a whole. Religion was, in its origin, an expression of this endeavor. After a time, a few persons with leisure and endowed by fortune with immunity from the rougher impacts of the world, discovered the delights of thought and inquiry. They reached the conclusion that through rational thought they could rise above the natural world in which, with their body and those mental processes that were connected with the body, they lived. In striving with the inclemencies of nature, suffering its buffetings, wresting sustenance from its resources, they were parts of Nature. But in knowledge, true knowledge which is rational, occupied with objects that are universal and immutable, they escaped from the world of vicissitude and uncertainty. They were elevated above the realm in which needs are felt and laborious effort imperative. In rising above this world of sense and time, they came into rational communion with the divine which was untroubled and perfect mind. They became true participants in the realm of ultimate reality. Through knowledge, they were without the world of chance and change, and within the world of perfect and unchanging Being.[9]

How far this glorification by philosophers and scientific investigators of a life of knowing, apart from and above a life of doing, might have impressed the popular mind without adventitious aid there is no saying. But external aid came. Theologians of the Christian Church adopted this view in a form adopted to their religious purposes. The perfect and ultimate reality was God; to know Him was eternal bliss. The world in which man lived and acted was a world of trials and troubles to test and prepare him for a higher destiny. Through thousands of ways, including histories and rites, with symbols that engaged the emotions and imagination, the essentials of the doctrine of classic philosophy filtered its way into the popular mind.

It would be a one-sided view which held that this story gives the entire account of the elevation of knowing and its object above practical action and its objects. A contributing cause was found in the harshness, cruelties and tragic frustrations of the world of action. Were it not for its brutalities and failures, the motive for seeking refuge in a higher realm of knowledge would have been lacking. It was easy and, as we say, "natural" to associate these evils with the fact that the world in which we act is a realm of change. The generic fact of change was made absolute and the source of all the troubles and defects of the world in which we directly live. At the very best, good and excellence are insecure in a world of change; good can be securely at home only in a realm of fixed unchanging substance. When the source of evil was once asserted to reside in the inherent deficiencies of a realm of change, responsibility was removed from human ignorance, incapacity and insusceptibility. It remained only to change our own attitude and disposition, to turn the soul from perishable things toward perfect Being. In this idea religion stated in one language

[9]Here and in the next paragraph one can recall, on the credit side, that "Theologians of the Christian Church" did have much respect for this material and changing world. Matter, as created, was good. There was a depth of meaning in the symbolism of the age and, more profoundly, in the doctrine of exemplary causality, which, far from minimizing the importance of this life and of the changing, material world, saw in them an intrinsic importance not only for their own being, but also as reflections of the divine. Cf. Blewett, *op. cit.*, Chap. 1, pp. 20-22, 27.

precisely what the great philosophic tradition stated in another.

Nor is this the whole of the story. There was, strangely enough, a definitely practical ground for the elevation of knowledge above doing and making. Whenever knowledge is actually obtained, a measure of security through ability to control ensues. There is a natural inclination to treat value as a measure of reality. Since knowledge is the mode of experience that puts in our hands the key to controlling our other dealings with experienced objects, it has a central position. There is no *practical* point gained in asserting that a thing is *what* it is *experienced* to be apart from knowledge. If a man has typhoid fever, he has it; he does not have to search for or pry into it. But to *know* it, he does have to search:—to *thought*, to intellect, the fever *is* what it is known to be. For when it is known, the various phenomena of *having* it, the direct experiences, fall into order; we have at least that kind of control called understanding, and with this comes the possibility of a more active control. The very fact that other experiences speak, so to say, for themselves makes it unnecessary to ask *what* they are. When the nature of an existence is in doubt and we have to seek for it, the idea of reality is consciously present. Hence the thought of existence becomes exclusively associated with knowing. Other ways of experiencing things exist so obviously that we do not *think* of existence in connection with them.

At all events, whatever the explanation, the idea that cognition is the measure of the reality found in other modes of experience is the most widely distributed premise of philosophies. The equation of the real and the known comes to explicit statement in idealistic theories. If we remind ourselves of the landscape with trees and grasses waving in the wind and waves dancing in sunlight, we recall how scientific thought of these things strips off the qualities significant in perception and direct enjoyment, leaving only certain physical constants stated in mathematical formulae. What is more natural, then, than to call upon mind to reclothe by some contributory act of thought or consciousness the grim skeleton offered by science? Then if only it can be shown that mathematical relations are themselves a logical construction of thought, the knowing mind is enstated as the constitutive author of the whole scheme. Realistic theories have protested against doctrines that make the knowing mind the source of the thing known. But they have held to a doctrine of a partial equation of the real and the known; only they have read the equation from the side of the object instead of the subject. Knowledge must be the grasp or vision of the real as it "is in itself," while emotions and affections deal with it as it is affected with an alien element supplied by the feeling and desiring subject. The postulate of the unique and exclusive relation among experienced things of knowledge and the real is shared by epistemological idealist and realist.

The meaning of a copernican reversal is that we do not have to go to knowledge to obtain an exclusive hold on reality. The world as we experience it is a real world. But it is not in its primary phases a world that is known, a world that is understood, and is intellectually coherent and secure. Knowing consists of operations that give experienced objects a form in which the relations, upon which the onward course of events depends, are securely experienced. It marks a transitional redirection and rearrangement of the real. It is intermediate and instrumental; it comes between a relatively casual and accidental experience of existence and one relatively settled and defined. The knower is within the world of existence; his knowing, as experimental, marks an interaction of one existence with other existences. There is, however, a most important difference between it and other existential interactions. The difference is not between something going on within nature as a part of itself and something else taking place outside it, but is that between a regulated course of changes and an uncontrolled one. In knowledge, causes become means and effects become consequences, and thereby things have meanings. The known object is an antecedent object as that is intentionally rearranged and redisposed, an eventual object whose value is tested by the reconstruction it effects. It emerges, as it were, from the fire of experimental thought as a refined metal issues from operations performed on crude material. It is the same object but the same object with a difference, as a man who has been through conditions which try the temper of his being comes out the same man and a different man.[10]

Knowledge then does not encompass the world as a whole. But the fact that it is not coextensive with experienced existence is no defect nor failure on its part. It is an expression of the fact that knowledge attends strictly to its own business: —transformation of disturbed and unsettled situations into those more controlled and more significant. Not all existence asks to be known, and it certainly does not ask leave from thought to exist. But some existences as they are experienced do ask thought to direct them in their course so that they may be ordered and fair and be such as to commend themselves to admiration, approval and appreciation. Knowledge affords the sole means by which this redirection can be effected. As the latter is brought about, parts of the experienced world have more luminous and organized meaning and

---

[10]The burden of this paragraph, as, indeed, of the entire selection, is Dewey's notion of knowledge. For him, knowledge is a "redirection and rearrangement of the real," it "marks an interaction of one existence with other existences ... a regulated course of changes," and the "known object is an antecedent object as that is intentionally rearranged and redisposed." This expresses an important function of human intellection. Dewey's hope is that, by the use of knowledge, more and more areas of life, individual and social, may be ever more intelligently controlled. In this project, anyone should be willing to admit the importance of his emphatic position. However, in the process, he makes this human endeavor the complete theory of human knowledge, the sum and substance of knowledge and truth. Then the question arises whether man has any knowledge of that "antecedent object," so that his arranging and, in general, his actions may be brought to bear on something which he already knows as it is. If not, how can the human operations be intelligently chosen and directed? Moreover, if truth is known by its "consequences," by what norm are the consequences to be evaluated. Cf. Blewett, *op. cit.*, Chap. 3, pp. 69-74, 77-79; Chap. 7, pp. 187-190.

their significance is rendered more secure against the gnawing tooth of time. The problem of knowledge is the problem of discovery of methods for carrying on this enterprise of redirection. It is a problem never ended, always in process; one problematic situation is resolved and another takes its place. The constant gain is not in approximation to universal solution but in betterment of methods and enrichment of objects experienced.

Man as a natural creature acts as masses and molecules act; he lives as animals live, eating, fighting, fearing, reproducing. As he lives, some of his actions yield understanding and things take on meaning, for they become signs of one another; means of expectation and of recall, preparations for what is to come and celebrations of what has gone. Activities take on ideal quality. Attraction and repulsion become love of the admirable and hate of the harsh and ugly, and they seek to find and make a world in which they may be securely at home. Hopes and fears, desires and aversions, are as truly responses to things as are knowing and thinking. Our affections, when they are enlightened by understanding, are organs by which we enter into the meaning of the natural world as genuinely as by knowing, and with greater fullness and intimacy. This deeper and richer intercourse with things can be effected only by thought and its resultant knowledge; the arts in which the potential meanings of nature are realized demand an intermediate and transitional phase of detachment and abstraction. The colder and less intimate transactions of knowing involve temporary disregard of the qualities and values to which our affections and enjoyments are attached. But knowledge is an indispensable medium of our hopes and fears, of loves and hates, if desires and preferences are to be steady, ordered, charged with meaning, secure.

The glorification of knowledge as the exclusive avenue of access to what is real is not going to give way soon nor all at once. But it can hardly endure indefinitely. The more widespread become the habits of intelligent thought, the fewer enemies they meet from those vested interests and social institutions whose power depends upon immunity from inspection by intelligence, in short, the more matter of course they become, the less need will there seem to be for giving knowledge an exclusive and monopolistic position. It will be prized for its fruits rather than for the properties assigned to it when it was a new and precarious enterprise. The common fact that we prize in proportion to rarity has a good deal to do with the exclusive esteem in which knowledge has been held. There is so much unintelligent appetite and impulse, so much routine action, so much that is dictated by the arbitrary power of other persons, so much, in short, that is not informed and enlightened by knowledge, that it is not surprising that action and knowledge should have been isolated in thought from one another, and knowledge treated as if it alone had dealings with real existence. I do not know when knowledge will become naturalized in the life of society. But when it is fully acclimatized, its instrumental, as distinct from its monopolistic, rôle in approach to things of nature and society will be taken for granted without need for such arguments as I have been engaging in. Meantime, the development of the experimental method stands as a prophecy of the possibility of the accomplishment of this Copernican Revolution.

Whenever anyone speaks about the relation of knowledge (especially if the word science be used) to our moral, artistic and religious interests, there are two dangers to which he is exposed. There exist on one hand efforts to use scientific knowledge to substantiate moral and religious beliefs, either with respect to some specific form in which they are current or in some vague way that is felt to be edifying and comforting. On the other hand, philosophers derogate the importance and necessity of knowledge in order to make room for an undisputed sway of some set of moral and religious tenets. It may be that preconceptions will lead some to interpret what has been said in one or other of these senses. If so, it is well to state that not a word has been said in depreciation of science; what has been criticized is a philosophy and habit of mind on the ground of which science is prized for false reasons. Nor does this negative statement cover the whole ground. Knowledge is instrumental. But the purport of our whole discussion has been in praise of tools, instrumentalities, means, putting them on a level equal in value to ends and consequences, since without them the latter are merely accidental, sporadic and unstable. To call known objects, in their capacity of being objects of knowledge, means is to appreciate them, not to depreciate them.

Affections, desires, purposes, choices are going to endure as long as man is man; therefore as long as man is man, there are going to be ideas, judgments, beliefs about values. Nothing could be sillier than to attempt to justify their existence at large; they are going to exist anyway. What is inevitable needs no proof for its existence. But these expressions of our nature need *direction,* and direction is possible only through knowledge. When they are informed by knowledge, they themselves constitute, in their directed activity, intelligence in operation. Thus as far as concerns particular value-beliefs, particular moral and religious ideas and creeds, the import of what has been said is that they need to be tested and revised by the best knowledge at command. The moral of the discussion is anything but a reservation for them of a position in which they are exempt from the impact, however disintegrative it may be, of new knowledge.

The relation between objects as known and objects with respect to value is that between the actual and the possible.[11] "The actual" consists of given conditions; "the possible" denotes ends or consequences not now existing but which the actual may through its use bring into existence. The possible in respect to any given actual situation is thus an ideal for that situation; from the standpoint of operational definition—of thinking in terms of action--the ideal and the possible are equivalent

---

[11]If value is to be contrasted with the present and actual and equated with the future and potential, it would seem to follow that nothing in the world and nothing already attained is of value. Also, does an "ideal," pursued and achieved, cease to be valuable because it becomes actual?

ideas. Idea and ideal have more in common than certain letters of the alphabet. Everywhere an idea, in its intellectual content, is a projection of what something existing may come to be. One may report a quality already sensed in a proposition, as when standing before the fire I remark upon how hot it is. When seeing something at a distance, I judge without sensible contact that it must be hot; "hot" expresses a consequence which I infer would be experienced if I were to approach close enough; it designates a possibility of what is actually there in experience. The instance is a trivial one, but it sets forth what happens in every case where any predicate, whether quality or relation, expresses an *idea* rather than a sensibly perceived characteristic. The difference is not between one mental state called a sensation and another called an image. It is between what is experienced as being already there and what marks a possibility of being experienced. If we agree to leave out the eulogistic savor of "ideal" and define it in contrast with the actual, the possibility denoted by an idea is the ideal phase of the existent.

The problem of the connection or lack of connection of the actual and the ideal has always been the central problem of philosophy in its metaphysical aspect, just as the relation between existence and idea has been the central theme of philosophy on the side of the theory of knowledge. Both issues come together in the problem of the relation of the actual and the possible. Both problems are derived from the necessities of action if that is to be intelligently regulated. Assertion of an idea or of an ideal, if it is genuine, is a claim that it is possible to modify what exists so that it will take on a form possessed of specifiable traits. This statement as it relates to an idea, to the cognitive aspect, takes us back to what has been said about ideas as designations of operations and their consequences. Its bearing upon the "ideal" concerns us at this point.

In this basic problem of the relation of the actual and ideal, classic philosophies have always attempted to prove that the ideal is already and eternally a property of the real. The quest for absolute cognitive certainty has come to a head in the quest for an ideal which is one with the ultimately real. Men have not been able to trust either the world or themselves to realize the values and qualities which are the possibilities of nature. The sense of incompetency and the sloth born of desire for irresponsibility have combined to create an overwhelming longing for the ideal and rational as an antecedent possession of actuality[12], and consequently something upon which we can fall back for emotional support in times of trouble.

The assumption of the antecedent inherent identity of actual and ideal has generated problems which have not been solved. It is the source of the problem of evil; of evil not merely in the moral sense, but in that of the existence of defect and aberration, of uncertainty and error, of all deviation from the perfect. If the universe is in itself ideal, why is there so much in our

[12]Incompetency, sloth, and irresponsibility are very strong words in the context and hard to admit in reference to "classic philosophers" from Plato to Hegel.

experience of it which is so thoroughly unideal? Attempts to answer this question have always been compelled to introduce lapse from perfect Being:—some kind of fall to which is due the distinction between noumena and phenomena, things as they really are and as they seem to be. There are many versions of this doctrine. The simplest, though not the one which has most commended itself to most philosophers, is the idea of the "fall of man," a fall which, in the words of Cardinal Newman, has implicated all creation in an aboriginal catastrophe. I am not concerned to discuss them and their respective weaknesses and strengths. It is enough to note that the philosophies which go by the name of Idealism are attempts to prove by one method or another, cosmological, ontological or epistemological, that the Real and the Ideal are one, while at the same time they introduce qualifying additions to explain why after all they are not one.

There are three ways of idealizing the world. There is idealization through purely intellectual and logical processes, in which reasoning alone attempts to prove that the world has characters that satisfy our highest aspirations. There are, again, moments of intense emotional appreciation when, through a happy conjunction of the state of the self and of the surrounding world, the beauty and harmony of existence is disclosed in experiences which are the immediate consummation of all for which we long. Then there is an idealization through actions that are directed by thought, such as are manifested in the works of fine art and in all human relations perfected by loving care. The first path has been taken by many philosophies. The second while it lasts is the most engaging. It sets the measure of our ideas of possibilities that are to be realized by intelligent endeavor. But its objects depend upon fortune and are insecure. The third method represents the way of deliberate quest for security of the values that are enjoyed by grace in our happy moments.

That in fortunate moments objects of complete and approved enjoyment are had is evidence that nature is capable of giving birth to objects that stay with us as ideal. Nature thus supplies potential material for embodiment of ideals. Nature, if I may use the locution, is idealizable. It lends itself to operations by which it is perfected. The process is not a passive one. Rather nature gives, not always freely but in response to search, means and material by which the values we judge to have supreme quality may be embodied in existence. It depends upon the choice of man whether he employs what nature provides and for what ends he uses it.

Idealism of this type is not content with dialectical proofs that the perfect is already and immutably in Being, either as a property of some higher power or as an essence. The emotional satisfactions and encouragements thus supplied are not an adequate substitute for an ideal which is projected in order to be a guide of our doings. While the happy moment brings us objects to admire, approve and revere, the security and extent in which the beautiful, the true and the revered qualify the world, depend upon the way in which our own affections and desires for that kind of world engage activities. Things loved, admired and revered, things that spiritualistic philosophies have seized upon as the defining characters of ultimate Being, are genuine elements of nature. But without the aid and support of deliberate action based on understanding of conditions, they are transitory and unstable, as well as narrow and confined in the number of those who enjoy them.

Religious faiths have come under the influence of philosophies that have tried to demonstrate the fixed union of the actual and ideal in ultimate Being. Their interest in persuading to a life of loyalty to what is esteemed good, has been bound up with a certain creed regarding historical origins. Religion has also been involved in the metaphysics of substance, and has thrown in its lot with acceptance of certain cosmogonies. It has found itself fighting a battle and a losing one with science, as if religion were a rival theory about the structure of the natural world. It has committed itself to assertions about astronomical, geological, biological subject-matter; about questions of anthropology, literary criticism, and history. With the advances of sciences in these fields it has in consequence found itself involved in a series of conflicts, compromises, adjustments and retreats.[13]

The religious attitude as a sense of the possibilities of existence and as devotion to the cause of these possibilities, as distinct from acceptance of what is given at the time, gradually extricates itself from these unnecessary intellectual commitments. But religious devotees rarely stop to notice that what lies at the basis of recurrent conflicts with scientific findings is not this or that special dogma so much as it is alliance with philosophical schemes which hold that the reality and power of whatever is excellent and worthy of supreme devotion, depends upon proof of its antecedent existence, so that the ideal of perfection loses its claim over us unless it can be demonstrated to exist in the sense in which the sun and stars exist.

* * *

A final word about philosophy is then in place. Like religion it has come into conflict with the natural sciences, or at least its path has diverged increasingly from theirs since the seventeenth century. The chief cause of the split is that philosophy has assumed for its function a knowledge of reality. This fact makes it a rival instead of a complement to the sciences. It has forced philosophy into claiming a kind of knowledge which is more ultimate than theirs. In consequence it has, at least in its more systematic forms, felt obliged to revise the conclusions of science to prove that

---

[13]This was a common enough view when Mr. Dewey wrote this work. It is not so prevalent among scholars today. Works which give indications of the opposite are the series of *Publications in Medieval Science* (Madison, Wis.: University of Wisconsin Press, 1952—), and James A. Weisheipl, O.P., *The Development of Physical Theory in the Middle Ages* (New York: Sheed & Ward, Inc., 1959). Cf. Blewett, *op. cit.*, Chap. 1, pp. 13-17, 20-22, 27-29.

they do not mean what they say; or that, in any case they apply to a world of appearances instead of to the superior reality to which philosophy directs itself. Idealistic philosophies have attempted to prove from an examination of the conditions of knowledge that mind is the only reality. What does it matter, they have said in effect, if physical knowledge recognizes only matter, since matter itself is mental? Idealisms in proving that the ideal is once for all the real has absolved itself from the office, more useful if humbler, of attempting that interpretation of the actual by means of which values could be made more extensive and more secure.

General ideas, hypotheses, are necessary in science itself. They serve an indispensable purpose. They open new points of view; they liberate us from the bondage of habit which is always closing in on us, restricting our vision both of what is and of what the actual may become. They direct operations that reveal new truths and new possibilities. They enable us to escape from the pressure of immediate circumstance and provincial boundaries. Knowledge falters when imagination clips its wings or fears to use them. Every great advance in science has issued from a new audacity of imagination. What are now working conceptions, employed as a matter of course because they have withstood the tests of experiment and have emerged triumphant, were once speculative hypotheses.

There is no limit set to the scope and depth of hypotheses. There are those of short and technical range and there are those as wide as experience. Philosophy has always claimed universality for itself. It will make its claim good when it connects this universality with the formation of directive hypotheses instead of with a sweeping pretension to knowledge of universal Being. That hypotheses are fruitful when they are suggested by actual need, are bulwarked by knowledge already attained, and are tested by the consequences of the operations they evoke goes without saying. Otherwise imagination is dissipated into fantasies and rises vaporously into the clouds.

The need for large and generous ideas in the direction of life was never more urgent than in the confusion of tongues, beliefs and purposes that characterizes present life. Knowledge of actual structure and processes of existence has reached a point where a philosophy which has the will to use knowledge has guidance and support. A philosophy which abandoned its guardianship of fixed realities, values and ideals, would find a new career for itself. The meaning of science in terms of science, in terms of knowledge of the actual, may well be left to science itself. Its meaning in terms of the great human uses to which it may be put, its meaning in the service of possibilities of secure value, offers a field for exploration which cries out from very emptiness. To abandon the search for absolute and immutable reality and value may seem like a sacrifice. But this renunciation is the condition of entering upon a vocation of greater vitality. The search for values to be secured and shared by all, because buttressed in the foundations of social life, is a quest in which philosophy would have no rivals but coadjutors in men of good will.[14]

Philosophy under such conditions finds itself in no opposition to science. It is a liaison officer between the conclusions of science and the modes of social and personal action through which attainable possibilities are projected and striven for. No more than a religion devoted to inspiration and cultivation of the sense of ideal possibilities in the actual would it find itself checked by any possible discovery of science. Each new discovery would afford a new opportunity. Such a philosophy would have a wide field of criticism before it. But its critical mind would be directed against the domination exercised by prejudice, narrow interest, routine custom and the authority which issues from institutions apart from the human ends they serve.[15] This negative office would be but the obverse of the creative work of the imagination in pointing to the new possibilities which knowledge of the actual discloses and in projecting methods for their realization in the homely everyday experience of mankind.

Philosophy has often entertained the ideal of a complete integration of knowledge. But knowledge by its nature is analytic and discriminating. It attains large syntheses, sweeping generalizations. But these open up new problems for consideration, new fields for inquiry; they are transitions to more detailed and varied knowledge. Diversification of discoveries and the opening up of new points of view and new methods are inherent in the progress of knowledge. This fact defeats the idea of any complete synthesis of knowledge upon an intellectual basis. The sheer increase of specialized knowledge will never work the miracle of producing an intellectual whole. Nevertheless, the need for integration of specialized results of science remains, and philosophy should contribute to the satisfaction of the need.

The need, however, is practical and human rather than intrinsic to science itself; the latter is content as long as it can move to new problems and discoveries. The need for direction of action in large social fields is the source of a genuine demand for unification of scientific conclusions. They are organized when their bearing on the conduct of life is disclosed. It is at this point that the extraordinary and multifarious results of scientific inquiry are unorganized, scattered, chaotic. The astronomer, biologist, chemist, may attain systematic wholes, at least for a time, within his own field. But when we come to the bearing of special conclusions upon the conduct of social life, we are, outside of technical fields, at

---

[14]"The search for values" is the work on which philosophy has been engaged, but it has not limited man or his values to the purely material or quantitative. It has recognized that man lives in different dimensions and that there are depths to his being which are inaccessible to the instruments and formulae of scientific investigation. And, since philosophy has investigated values on different levels, it has not been concerned exclusively with the absolute and immutable.

[15]One hopes that this has always been the endeavor of philosophers, and one cannot help wondering how much commitment to Naturalism has influenced Dewey in his position on spiritual values and on the successes and failures of the history of Western thought and culture.

a loss. The force of tradition and dogmatic authority is due, more than to anything else, to precisely this defect. Man has never had such a varied body of knowledge in his possession before, and probably never before has he been so uncertain and so perplexed as to what his knowledge means, what it points to in action and in consequences.

Were there any consensus as to the significance of what is known upon beliefs about things of ideal and general value, our life would be marked by integrity instead of by distraction and by conflict of competing aims and standards. Needs of practical action in large and liberal social fields would give unification of our special knowledge; and the latter would give solidity and confidence to the judgment of values that control conduct. Attainment of this consensus would mean that modern life had reached maturity in discovering the meaning of its own intellectual movement. It would find within its own interests and activities the authoritative guidance for its own affairs which it now vainly seeks in oscillation between outworn traditions and reliance upon casual impulse.

The situation defines the vital office of present philosophy. It has to search out and disclose the obstructions; to criticize the habits of mind which stand in the way; to focus reflection upon needs congruous to present life; to interpret the conclusions of science with respect to their consequences for our beliefs about purposes and values in all phases of life. The development of a system of thought capable of giving this service is a difficult undertaking; it can proceed only slowly and through coöperative effort. In these pages I have tried to indicate in outline the nature of the task to be accomplished and to suggest some of the resources at hand for its realization.

12

The Meaning and Function of Concepts

Jacques Maritain (1882-)

The following pages contain a consideration of the very activity of knowing—an activity which has no parallel in the material world, and which, because of its uniqueness, may be referred to as involving mystery. In the selection, M. Maritain emphasizes the meaning of *intentional* existence, the meaning of *object* and of *thing*, the role of the species, and the concept as a formal rather than instrumental sign. These are views basic in a scholastic Realism, and the very logic of the situation of knowing is shown to lead inexorably to their admission. However, modern philosophies, as the author clearly indicates, have not really handled knowledge from this point of view and are actually incapable of doing so with any success, since they have lost from view the true nature of idea and of intentionality and have conceived the function of knowledge "upon the pattern of events in the material world." M. Maritain ends with a look at the knowledge of singulars and of beings of reason.

CRITICAL REALISM[1]

"Thus, that there may be a remedy for such imperfection, another mode of perfection is encountered in created things, and according to that mode the perfection that is the property of one thing, is itself also encountered in another thing. Of that kind is the perfection of the knower as such, because insofar as the knower knows, the thing known exists within him in a certain way.... And as a consequence of that mode of perfection it is possible for the perfection of the whole universe to exist in a solitary particular thing."

III. CONCERNING KNOWLEDGE ITSELF

22. This text of St. Thomas introduces us into the very mystery of knowledge. It is time we asked in what this mystery consists. What is the inner nature of that which we call knowing? It must be confessed that modern philosophers do not even begin to treat that question because they cannot make up their minds to ask it. Neither Descartes, nor Kant, nor the Neo-realists, nor even the phenomenologists (except, it seems, Nicolai Hartmann, who has at least profoundly felt the antinomies with which it is pregnant) have faced it squarely. It is the peculiar merit of St. Thomas and his great commentators to have frankly formulated this problem, for it is the most important of all the problems of neotic, and one that can only be treated as it should by bringing into play the most delicately refined metaphysical equipment. And it is to their credit not only to have formulated the question, but to have given it its profoundest solution as well. Before tackling it, they warn us that we must raise our minds, because we are entering quite a different order of things, *et disces elevare ingenium, aliumque rerum ordinem ingredi*. Errors, that are so frequent in this realm, arise from the fact that too often we confuse a spiritual event, like knowledge, with the material events by which our ordinary experience is nurtured.

Permit us, *brevitatis studio,* to set forth at this juncture a very concise résumé in seven points of the Thomistic doctrine on the nature of knowledge. The advantage of condensations of this kind is to force one to a synthesis in which only what is essential is stated. [I]. There is a vigorous correspondence between knowledge and immateriality. A being is a knowing being to the extent that it is immaterial. [II]. Why is this so? Because, by an apparent scandal to the principle of identity, to know is to be in a certain way something other than what one is: it is *to become a thing other than the self,* "fieri aliud a se," *to be or become the other as other,* "esse seu fieri aliud in quantum aliud." Now this presupposes, on the one hand, that the subject capable of knowing

[1]Reprinted with the permission of Charles Scribner's Sons from *The Degrees of Knowledge* by Jacques Maritain, newly translated from the fourth French edition under the supervision of Gerald B. Phelan. Copyright © 1959 by Jacques Maritain. Chap. 3, Sect. 3, pp. 111-135.

emerges above matter (which restricts or encloses things exclusively within their own being); and, on the other hand, that there is a kind of union, transcending every union of a material sort, between the knower and the known. For when matter receives a form, it is to constitute a third term with it, a *tertium quid,* i.e., informed matter. Thus, a material being can become *other*, i.e., it can itself change or be modified, but it cannot become *the other.* Whereas the knower, even while maintaining his own nature intact, becomes the known itself and identifies himself with it, the knower being thus incomparably more *one* with the known than the matter with the form. [III]. *To know* is to the sense and the intellect—taken as cognitive functions—as *to exist* is to the essence—to the quidditative function. It is a kind of existence that defines knowledge. To know does not consist in making anything nor in receiving anything, but in existing in a way better than by the simple fact of being set outside nothingness. Knowing is an active, immaterial superexistence whereby a subject not only exists with an existence limited to what that subject is as a thing enclosed within one genus—as a subject existing for itself—but with an unlimited existence in which by its own activity it is and becomes itself and other things.

That is why existence and knowledge in God, because He is infinite, are purely and absolutely the same thing. There is no distinction, not even a virtual distinction, between *esse divinum* and *intelligere divinum*. His existence is His own very act of understanding.

Once we have arrived at this stage, we understand that the formula "to become the other as other" does, indeed, really define knowledge, but knowledge considered in what especially characterizes human knowledge, which is first turned to the other. An angel knows itself before knowing things; God knows Himself—He is the only object worthy of specifying His intellect, and He knows things—both possible or created—within His own essence. To give a definition of knowledge that is suited to its complete analogical amplitude, we would have to say that to know is to be or to become a thing—either oneself or other things—otherwise than by existence actuating a subject. An angel, in knowing, is itself and other things otherwise than by its proper existence as a limited subject; by His knowledge, God is Himself and things otherwise than by an existence that would actuate a subject.

IV. The act of knowing is none of the actions we customarily observe round about us; it is not part of the category "action"—nor of the category "passion"—in Aristotle's table. Taken purely in itself, it does not consist in the production of anything, even within the knowing subject. To know is to advance oneself to an act of existing of supereminent perfection, and that, in itself, does not involve production.

In fact, there is a production of an image in sensitive knowledge and of a mental word, or concept, in intellectual knowledge; but that inner production is not formally the act itself of knowing. It is at once a condition and a means, and an expression of that act.

That is why the ancients said the act of knowing is a properly immanent action, a perfectly vital action, belonging to the category "quality."

V. Wherever it is a matter of a knowing being other than God—for, by Himself, He is in supereminent fashion all things—we are forced, if we would conceive a knowledge without absurdity, to introduce the notion of a very special kind of existence, which the ancients called *esse intentionale,* intentional being, and which is opposed to *esse naturae,* i.e., to the being a thing possesses when it exists in its own nature. For after all, the scandals suffered by the principle of identity can only be apparent, and it is certain that, if it is proper to the knower to be another thing than what it is, we must needs, to avoid absurdity, distinguish two ways of having existence; we have to conceive of an *esse* that is not the proper act of existing of the subject as such or of its accidents.

In what manner is the knower the known? It cannot be what it is not in virtue of its own natural being.

How does the thing known exist in the knower? The tree or the stone does not exist in the mind, according to its natural being.

Another kind of existence must, then, be admitted; an existence according to which the known will be in the knower and the knower will be the known, an entirely tendential and immaterial existence, whose office is not to posit a thing outside nothingness for itself and as a subject, but, on the contrary, for another thing and as a relation. It is an existence that does not seal up the thing within the bounds of its nature, but sets it free from them. In virtue of that existence, the thing exists in the soul with an existence other than its own existence, and the soul is or becomes the thing with an existence other than *its* own existence. As Cajetan tells us, *intentional being* is there as a remedy for the imperfection essential to every created, knowing subject, to wit, the imperfection of possessing a limited natural being and of not being, of itself, everything else.

In another order than that of knowledge, in the order of efficient activity, is it not equally necessary to admit an intentional manner of existing—the way, for instance, in which artistic power *passes* into the painter's hand and brush? For the whole picture is the work of the brush; there is nothing in the picture that is not really caused by the brush. And yet the beauty and intelligible brilliance, the spiritual values with which the picture is charged, far surpass everything of which the brush's proper causality, bound up as it is with the material universe, is capable. A causality higher than its own, a causality superordered to it, must, then, pass through the brush. Examine everything "entitative" or existent in the brush, *secundum esse naturae,* and you will not find the painter's art; you will only find the substance and qualities of the brush whereby it is moved by the hand. Yet the art passes through it. Examine everything entitative about the medium that transmits sensible quality and you will only find the properties and movements—the wave movements and others—that the physicist sees in them. You will no more find quality there than you will find the soul under the scalpel. Yet quality passes through it, *secundum esse intentionale,* since the sense will perceive it when the wave or vibration reaches the organ. It is like a dream of a materialistic imagination to want, with Democritus, to have quality pass through the medium entitatively, or, since it is not there entitatively, to deny, with the votaries of modern "scientism," that it could pass through it at all. Even when *esse intentionale* has nothing to do with the world of knowledge, it is already a way for forms to escape from this entombment in matter. The scholastics often gave the name *esse spirituale* to this existence (which is not for itself), this tendency-existence whereby forms, other than their own, come upon things. We think it would be of great interest to philosophers to study the role that *esse intentionale* plays in the physical world itself, wherein there undoubtedly arises from such existing, that sort of universal animation whereby motion puts into bodies more than they are, and colours the whole of nature with a semblance of life and feeling undoubtedly derived from it. However this may be, what is important for us at this moment is its role in knowing and in the material operations of knowing, the intentional presence of the object in the soul and the intentional transformation of the soul into the object, both a function of the immateriality—imperfect for sense, absolute for intellect—of the cognitive faculties.

VI. What is the means by which the union of the known and the knower is affected? What is the medium thanks to which the thing known exists intentionally in the knower and thanks to which the knower becomes intentionally the thing known? It is the whole world of intra-psychic immaterial forms that exist in the soul as vicars of the object. These the ancients called likenesses or *species*. The word "species" has no equivalent in our modern languages, and we feel that the most suitable expression to render it would be presentative or objectifying form. For the philosophers, the notion of *species* is not, any more than the notion of *esse intentionale*, an explanatory factor already known and already clarified by some other means. Species are, as it were, the abutments upon which an analysis of the given leans for support, the reality of which the mind, by that very analysis, is compelled to recognize—with certainty, if the analysis itself has proceeded correctly and under the constant pressure of intelligible necessities. Some determination must, of necessity, actually supervene upon the knower, thanks to which a thing that is not the knower will exist in him *secundum esse intentionale* (not as an accident in a substance) and by which the thing will be able to exist with the very same active superexistence which is the existence of the knower that has become the thing known. The species is nothing but that internal determination.

In the case of sensitive knowledge, the external sense, which is in a state of vital tension and has only "to open up" in order to know (everything is ready for it beforehand and, on that account, is like an already acquired intellectual *habitus*), receives from the thing—acting upon the organ through its qualities and thereby offering itself to be sensed (we say: "sensible in act")—a *species impressa*, a presentative form impressed upon it—let us say a "received presentative form"—thanks to which it is specified as though by a seed that has entered into its very depths. The sense, having thus intentionally become the sensible thing in initial or "first" act (for the sense and the sensible thing are then but one and the same principle of operation), becomes it in terminal or "second" act in its immanent action itself, and exercises one and the same act with the sensed thing—not without at the same time producing an image of that sensed thing, a *species expressa* of the sensible order, in the imagination and memory.

The intellect, for its part, knows things by forming them in a fruit which it conceives in the bosom of its own immateriality. Following Aristotle, Thomists recognize in the intellect an active light (the "agent" or acting intellect) which, using sensible representations and setting free the intelligibility they contain in potency (and this is possible only by leaving aside individuating characteristics vested in the sensible as such), specifies the intellect with the help of a *species impressa*, a "presentative form" abstracted from the sensible and "received" by it. Then the intellect is in initial or first act. Precisely as principle of action the intellect has intentionally become the object, which, through its *species*, is hidden in it as a fertilizing seed and co-principle of knowing (just as the intellect, the sufficient principle of its own action, already is, itself). In this way, the intellect itself actuated by the *species impressa*, and then producing within itself a *species expressa* of the intelligible order, an "elaborated" or "uttered" "presentative form" in which it brings the object to the highest level of actuality and intelligible formation, becomes the object in final act. If the distinction between first and second act is thus once more encountered in knowledge, it is because knowledge, as we have already said, constitutes unto itself alone a whole metaphysical order apart, wherein meet in common both the distinction between essential form and existence in the line of being and the distinction between operative form and the operation in the line of action—now transposed on to one and the same line, the line of knowing. Is not knowing at once existence and (immanent) action? By its faculties of knowing the soul first (intentionally) becomes the object in first act so as to then become the object in second act, even as nature exists before acting.

VII. As regards the *species* or presentative forms, two roles or functions of quite different orders must be carefully distinguished. On the one hand, these immaterial forms, these *species*, are modifications of the soul, and by that title they determine the faculty in the same way as any form determines a subject; but these modifications of our proper natural being, these modifications of the entitative order are only the prerequisite conditions for knowledge. In no way do they constitute knowledge.

On the other hand, precisely as means of knowing, presentative forms are purely and formally vicars of the object, pure likenesses of the object (i.e., in the soul, they are the object itself divested of its proper existence and made present in an immaterial and intentional state). By this title they do not determine the faculty as a form determines a matter or a subject. They determine it according to a wholly immaterial and suprasubjective union in virtue of which one becomes the other intentionally, first in initial act and then in second act through its vital operation. This entirely immaterial informing, wherein the soul receives or submits only in order to exercise its own vital activity—only in order to bring itself in act to an existence that is not limited to itself alone—is that which constitutes knowing.

23. In short, knowing appears to us to be an immanent and vital operation that essentially consists, not in making, but in being; to be or become a thing—either itself or other things—in a way other than by an existence that actuates a subject. This implies a union quite superior to the union of matter and form which together comprise a *tertium quid*, and it supposes that the known object is intentionally made present to the faculty thanks to a *species*, a presentative form. Finally, intellectual knowledge is accomplished thanks to a mental word or concept, a presentative form uttered by the intellect within itself, and in that form the intellect intentionally becomes, in terminal act, the thing taken in this or that one of its intelligible determinations.

The Concept

24. Thomists distinguish between two kinds of essentially different *signs:* what they call *instrumental sign,* and what they call *formal sign.* An instrumental sign is anything that, being itself first known, makes some other thing known consecutively: a streak of smoke we see rising into the sky, a portrait painted on canvas that we see in a gallery—both are objects upon which our knowledge first bears, only to pass from thence to other objects that are known thanks to them—to the fire of which the smoke is the effect, to the sitter of whom the portrait is the image and the sign.

A formal sign is a sign whose whole essence is to signify. It is not an object which, having, first, its proper value for us as an object, is found, besides, to signify another object. Rather, it is anything that *makes known,* before being itself a known object. More exactly, let us say it is something that, before being known as object by a reflective act, is known only by the very knowledge that brings the mind to the object through its mediation. In other words, it is not known by "appearing" as object by "disappearing" in face of the object, for its very essence is to bear the mind to something other than itself. All that we have established up to this point enables us to understand that the *species expressae,* or the elaborated presentative forms which intervene in knowing, are formal signs, not instrumental signs. A remembrance, or presentative form retained in memory and used by the memory *hic et nunc,* is not *that which* is known when we remember. It is the *means* by which we know. And what we know by that means is the past itself, the thing or event woven into the web of our past. The concept or mental word is not *that which* is known when our intellect is at work; it is the *means* whereby intellection takes place. And what we know by that means is the very nature or intelligible determination of an actually or possibly existing thing. Presentative (elaborated) forms are the only realities that correspond to the notion of "formal sign." This notion has been "made to measure" according to the exigencies of an analysis that respects the proper nature of knowledge. It belongs there and there only. All other signs of which we have experience are instrumental signs. That is why, the moment one neglects or forgets the irreducible originality of matters affecting knowledge, presentative signs are so easily confused with instrumental signs, just as the immanent activity of sensation and intellection are confused with the transient activity proper to the world of bodies. And, at once, knowledge is destroyed.

St. Thomas, refuting beforehand certain idealistic positions, takes great pains to warn us that the *species* or presentative forms are not the object we know, but pure means of our knowing. They only become the object of knowledge reflexively, and thanks to the production of a new concept. If our knowledge, he explains, stopped at those forms, if it were our representations that we know, then, on the one hand, all the sciences would be absorbed into a single science—and it would be psychology—and, on the other, contradictories would be true—since a true judgment would then be a judgment in conformity with our representations; a person judging that 2 + 2 equals 4 and one judging that 2 + 2 does not equal 4, would be equally right, since each is expressing his respective representations. Thus, presentative forms, concepts in particular, are pure means of knowing; scholastics called them *objectum quo,* mental objects *by which* knowledge takes place. What is known through these immaterial *species,* they called *objectum quod* the object *which* is known.

25. If we should group together in a synoptic chart [see the following page] the various elements that concur in an act of intellectual knowledge, we get a schema whose scholarly aspect demands an apology but which, none the less, will help us to clarify distinctions that are, in our opinion, of capital importance.

We have distinguished two features in the concept: an entitative function, by which the concept is a modification or accident of the soul, and an intentional function, by which it is a formal sign of the thing and in which the object is grasped by the mind. That object grasped by the mind by and in the concept is the thing itself, taken under this or that one of its determinations, for that thing has been transported—though stripped of its own existence—within the mind, first by means of sensation and then by abstraction. For the first three terms of this chart are all within thought: it is in the bosom of thought that the object is attained; it is known in the core of the intellect. (That is why the ancients often called it *conceptus objectivus.*) Only the thing, taken in its own proper existence (either actual or possible), is extramental or metalogical. But what is capital in this regard is that while existing in two different states (I° in the concept, in a state of abstraction and universality which allows it to be handled, divided, compared by the mind, and to enter into the concatenations of discourse; 2° in the thing, in a state

	IN THE MIND			OUTSIDE THE MIND
	concept (QUO)		thing (QUOD)	
Saint Thomas Aquinas	as modification of the subject	as species (formal sign)	as object (formal object)	as thing (material object)
		here ← an intentional existence	possessing	→ there an existence of nature
	idea (QUOD)			ideated (QUOD)
Descartes	"formal" reality of the idea	[the intentional disappears]	"objective" reality of the idea	thing which the idea resembles
Berkeley			idea-thing	no thing
Kant			constructed phenomena	unknowable thing-in-itself
	IN ABSOLUTE THOUGHT			
Hegel		[productive spontaneity]	the mind's self-objectivation	no thing-in-itself except thought itself
	IN INTENTIONAL AWARENESS			
Phenomenologists and Critical Realists		[the intentional reappears]	object-essence	no thing-in-itself
	IN KNOWLEDGE			
American Neo-Realists				thing immanent to thought qua thing

of individuality and concreteness), nevertheless the *object* and the *thing* do not constitute two known terms, two *quod's*, but only one. One and the same term of knowledge, one and the same *quod*, exists for itself as thing, and is attained by the mind as object.

The *thing* may be Peter, for example. He exists outside the mind in a certain place; he is not only man but also animal, substance, etc., philosopher or musician, well or ill. The *object* may, for instance, be the object-of-thought "man," which in Peter, and outside the mind, has a natural existence, and in the concept and within the mind, an intentional existence (and as known, or placed before the mind, it has only an ideal existence or existence of reason). It is essential to the concept to be abstract and universal. It is essential to the extramental thing to be singular and concrete. The object, on the contrary, existing as it does in the thing, with an existence of nature (singular and concrete, and proper to the thing), and also existing in the concept with intentional existence (abstract and universal, and proper to the concept), is in itself indifferent to one state or the other. It is posited before the mind in a state of abstraction and universality that comes to it from its existence within the concept, wherein it is grasped by the mind; that state, however, is not essential to it, since in a judgment—for example, when we say "Peter is man"—I identify the individual Peter and the object of thought, man.

26. As concerns the concept or mental word which I have in mind when I think "man," it is said to be a sign of the thing, a likeness or vicar of the object, an interior term wherein the object is perceived intellectually (*terminus in quo*). But in this connection, let us be on our guard against that sort of materialization or spatialization which language brings with it, unless we are on the watch for it. The object does not in any way exist in the concept as a material content exists in a material container; the concept is emphatically not a material thing enveloping another material thing. It is an immaterial "word," an utterance of the mind expressing the object. For the concept "to contain" is purely and simply to know. The object exists in the concept and is grasped in it in the sense that by the very fact of emitting the concept, and fulfilling itself in this spiritual production, the immanent act of understanding immediately attains the object and attains it, clad in the conditions of the concept. And that itself is possible only because the concept is a sign, vicar or likeness of the object only insofar as it is a formal sign, as we have pointed out above.

And what does this mean if not that the notions "vicar" or "likeness" or "image" must in this case be purified of everything that would make of them things that first come before the mind's eye, like a portrait falling under the gaze of the eyes of the body. But then, if the concept is not a thing that resembles the object, what is left for it? As something existing intentionally in the soul and bringing the object to the ultimate level of spirituality there in the soul, as something *making known*, it remains for it to be what the thing or object is as it is *known*. The concept and thing make two from the point of view of entity; but as formal sign, and in the pure line of knowing rather than being, we must say that it and the object do not make two. The fruit of understanding in act, it has as its intelligible content the object itself. But this intelligible content set, as object, before the mind, is vitally expressed as concept by the mind and has, as its proper existence, the act of intellection itself. As for its intelligible constitution, the concept is therefore identical with the object—not, certainly, as if it were *that which* is known: that is not what I mean; rather I mean precisely this: it is identical insofar as it is the inner sign and term *by which* the intellect becomes, in ultimate act, what it knows. A moment ago we said the formal sign is not something that is first known and afterwards makes known another thing. We now understand that it is something known precisely insofar as it makes known, and in the very act of making known. The immanent reason of the presentation of the object to the intellect in act, the concept or mental word is steeped in intellectuality in act; to be thought in act, to terminate understanding in act, is, for the concept, an intrinsic denomination, since it is in the concept that the object, like the intellect, is in the ultimate act of intellectuality. But it is not as object that it is thought and known; it is not as term signified that it is *intellectum in actu*, grasped and shot through with actual understanding. It is a signifying term.

27. Finally, the concept in its entitative role and as modification of the subject, and the concept in its intentional role and as formal sign, are not two distinct things (indeed, intentionality is not exactly a thing-in-itself but, rather, a mode). These are two formal aspects or two distinct formal values of the same thing, the intentional role being of importance only to knowing, the entitative function, to the being of nature (in this case, of the soul itself). Just as the divine essence, being understanding in pure act, has itself the value of *species impressa* and *species expressa* for the intellect of the blessed, and just as the angel's substance is itself *species impressa* for the angel's intellect, so the entity of the concept is itself, in us, the formal sign of the object. As thing or entity, the concept is an accident, a quality or modification of the soul; but arising, as it does, within the soul as a fruit and an expression of an intellect already formed by the *species impressa*, already "perfect," and under the influence of that created participation in the divine intellectual power, that focus of ever-actual immateriality, the highest point of spiritual tension naturally present within us—which must be called the active intellect (*intellectus agens*) and from which the intellect which knows derives all its formative energy—this quality, this modification of the soul which is the concept, has (as all objectifying forms do) the privilege of transcending the entitative, informing activity it exercises and of being present in the faculty after the manner of a spirit. It is from the intellect itself, from the intellect in vital act, that that quality holds this privilege, as though the intellect gathered together its own spirituality into this active point, there to bring it to a maximum. Thus, the concept exists in the intellect not only in an entitative manner and as an informing form, but also as a spiritual form, not absorbed in actuating a subject so as to form a *tertium quid* with it, and therefore actuating, on the contrary, or rather, terminating, the intellect intentionally and in the line of knowing, in that it expresses the object and renders it transparent.

On the other hand, the form that the intellect, once it has been placed in first act by the *species impressa,* engenders within itself, under the uninterrupted irradiation of the agent intellect, is truly, as we have said, the object's pure likeness, spiritually on fire, or rather the object itself now made spirit and *intentionally* present (not as object but as sign): because its entire specification comes from the object. The intellect that illumines and the intellect that knows are by themselves equally undetermined. Thus, the concept (in its intentional role) and object are indistinguishable, save that one makes known and the other is known, one is sign and the other is signified, one exists only in the mind and the other exists at the same time in the mind and in the thing.

Thus, we see that the intuitivity proper to the intellect consists (at the lowest stage) in the abstractive perception performed by means of the concept, and that, for the things that fall, in the very first place, within the grasp of our intellect, that perception is absolutely infallible. It delivers to us those first principles which are known of themselves and command the whole development of knowledge. And yet, since our intellect has thus to form its own objects for itself and, in proportion as it advances in knowledge, actively draw, from the same presentative form (*species impressa*) it has received, various concepts that set forth the various aspects of the same intelligible nucleus according to the various directions of attention that prevail within the mind--(for things are not merely brought to actual intelligibility in the *species impressa;* within the bosom of the intellect an inventory of them is taken and they are sorted out in many ways in order to be brought to the final degree of actual intellection in the concept); we also see that the conceptual task is highly complicated and slow moving; we see that it proceeds from the indeterminate and generic to the determined; we see that it admits of a large measure of construction and artifice; we see that it makes us take very indirect or "confused or partial or derivative or negative" views of things, and finally that it runs the risk of error in proportion as it advances—not only from the fact of judgment and reasoning but from the fact of abstractive perception as well, because when our intellect is already busied with forms, the new concepts it engenders (whose formation no longer depends on the thing alone, but on objects already possessed and in virtue of which the new object is placed before the mind) can be formed awry. Undoubtedly, they always present to the mind some aspect of the real—or some being of reason based on the real—when they are not pseudo-concepts giving the mind a complex of contradictory elements (such as the greatest whole number or the most perfect world); yet they may be capable of being cut up or recast n such arbitrary fashion that the gain will be very slight, if not illusory. Thus, we witness that certain concepts used by science, oftentimes for quite a long while—and, indeed, not absurdly—disappear forever and leave no trace; the ancient chemistry had its phlogiston, and in the sociology that came from Auguste Comte, as well as in our modern psychology, concepts that are quite as perishable are to be found.

Idealistic Positions and Attempts at Reaction

28. Well, after that, if we come back once more to our diagram, we can easily discern for ourselves the classical moments in modern idealism. The latter is characterized, truth to tell, by a radical misunderstanding of the true nature of the idea and of the intentional function of knowledge, thenceforth conceived upon the pattern of events in the material order. Descartes clearly saw that the known object is known within thought; his capital error was to have separated the *object* from the *thing,* believing as he did that the object is in thought, not as an intelligible entity rendered present to the mind through an immaterial form—and with which the mind is intentionally identified—but as an imprint stamped on wax. Henceforth, the intentional function disappears; the known object becomes something of thought, an imprint or portrait born within it; understanding stops at the idea (looked upon as instrumental sign). This idea-portrait, this idea-thing, has as its double a thing to which it bears a resemblance but which is itself not attained by the act of understanding. They are two separate *quod's,* and the divine veracity is needed to assure us that behind the *idea-quod* (which we attain), there is a *thing-quod* corresponding to it. Of itself thought attains nothing but itself.

Thenceforth, the idea becomes—as, later, Locke will say—the immediate object of thought.

Berkeley will see, not unreasonably, that under these conditions there is no legitimate reason for keeping the thing as a double of the idea, and he will believe he is returning to the evidence of common sense in affirming that we immediately perceive objects, but that those objects are themselves our ideas.

Finally, Kant will once more admit, with Descartes, a *thing* (das Ding an sich) hidden behind the *object.* But because he looks upon the object as something constructed by the mind's activity in accordance with its *a priori* laws, will arrest our knowledge at the phenomenon that is thus constructed, the thing in itself remaining unknowable.

All these philosophers equally disregard the proper nature of knowledge. They envisage the operation of knowing after the pattern of material operations; they regard an activity which is essentially immanent, as an activity *ad extra.* For Cartesian innatism, thought is essentially passive; it is a certain matter that has received an imprint. The same is true for the empiricists who will look upon that imprint as caused in thought not by God but by things. Kant sought to restore the activity of thought, but always according to the same type of a transient or productive activity imposing a form on matter. This time, however, the form belongs on the side of the mind; concepts are empty forms and it is sensible matter that is subsumed and organized by those forms. The inexhaustibility of the thing as a subject to be known will pass, by virtue of the "Copernican principle," to thought as generative of the object, and thought itself will appear to be an indefinite process of fabricating the object.

Indeed, once the intentional function disappeared, knowledge became perfectly unintelligible. For in the entitative order it is clear that a thing cannot be something other than what it is. Thus, our idealists deem it absurd to look for an *outside* of thought, as they say. Everything is absorbed within thought, and, for thought, to know is henceforth to develop itself as a plant or an animal, a lichen or a polyp vegetates and grows.

As to present-day reactions against idealism, reactions that seem to us seriously incomplete, they appear under two main aspects. On the one hand, the Neo-realist school, by insisting on the thing's immanence within knowledge, seems to disregard any distinction at all between *thing* and *object*, and encloses the extramental thing itself within the mind. And that has every appearance of being a contradiction.

On the other hand, a much more important group—and in spite of their differences we might at once attach to this group such thinkers as Russell and Whitehead, along with those who have chosen the name "Critical Realists," as well as the Phenomenologists in Germany—stops knowledge short at an *object* which is no longer a product of the mind, as it is for the idealists, but rather an *essence*, an *irreducible datum*, an intelligible entity independent of the mind, or at least exhibited to it in an intuition. But such an object-essence remains for them, as it did for Kant and for the whole modern tradition, still separate from the transobjective subject or the extramental thing. The latter is only hypothetical or problematical and, indeed, it would be better—in virtue of the principle of economy and Occams' razor—to do without it. Or else that extramental thing will be held by others to be "absurd"; and they, remaining, without realizing it, to a certain extent dependent upon Hegel—while still vigorously reacting against his panlogism (yet it was from him they learned to confuse logic with ontology)—will be forced, as Hegel was, to resorb the thing into idea. And they will attribute to the object, taken as separated from any transobjective subject, characteristics that can, in reality, come to it only from that subject. And when I say "in reality," I do not mean that reality for itself which Hegel granted to the Idea, but rather the characteristic of not being producible by the mind, the irreducible consistency of essence.

All this makes the object to be something absolutely irrational, for the object is neither an aspect of a thing nor a modification of the mind; and it also makes knowledge to be a completely unintelligible process, neither vitally immanent nor productive. Moreover, even though it be not productive or transformative, as Kant would have it be, that process still remains, properly speaking, without a term: not "without a term" in the very true sense that knowledge continues to go on penetrating things by adding truth to truth, but in the sense that, in not laying hold of any thing that regulates it, it can—in spite of the ephemeral constructions reared by the theoricians of this idealism redivivus—only overreach itself endlessly by substituting one truth for another and forever attain nothing.

The Universe of Existence and the Universe of Intelligibility

29. Everything we have said of the concept presupposes the Aristotelian theory of *abstraction* according to which the intellect actively draws from sensible data, from things as the sense first lays hold of them, this or that content which is potentially intelligible in those data—an operation which is possible only if individuating notes, invested in the sensible as such, are left aside. It is this intelligible content which the intellect actualizes and expresses in the concept—and which is the object known by it. If, with Aristotle and St. Thomas, *thing* and *object* are distinguished in this fashion but not separated, and if, while maintaining their unity, allowance is made for what comes from the thing and for what comes from the mind in knowing, then it is clear that from the things which exist outside our mind and constitute what may be called the universe of existence, the mind draws forth a world of objects composed of abstract and universal concepts which we may term the universe of intelligibility or of human knowledge. And that universe is, on the one hand, detached from the universe of existence, in order that it may be known. It is, on the other hand, identified with it, in order that it may itself subsist. Thus, we really do attain the things of the world of existence when we attain the world of intelligibility, but we do not attain them in their singularity nor in the contingency proper to the flux of their singular occurrences. Our senses attain them in that way; our scientific knowledge attains them directly only in the universal natures and universal determinations which are the scene of intelligible necessities. And, as Cajetan says in a text we have cited above, it is by turning back, with the aid of the senses, to the singular and contingent things wherein the universal is realized, it is by reintegrating the intelligible in the thing that exists—whether it be a sensible existent or a spiritual one—that the intellect completes its grasping of the real. (One of these, the sensible existent, is at the root of all our knowledge. The other, the spiritual existent, is known—whether it be reflexively experienced, when the soul knows itself through its own acts, or attained through reasoning, when it knows God and spirits—by analogy with sensible existents, to which our mind has to refer in some way or other even in its knowledge of the suprasensible.)

30. Let us not, indeed, forget that even though the singular as such is not the object of science and cannot be directly grasped by the human intellect, it can still be grasped by it indirectly in reflex concepts; and also that science comes to its term in the singular (as transobjective subject), thus completing the circle of its intelligible movement. That is why we need the sense not only in order to derive our ideas from things, but also to resolve our judgment, for in one way or another judgment (even

when it does not have to be verified in the sensible) has to be made in the senses, *sicut extremo et ultimo, ad quod resolutio fiat,* because judgment has to do with existence (actual or possible), and the "sensible and visible thing" is for us the paradigm of the existent.

For St. Thomas, a science of nature that would not return to the singular, real entity would not be a science but a dream. And, analogically, the same thing is true of metaphysics—which also goes back to the singular—and mathematics, insofar, at least, as it comes back to a singular that can be intuitively constructed and in which their basic entities have an imaginable existence. Indeed, "the term in which the knowledge of nature is completed, is the thing attained by the senses, and especially by sight. Just as the cutler seeks a knowledge of 'knife' only for the work he has to do—I mean in order to make this particular knife—so, too, the scientist seeks to know the nature of 'stone' or 'horse' only in order to know the reasons of the things that fall under the senses. And as the craftsman's judgment about the knife would be faulty if he did not know the work it was to do, so also would the scientist's judgment about the things of nature, if that which falls under his senses were unknown. Moreover, everything our intellect knows [even mathematical beings and metaphysical realities] in the present state of union with the body, it knows by referring it in some way to the sensible things of nature. Moreover, it is impossible for the judgment of the intellect not to be faulty in us when the external senses are fettered by sleep."

31. Indeed, we do not derive a *single* world of intelligibility by abstracting from the world of existence; there are as many universes of intelligibility as there are degrees of immateriality or immaterialization of the object.

Being of Reason

32. Our mind not only draws out of the sensible such and such intelligible natures realized in the world of existence; it not only sets before itself those natures whose notion is born to it from the consideration of those natures, and which can all exist; in short, it does not conceive only real beings, i.e., *beings capable of existing.* It can also construct in the image of these natures, *ad instar entis,* objects of thought that are *incapable of existing* outside the mind (for example, genus and species, subject, predicate, etc.), which the ancients called beings of reason, *entia rationis.*

Our mind does not create these objects of thought—which do not deserve the name essence, since essence is the capacity for existing (*esse*)—out of whole cloth. It makes them out of elements that are essences or intelligible aspects first grasped in things: for example, it makes the object of thought "nothing," from "being," to which it adds negation. In themselves they are never anything but simple non-essences (*negations* or *privations*)—a chimera is a non-being conceived in the likeness of an animal—or *relations* which, even though they cannot exist outside the mind, still have the same intelligible content and the same definition (προς τί) as real relations. Such objects are not things, and yet they are not *pure objects* separated from any trans-objective subject as the "phenomena" of the moderns are, for they are conceived in the image of those subjects (of which they presuppose a previous knowledge) and are constructed with elements borrowed from the real. Far from being separated from what is real, they are bound to it on these two counts. The real (actual or possible) remains their root or their occasion. They derive all the objective consistence they have from the real. If we can make judgments about them, it is because we treat them *as though* they were things: "ratio de eis non entibus negotiatur quasi de quibusdam entibus, dum de eis affirmat vel negat aliquid"; and if the mind can be true or false in respect to them, it is by indirectly referring to the real which served as their occasion or basis. Do away with the nature of the circle and of the square, and you can no longer say a square circle is unthinkable; get rid of every nature that is knowable in various degrees of determination, and you can no longer say that a species is part of genus.

If, as the critical realism of Aristotle and St. Thomas teaches, intelligible, extramental being is the first object of our intellect, and if the real existent is first given to us by the senses—whence our intellect draws its ideas—then we are assured that our first intellectual apprehensions do not bear upon beings of reason. *Ab actu ad posse valet consecutio*: since there are ants, the ant is possible. And as for the possibility of being in general, it is certified for us—even independently (*de jure*) of any perception of actual existence—by the very first judicative intuition of our intellect, for it affirms precisely that being is not non-being. But in a philosophy which starts only with thought, a philosophy according to which the mind attains at first only itself, how can we be sure that all our objects of thought are not beings of reason? That is where the Evil Genius plants his barb. That problem was crucial for Descartes (and for Leibniz, too). By the force of that violent splitting in two, that lived contradiction which is at the heart of idealism, must we not at last ask ourselves if being itself—in the likeness of which being of reason is thought and which is, in fact, conceived at first blush as a (possible) reality—must we not ask ourselves, I say, whether being itself is not a being of reason?

33. God does not make beings of reason. It is a mark of the weakness of our abstractive intellect that it is not able, in many cases, to conform itself to the real except by forming beings of reason. We can lay hold of defects in being only by conceiving them in the likeness of being. "Tunc efficitur ens rationis, quando intellectus nititur apprehendere quod non est, et ideo fingit illud, ac si ens esset." At this point, let us note that if there are beings of reason (like the square circle, the largest whole number, a chimera, the best possible world), which cannot exist because they are intrinsically contradictory—these are the thieves and forgers among beings of reason—there are, on the other hand, many others, the honest beings of reason, which cannot exist either, not because they themselves

are composed of incompossible characteristics, but only because to posit them in existence would be incompatible with one of their objective notes. The notion "predicate" is not an absurd one, but it would be absurd to attribute existence outside the mind to a predicate, for it is defined by a certain function which a thing has precisely inasmuch as it is known.

Since these beings of reason imply in their very notion a relation to something real which is attained by the mind, they are said to be *founded on reality*. It thus happens that a being of reason, which cannot exist outside the mind as it itself is presented to the mind, i.e., as a being, does make manifest, by reason of its foundation in the real, that which exists outside the mind, and it has not even been constructed except for that purpose. To say that Neptune is observed by an astronomer is to put a relation of reason in Neptune, but it is a *real* fact that the astronomer does observe Neptune. Evil is a being of reason in the sense that to think of the lack of a good that should be in a subject, I am compelled to conceive that lack as if it were something. But evil does exist in a very real and very positive way, in the sense that the subject in question is indeed deprived or despoiled of a good that should exist in it. The physician does not find deafness in the ear and he does not seek to destroy it as he strives to destroy a colony of bacteria. Yet to be deprived of the sense of hearing is actually something real; the being of reason "deafness" is based on a very real disturbance in the inner organization of the ear.

Moreover, such and such objects of thought can be affected by the mark of unreality characteristic of a being of reason in very different degrees. Evil and deafness, while referring to the very real fact that a subject is deprived of some good due it, are non-beings as objects posited before the mind in the manner of substance or a quality. A geometric surface is a possible being (if it is a Euclidian surface) affected by a condition of reason that prevents it from existing in nature with the absolute lack of thickness its definition implies. Motion is the reality *par excellence* of sensible nature; but we can only conceive it by retaining in memory that part of it that has already flowed by so that "if the soul did not exist time and motion would not exist," meaning they would not exist with that unreal consistence (a condition of reason) which our apprehension bestows upon them. As we shall see in the next chapter, it is very important to consider the role played in our knowledge by beings of reason, founded *in re*.